Alzheimer's

A Daughter's Testimony

KISHA INGRAM

PAGE PUBLISHING, INC.
Conneaut Lake, PA

First originally published by Page Publishing 2021

Cover Design by Kobi Taliaferro

ISBN 978-1-6624-5642-8 (pbk)
ISBN 979-8-88793-998-8 (hc)
ISBN 978-1-6624-5643-5 (digital)

Printed in the United States of America

Dedication

This book is dedicated to my mother, Joanne, who has always been a fighter and advocate of self-determination. To the millions of individuals who suffer from Alzheimer's and to the many families that are impacted because of this terrible disease, I pray that you take comfort in knowing you are not alone! I implore you to take something positive from my testimony and think about sharing your own testimony with others. Writing this book was therapeutic for me; it really allowed me to express my feelings in a way that I have never done before. I pray that you find the strength to move forward, and I thank you for supporting me.

Contents

Contents

Introduction

As the only child of a mother who has Alzheimer's, it is very overwhelming at times to take care of her as she goes through the different stages of this disease. Alzheimer's causes the memory to deteriorate as time goes on, and from one stage of this disease to the next, it will cause her to lose all mental functionality at some point.

As a daughter, it's hard for me to express how I feel because it's an emotional roller coaster. Emotions transition from sadness to fear, anger to happiness, and triumph to pain, which sometimes lead to frustration and depression at times because she doesn't want to be a burden on me. However, she is my mother, and I want to be there for her and support her every step of the way, no matter what stage of Alzheimer's she is in.

I know it will be difficult as time goes on, but through it all, I want to do right by my mother and give her the love and support that she has given me while growing up.

Throughout this book, you will read my testimony and hopefully feel how loving and supportive my mom has been. You will also learn about how she transitions through a life-altering state, living with this progressive disease, and how it changed the outlook we had on life. Being an advocate for my mother has its challenges, but as you read, you'll see that I've learned how to meet each challenge head-on!

Like any other illness, my mother has her good days and bad days. Surviving the day-to-day changes can be very difficult at times. Often, I feel as though I cannot look beyond my day-to-day tasks because I need to focus on her wants and needs.

My life is stressful, and getting accustomed to the fact that I'm my mother's caregiver is hard for me. It's not easy to identify myself in this role; nevertheless, this is my journey, and I must take the bitter with the sweet. As I take you on my journey, I want you all to be encouraged. If someone you love is diagnosed with Alzheimer's, love and support them throughout their journey as this battle is not easy.

Chapter 1

Superwoman

As a single mother, she weathered through so many storms. Fighting to have a social life outside of work and taking care of me was not easy. A day off was not a day off because of all the errands and things that needed to be done. After she and my biological father separated, I can remember her looking different. Maybe she felt a sense of failure because her marriage had failed, and now, she was a single parent. Sacrificing and going without to ensure all my needs were met was her norm. It's a single mom's instinct to feel like she needs to do it all, but luckily, she had a great support system. My auntie did not let her do it alone. During my grammar school days, I would spend time after school at my auntie's house until my mom returned home from work. My cousin would help me with my homework when I needed it. So you see, it really does take a village.

Growing up, I never thought about having to take care of my mom. As a young girl, I saw my mom as a superwoman, a woman who walked through every trial and obstacle she faced with grace. She worked hard and loved helping others. She may not have been deemed perfect to the rest of the world; however, she was perfect to me. To see my mother in her present state makes me sad. Although she may have had her ups and downs in life as we all do, to watch her mental health decline breaks my heart.

I often think about superwoman when I think about growing up. My mother encouraged me to educate myself, do what I love, and work in a field that would bring me joy. When I think about her vibrant spirit, how she was always eager to help others, and how she cared for me, I find strength for the journey. What she instilled in me taught me independence and to be okay with my choices, no matter what others thought about them. Thinking about my younger years with my mom gives me the hope to persevere throughout this season in my life. A superwoman is not just about being able to do everything; a superwoman means doing your best and taking care of your responsibilities regardless of life's circumstances. I want all my readers, who may be going through a tough season of watching their loved ones suffer from a sickness, to be encouraged! Hold on to the memories of them being healthy because I believe this will help you get through the journey.

I want to make sure that I'm with my superwoman throughout her journey and that we give her the best we have to offer. While I want to make sure my mom enjoys her later years, it's difficult sometimes to get her out of the house. Once my husband and I planned to take her on a cruise but realized that because of her memory, it would not be a good idea. We realized that being surrounded by so many people presented new possibilities at this stage in her life, possibilities we didn't have to consider before. The potential to get lost was greater than ever, and her new reality prevents her from enjoying herself. I couldn't bear to see that, so we had to make a difficult decision. Instead of her going on the cruise, she stayed with my auntie while we were gone. To this day, I still feel so guilty about this; but making my mom comfortable throughout her journey is always my intention, and it should be your intention as well as you care for your loved ones.

Leaning on God was the only choice my mother had when I was growing up. My biological father decided to move out when I was a child. He moved in with another woman while he was married to my mom. Though I'm sure the situation was difficult for her, she still gave me the love and support I needed growing up. Although this was a painful and tough predicament to be in, my mother persevered during this difficult time. She kept pushing! Doing what was needed to be done was the only option for her. Taking me where I needed to go, loving me unconditionally, and spending time with me was the best gift a mother could give a daughter. That's why I call her my superwoman!

After my biological father moved out, suddenly it was entirely on my mother to figure out how she was going to adjust to her new norm. She learned to cope with the reality that no matter how burned out she felt, she had to make sure everything got done. She was forced to rely on herself and God because of the broken marriage. She took on a level of responsibility that she wasn't prepared for, but it empowered her to be stronger through her agony of being a single mother.

As the years went on, my mother remarried. My stepfather was more of a father figure to me up until he passed away. He was a sweetheart; he was kind-hearted and would give me the world.

When he got sick (kidney failure), I would take him to his dialysis appointments. We would laugh and joke all the time in the car; he was so funny. His illness persisted, which later resulted in the amputation of a leg. This was very challenging for my mother and me because he was so loving and caring to us. It was hard to see him unable to really do for himself. My stepfather eventually passed away in June 2000. We buried him on my birthday. To this day, I have periods of sadness on my birthday because I think of him. I honor my mother for this period in her life. She took on another challenging role as a wife as well as kept every other aspect of her life intact, and that is why *Superwoman is her name.*

Chapter 2

Without a Father

As far back as I can remember, just about every female friend I had lived with both parents in the home. I always think about how their fathers made me feel as though I was their daughter and, I guess, to a certain degree; that's why I really didn't feel as though I was missing out on anything. Yes, my friends had their dads all the time, and I only saw their dads maybe on the weekends; but it seemed like they cherished our time together just as much as I did. We would laugh, joke, and cry together as a family. I also think that's why my mother always made sure to keep my circle of friends small. I believe, subconsciously, she wanted me to value these relationships as well as understand that we really did have a village around us that supported us and understood that she was raising me as a single parent (before remarrying my stepfather). While my friends and I never discussed it much back then, I think they, too, understood how important it was to make me a part of their families.

As an adult, I hear so many individuals, men and women, play the blame game. They use the excuse that because their fathers were not in the home with them growing up and did not help raise them or spend time with them, their lives are not what they should be. The emotional aspect of being rejected and insecure tends to become overwhelming factors in their lives. I've always wondered if girls that do not grow up with a strong father figure in the home also grow up with trust issues or lack of self-esteem.

I wonder if women who have not experienced having a father in their lives find it complicated to love others. Do they not know how to receive love because they have not experienced that nurturing, caring, and secure attachment from their father?

I must admit, it's funny I have a different perspective than most individuals I know who suffer due to an absent father. My biological father was married to my mother and was living in the home until I was five years old. Afterward, my father and my mother split; he moved in with another woman who lived about a mile from us, and they later married. He would visit me sometimes, and I would see him on the weekends if he decided he wanted to keep his promise to me. Overall, I can say that he was not a real father figure.

At the time, I wasn't really in tune with my feelings of not having my biological father around consistently. Now as I think about what a father and daughter relationship should consist of, I can say that he truly missed out on being a part of my life. I really don't think he took the time to think about our relationship. He had moved on, and he was now taking care of someone else's children. At the time, I hadn't given it much thought; but as I got older, I started to think to myself, What kind of man would decide not to take care of his own kids but take care of someone else's? I also started to think about why he and my mother didn't work out. Was it because of me? Was it my mother? What really happened to destroy their relationship? I had so many thoughts behind why my biological father made the choices he made, choices that would ultimately negatively impact how I feel about him today.

I often reflect on our relationship growing up. Though he attended my eighth-grade and high school graduations, the in-between time consisted of an absent father. He wasn't there to talk to me about boys and explain how they should treat me. My mother provided her wisdom on the issue. He wasn't there to talk to me about life or tell me how much he loved me or how beautiful he thought I was. Those things matter to a young girl. After graduating from high school, there was no communication with him until my mom encouraged me to reach out and have an honest conversation about my feelings with the hopes of building and repairing the relationship.

Let me say the conversation did not go well.

When I reached out to him, I tried my best to have an open mind. However, the conversation shifted as his lack of accountability for being an absent father hijacked the conversation. He went into a rant about how my mother planted negative thoughts in my head about him. Once he started blaming my mother for not being able to see me as often as he would have liked to, I asked him what is the excuse now. I'm an adult? The conversation infuriated me to the point where I cut him off and decided not to invite him to my first wedding.

Today we do not communicate at all. I attended my niece's wedding, (the daughter of my step-sister by my biological father), which he also attended. I was so mad at my step-sister because she had placed us at the same table, knowing that I did not want to communicate with him. He tried to talk to me and even tried to take a picture with me. I could not allow that! I don't deem him as my father! That chapter of my life is closed, and I'm okay with that.

Some may think it's harsh to have these feelings, but I can honestly say I don't know what my life would be like today if he was in it. Would I be where I am today had I not gone through this storm? The idea of my biological father not supporting me during this challenging season of my life makes me appreciate my mother even more.

Chapter 3

Congratulations

After working tirelessly for thirty-three years, my mom was finally able to retire from Northwestern Memorial Hospital. She worked as a unit secretary for multiple departments and was adored and respected by everyone. Although she was going to miss working with her coworkers and the relationships she had built over the past thirty-three years, she was so excited about retiring. It's funny I had watched my mother, for so many years, get up without an alarm clock and travel to work so that she could provide me with the best life possible. The time had finally come for me to return the favor.

I was blessed to have a mother who always had my back and was always there when I needed her. Now I couldn't shower her with gifts or money, but I could shower her with my gratitude and appreciation. As I thought about how I would celebrate my mom, I wanted to make sure it was something that I knew she would enjoy and would always remember. After careful consideration, I decided to give her a surprise celebration for her sixty-fifth birthday and her retirement. I knew my mom had never had a surprise party, and I wanted to make sure that she wouldn't catch on so there was a lot of sneaking around that had to happen. I had to make copies of her phonebook to contact her friends and family. I would go by the house when she was at work so she wouldn't suspect anything; it was a lot of work. I had to consider all the guests of honor that she would enjoy and figure out how I was going to get the honoree to the party. Creating some ideas that would not give the surprise away was no easy task. We ended up coming up with a fake dinner event to distract her. I had to make sure this party was kept a secret, so I enlisted some of my friends to help me bring forth a fantastic birthday and retirement celebration. I also asked my cousins, aunts, and friends of my mother to help with the planning process.

I was nervous about my mother finding out about her party as it was hard for me to keep it a secret. I was hoping none of my family or her friends would slip up and tell her about the surprise. Before I knew it, I had over seventy-five people coming for this gracious event and would have been devasted had she discovered what was going on. The day finally came, and everything went off without a hitch. One of her best girlfriends, whom she had worked with in the past, picked her up and drove her to the party. She was under the impression that she was going to dinner. However, her friend advised her that they needed to make one stop. Lo and behold, we were there to surprise her.

My mother was clueless about the party. I was so nervous standing in the entryway with the camera while waiting for her to come through the doors. She had no idea what was going on. The look on her face was priceless! From time to time, I take those pictures out and begin to reflect. Those pictures were the beginning of the next phase of life. I can't help but remember how happy she was and how great we thought life was about to be for her during this next phase in her life! We danced, laughed, and had a joyous time that day; and it was all for my mom!

Chapter 4

The Signs

As we celebrated my mother in anticipation of the next phase of her life, the joy she had as a result of everyone coming together brought me great joy as her daughter. She was looking forward to retiring and vacationing with her friends. We hoped that she would go on many trips to places that she had never been. She would get to sleep in and simply do what she loved. I envisioned one thing, but things sure didn't go that way.

I think she wanted to just be happy. I think at the time, she felt that she could not be alone. By this time, it had been eleven years since my stepdad had passed, and she was looking for companionship.

My mom remarried and relocated to Mississippi. Things were going great. She had lived there for only a year before having to return to Chicago after I got diagnosed with multiple sclerosis. This was a devastating period in our lives, and we needed one another. My mother provided me with the emotional support I needed after being diagnosed, and as always, she made sure she was by my side as I embraced my new normal.

When my mom came to visit, I noticed some patterns of forgetfulness regarding things she would never forget to do for herself or others. I could tell something was not right; she was different. As time went on, I noticed she was forgetting things more often than usual. At first, I just chalked it up to getting older; hell, sometimes I forget things I'm supposed to do, especially when there's a lot that needs to be done. After a while it got worse and she was having a difficult time concentrating. She was moody at times, and there was a change in her personality. I decided to talk to her about going to the doctor so they could run some tests and see what was going on. She was in denial and stated there was nothing wrong with her. Sometimes parents can be stubborn, especially regarding things that make them uncomfortable or that imply something might be wrong regarding their health.

Most parents I know would typically ignore the issues or struggles they may have, however, it was important that I share with her, that ignoring these health issues will not make them go away; it will only get worse

I also tried to tell my mother's husband to take her to the doctor to find out what was happening, but in the back of my mind, I already knew what was happening. My grandmother died with Alzheimer's, and it was beginning to be clear to me that my mom was starting to suffer from this same terrible disease. I couldn't help but think, Why my mother? Out of the five siblings, why was my mom the chosen one? Trying to come to grips with this reality, I felt as though my mom's husband was not supportive of getting her the help she needed. I remember one time, I tried to obtain her doctor's information from him; after he gave me the information, he told my mom that I asked him for it. My mom called me and went off on me, asking me why I wanted this information and again began to tell me that there was nothing wrong with her. To this day, I'm not sure why; but I often ask myself, Did my mom's husband not care about her well-being, or was it because he didn't know how to care? Marriage is hard, and having to make decisions for your spouse can be overwhelming, but I've learned that this is what you sign up for! You can't let fear get in the way of you getting the help your spouse needs to live a better life. My mother's husband made the selfish decision to ignore the signs! While there is no cure for this disease, early detection and medication could have potentially slowed down its progression.

Chapter 5

The Anger and Resentment

The signs of my mother having Alzheimer's was hitting me in my face! I had already watched my grandmother go through all the stages of this disease. It was a hard experience to embrace. When a person is suffering from a disease like Alzheimer's, they need extra support, and you need to have tough skin to deal with the day-to-day changes that occur. Someone must always be watching them because of their difficulty of concentration and memory loss.

The anger

My mother lived with her husband in Mississippi for seven years, and for at least four of these seven years, I could tell my mother was in a bad space and unhappy! Not to mention her memory was fading as time went on. Her illness started to progress, and because my mother did not have a supportive husband, this made life harder for her!

Everyone was aware of my mother's illness, including her husband, my aunts, and cousins. And although he knew, my mother's husband did not take the initiative to get her the help she needed. He would leave my mother in the house alone with no one to watch her or check on her. He would go out of town traveling to Chicago, to Las Vegas, and wherever else he felt like traveling to with no regard for my mother's wellbeing. My anger grew as time went on.

Once he allowed my mother to travel on a Greyhound bus to Minnesota to visit my Auntie. I couldn't understand why he would do something like this knowing my mother's condition. This was a huge mistake to let my mother travel alone on a bus that made stops along the way. My mother had a hard time with her surroundings due to her memory loss and difficulty concentrating. I was enraged with anger and helpless at the same time because her husband did not accompany her on the trip or at least call me to let me know my mother was traveling alone to Minnesota. During her trip, my mother called my auntie and told her the bus had made a stop but that she didn't know where she was. This was terrifying. Thankfully, my mother arrived in Minnesota without incident.

After this occurred, I knew it was time for me to make some decisions for the well-being of my mother. I felt he either did not love my mother or he did not want the responsibility of caring for my mother in a time where she needed him most.

Resentment

As time went on, I came to terms with the fact that he failed at being a supportive husband, and I resent him for that. He did not have to do this to my mother. He could have called me if he did not want the responsibility of taking care of his wife; instead, he put my mother in a dangerous position.

During this time, I also started resenting my biological father. New and returning emotions had surfaced. These emotions started consuming me while I was in the process of getting my mother in a safe and comfortable place. I was angry with my biological father while thinking if he would have been faithful to my mother when they were married, maybe they would still be together. Maybe he would have been a more supportive husband for her during this time as well as a more supportive father to me. The attention and love needed from a person who has Alzheimer's are so critical because in the late stages of this disease, the person will not know who you are. Nevertheless, it is my mother, and I do not want to live with regrets of not being there for her every step of the way.

Chapter 6

The Transition

On the weekend of Memorial Day 2018, we drove to Arkansas for my husband's annual family picnic. It was my second time attending this event, and I looked forward to having some much needed fun after going through an emotional roller coaster about my mother's well-being. The first time in Arkansas, I really couldn't enjoy myself as I was still recovering from surgery, my mobility was limited. Four months before going to the family picnic, my husband and I discussed that we would drive from Arkansas, after the weekend's activities, to Mississippi to pick up my mother. Her husband's children called me and made it very clear that their father could no longer care for my mother.

His daughter informed me, and I quote, "Your mom has a debilitating illness that with God's intervention will not improve." I will be honest, I was upset by this statement; I was hurt that she said this to me. I was hurt that she said this to me, I couldn't believe someone would say something like this. How could someone be so hurtful and disrespectful? At this point, all I could do was concentrate on removing my mother from this situation. When we arrived in Mississippi, we were exhausted and wanted to get a good night's sleep. The plan was to start the drive to Chicago early in the morning. Upon arrival and to our surprise, my mother's belongings were not packed—absolutely *nothing*! I was livid! Her husband had no excuse for it except to say that my mother wouldn't allow him to touch anything. For the next four hours, I worked to put my mom's belongings in garbage bags; yes, you read correctly *garbage bags*! At this point, I felt as though he was throwing her out like trash! By the time I put everything in the truck, there was hardly any room for anyone. My mother wanted to take her dog, Corky, but there was no room for him. Throughout this ordeal, my mom would try to help me pack. She kept forgetting things she had already told me, which slowed down the process of getting things together. To this day, her estranged husband doesn't understand why I feel the way I do, and it's sad.

I had a conversation with my auntie, and she agreed that my mother could come and stay with her. I'm not sure why, but my auntie decided that it would be in the best interest of my mom to get medical attention before moving to Minnesota. At first, I was upset; but after careful consideration, my husband and I decided that it would be best for my mom to stay with us. Let me be clear, I wasn't upset that my auntie changed her mind. I was upset because it seemed so sudden as we had numerous conversations regarding the move. I was caught off guard and unprepared. This left us scrambling to get her room prepared. I will say this: as I go through this tough season of battling with my own illness and taking care of my mother as she suffers from Alzheimer's, I'm grateful for the support system that I have, and I can honestly say that I'm blessed and highly favored to have a husband and in-laws who are going through this journey with me. They truly care about our well-being. They have been good to me and have been instrumental in making the transition as smooth as possible. They are loving and understanding, and I appreciate how they have helped me adjust to our new norm.

At the onset of my mother's move with my husband and me, she experienced horrible episodes where she would call her estranged husband, asking him to come get her. Keep in mind, she has difficulty with remembering she lives in Chicago now. She would think that she was staying in an apartment down the street from him, and she would tell him he needed to come get her and bring her home. It took a long time to get her out of the habit of contacting him and asking him to bring her home. While she continues to have different episodes, I've gotten better at handling them. At first, I would break down and cry. My husband would have to comfort me, telling me it would be okay. It breaks my heart to see her in this condition. There are days when we get to laugh and joke while she's in good spirits, but then there are other days when she is not so good. On those days, she's combative, angry, sad, and confused. A host of emotions can happen all in one day. In these instances, we continue to push through because tomorrow is a new day. It's sad to say, but my mom will most likely not remember the emotions she endured yesterday.

In this tough season of my mother's life, part of me does not want her talking to her estranged husband because he didn't honor his vows; however, she still wants to keep in contact with him. I don't think he fully understands the situation and how continuing to speak with her disrupts her life. Right now, to this day, she has episodes where she forgets where she is or how long she has been with us. I tell my husband all the time that it's as if it's *Groundhog Day* and she's repeating the same day over again.

After my mother came to live with us, I immediately made doctor's appointments for her so I could get her on some medication to help her with her Alzheimer's. It's sad to say that the medication won't cure, and in my mom's situation, I don't really think it helps due to the progression of the disease. She has her good days and bad days, but we try to inject laughter into her daily routine as much as we can. When I talk to certain people, they state that I need to get my mother out of the house to keep her mind engaged. I must take a step back to make sure my words don't come out harsh, but it is not easy. People just don't understand. You have someone who doesn't remember what she did two minutes ago and gets depressed about it because of her condition. This often makes her feel lonely even though she has us. The reality is her life has completely changed from being independent to dependent. I would tell anyone who is caring for loved ones with this horrible disease to try not to take anything personally, for their minds are no longer theirs, and they need your help to get through the day.

Chapter 7

Living with Alzheimer's

I guess it's true what they say: you truly find out who has your best interest at heart during hard times. It's really been an eye-opening experience as we help my mom transition to this new way of life and living with us. Relationships with friends and family have changed. Some don't reach out to even ask how she's doing, nor do they reach out to ask how I'm doing. My godmother has been there for me. If she is not busy, she will come and take my mom to the casino or just hang out. As I discussed earlier, my mom has been independent her entire life, and now she must depend on us to watch out for her. While my mom is not yet at the stage of not being able to bathe or feed herself, it's still a very hard transition to go through because she can't be left home alone. But because she can't be left home alone, I must depend on my husband, mother-in-law, and sister-in-law to help me look out for her well-being. Our lives have changed significantly! My husband and I don't go out much; and if we are invited out, I encourage him to go without me because it's my mom, and I don't want to stop him from going out and living his life.

As stated earlier, my mom has her good days and her bad days. In the beginning, we would leave the house for a couple of hours, believing that she would be okay as my in-laws live upstairs. We were wrong! One day, my husband and I decided to visit some friends, who live about fifteen minutes from us. An hour into our visit, my mom called, telling me she thought she saw someone in the bathroom window trying to get in. This was the day I knew we couldn't leave her totally alone. I became so emotional that my husband had to calm me down. Just in case you're wondering, she was seeing shadows of the trees in the window. There are still some days where she asks how long she has been in Chicago, and she can't believe it when I tell her it's been over two years.

A while ago, my mom had to be hospitalized; we had gone out to celebrate my sister-in-law's sixtieth birthday. Initially, I didn't want to go as I knew this would disrupt my mother's daily routine of sleeping and eating. She sleeps mainly throughout the day and then stays up until three or four in the morning. Because her day was disrupted, she really hadn't had much to drink or eat. By the time we got to the restaurant, she started to complain about a headache. Once we were seated, after waiting for fifteen minutes, she started to experience what I believed to be stroke-like symptoms. The ambulance was called, and she was taken to Northwestern Memorial Hospital, where they conducted a series of tests. Luckily, she was only diagnosed as being a little dehydrated. The doctor kept my mom overnight for observation. Throughout the night, she was combative with me, asking me questions as to why she was there over and over. She took off her heart monitor twice and said she was leaving. It was a rough night, to say the least. The next day, after she was discharged, my husband picked us up. While riding home, I heard her on the phone with her estranged husband, asking him to bring her keys to her house because she was headed home. She didn't remember she lived with us, nor did she remember being in the hospital, and we were just minutes from leaving. I can say that being an only child is tough. Not having siblings who can share the responsibility of taking care of a parent can be overwhelming. Because my mom's siblings live in different states, I really can't rely on them to assist either. I take full responsibility for caring for my mom. It's my job as she took care of me growing up, so I owe her that. It does get hard, and there are days where I cry uncontrollably because I feel so overwhelmed. I never want my mom to think that she is a burden or that I'm trying to put her off on someone else, but unfortunately, I must work and figure things out. Every day is different; she has her good days where we laugh, and she has her bad days where she is confused and combative. In those bad days, she also seems so depressed; it's like she knows something is wrong with her, but unfortunately, she can't remember. Every day, I give her medication that I can't tell her the truth about what it's for because she won't take it because she does not believe she has memory issues. It's heartbreaking to see my mother like this. My husband always tries to encourage me to embrace the good times we have because that's creating memories. I guess until you live with someone with this terrible disease, you really don't know what it's like. I hate to think about it down the road as I know it will get worse. There will be a day where my mom doesn't remember who I am, and I'm not sure I will be able to handle it daily. As I'm sitting here, typing this, tears are coming down my face as I can't bear to think about the future. In the end, all I can do is provide her with the love and support that she has always given me and hope that I live up to her standards of what being a good daughter is.

Acknowledgments

I would like to give honor to God for all the continued blessings he has given me and all that he has in store for me. I want to take the time to thank my husband, Jerry, for loving me and my mother; having my back; and helping me support my mother. I love you, baby.

I would like to express my love and gratitude to my in-laws, Donna and YaYa, who are with me on this journey and have supported me throughout this transition. I truly appreciated you all. I would like to express my love and gratitude to my godmother, Mary, for her continued support in this challenging season of our lives. I truly appreciated you. For all others who lend a helping hand or offer words of encouragement, you too are truly appreciated.

About the Author

Kisha Ingram was born and raised on the south side of Chicago in the Englewood neighborhood. Growing up, she never imagined carrying for her mother in this capacity. Learning to care for a parent is not easy; it requires patience, time, and support from others to help with such an important job. Kisha relies heavily on the support of her husband and in-laws to create a warm and welcoming environment to help care for her mother who suffers from Alzheimer's. Every day she strives to be the best wife, daughter, and friend she can be to live a calm life. Kisha also continues to pray that if only for one minute of the day, her mom realizes that she loves her and works hard to live up to her expectations as a daughter.

CPSIA information can be obtained
at www.ICGtesting.com
Printed in the USA
BVHW041341020623
665282BV00002B/62

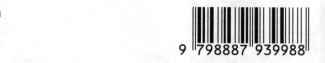

Rebalancing U.S. Forces

Basing and Forward Presence in the Asia-Pacific

Edited by
Carnes Lord and Andrew S. Erickson

Naval Institute Press | Annapolis, Maryland

Naval Institute Press
291 Wood Road
Annapolis, MD 21402

Library of Congress Cataloging-in-Publication Data
Rebalancing U.S. forces : basing and forward presence in the Asia-Pacific / edited
by Carnes Lord and Andrew S. Erickson.
    pages cm
  Includes bibliographical references and index.
  ISBN 978-1-61251-465-9 (hardcover : alk. paper) — ISBN 978-1-61251-464-2
(ebook) 1. Military bases, American—Pacific Area. 2. United States—Military
policy. 3. United States—Military relations—Pacific Area. 4. Pacific Area—
Military relations—United States. I. Lord, Carnes, editor of compilation. II.
Erickson, Andrew S., editor of compilation. III. Erickson, Andrew S. Guam and
American security in the Pacific. Contains (work):
  UA26.P3R43 2014
  355'.03307305—dc23
                        2013047470

♾ Print editions meet the requirements of ANSI/NISO z39.48-1992 (Perma-
nence of Paper).
Printed in the United States of America.

22 21 20 19 18 17 16 15 14   9 8 7 6 5 4 3 2 1
First printing

Maps 1–6 created by Christopher Robinson.

Contents

Illustrations

Acronyms and Abbreviations

A2/AD	anti-access/area denial
AFRICOM	U.S. Africa Command
ANZAC	Australia–New Zealand Army Corps
ANZUK	Australia–New Zealand–United Kingdom
ANZUS	Australia–New Zealand–United States
AOR	area of responsibility
APS	Afloat Prepositioned Stocks [Army squadron]
ASEAN	Association of Southeast Asian Nations
AUSMIN	Australia–United States Ministerial Consultations
BIOT	British Indian Ocean Territory
BMD	ballistic missile defense
C4ISR	command, control, communications, computers, intelligence, surveillance, and reconnaissance
CARAT	Cooperation Afloat Readiness and Training
CCP	Chinese Communist Party
CENTCOM	U.S. Central Command
CFC	Combined Forces Command
CIA	Central Intelligence Agency
CNMI	Commonwealth of the Northern Mariana Islands
CNO	Chief of Naval Operations
COMLOG WESTPAC	Commander, Logistics Group Western Pacific
CONUS	continental United States
CSL	cooperative security location
CTS	Combat Training Squadron

DMZ	demilitarized zone
DoD	Department of Defense
DPRK	Democratic People's Republic of Korea
DSP	Defense Support Program
EEZ	exclusive economic zone
EUCOM	U.S. European Command
FISC	Fleet Industrial Support Center
FOS	forward operating site
FPDA	Five Power Defence Arrangements
GEODSS	Ground-Based Electro-Optical Deep Space Surveillance
GPR	Global Posture Review
IMU	Islamic Movement of Uzbekistan
ISR	intelligence, surveillance, reconnaissance
JCTC	Joint Combined Training Centre [Capability]
JHSV	joint high-speed vessel
JI	Jemaah Islamiah
JSDF	Japan Self-Defense Force
K2	Karshi-Khanabad [Uzbekistan]
KMAG	Korea Military Advisory Group
LCS	littoral combat ship
LPP	Land Partnership Plan
MAGTF	Marine air-ground task force
MIDET	Marine Inspection Detachment
MLP	mobile landing platform
MOB	mobile offshore base
MoU	memorandum of understanding
MPF	Maritime Prepositioning Force
MPSRON	maritime prepositioning squadron
MSC	Military Sealift Command
MSCFE	Military Sealift Command Far East
MSFSC SSU	Military Sealift Fleet Support Command Ship Support Unit Singapore
NAVFAC	Naval Facilities Engineering Command
NCIS	Naval Criminal Investigative Services
NCTAMS	Naval Computer and Telecommunications Station
NCTAMS DET DG	NCTAMS Detachment Diego Garcia
NDAF	Navy, Defense Logistics Agency, and Air Force
NGO	nongovernmental organization
NPT	Non-Proliferation Treaty

NRCC	Navy Regional Contracting Center
NRCS	Navy Region Center Singapore
NSA	National Security Agency
OEF	Operation Enduring Freedom
OPCON	operational control
OSD	Office of the Secretary of Defense
P-3	Lockheed P-3 (patrol) Orion four-engine turboprop anti-submarine and maritime surveillance aircraft
PACOM	U.S. Pacific Command
PBY Catalina Flying Boat	Consolidated Patrol Bomber Catalina American flying boat
PLA	People's Liberation Army
PLAN	People's Liberation Army Navy
PRC	People's Republic of China
QDR	Quadrennial Defense Review
RAAF	Royal Australian Air Force
RAN	Royal Australian Navy
RGS	relay ground station
ROK	Republic of Korea
RSOI	reception, staging, onward movement, and integration
SCO	Shanghai Cooperation Organization
SLOC	sea line(s) of communication
SM-3	Standard Missile-3
SMA	Special Measures Agreement
SOF	special operations forces
SOFA	status of forces agreement
SSA	space situational awareness
SSBN	nuclear-powered ballistic-missile submarine
SSGN	nuclear-powered guided-missile submarine
SSN	nuclear-powered attack submarine / fast-attack submarine
THAAD	Terminal High-Altitude Area Defense
TLAM	Tomahawk land-attack missile
TMD	theater missile defense
TRANET	U.S. Navy Doppler Tracking System
UAE	United Arab Emirates
UAV	unmanned aerial vehicle
UKUSA	United Kingdom–United States of America Agreement
UN	United Nations
UNC	United Nations Command

USAG	U.S. Army Garrison
USFK	U.S. Forces Korea
VLF	very-low frequency
WMD	weapons of mass destruction
YRP	Yongsan Relocation Program

Foreword

This edited volume incorporates the work of Naval War College faculty and outside scholars on a subject that is of current strategic interest to the United States and other nations, namely U.S. basing in the Asia-Pacific. The subject of basing for the U.S. Navy has been a topic of study at the College almost since its first class convened in 1886. Alfred Thayer Mahan recognized the value and necessity of overseas naval bases. In the 1890s and early 1900s the United States was "strategically balanced" toward the Caribbean due to the potential importance of a completed Panama Canal and the strategic imperative of the time—enforcing the Monroe Doctrine. Mahan envisioned the establishment of key bases in Cuba and elsewhere to allow the Navy to cover the Atlantic approaches to the canal. With the rise of the Japanese empire and the gaining of Pacific territorial possessions as a result of the Spanish-American War, the U.S. Navy gradually rebalanced to the Pacific, establishing major bases at Subic Bay in the Philippines and at Pearl Harbor in Hawaii.

Even before World War I, the Navy began to regard imperial Japan as a potential enemy, and the Naval War College began conducting games and studies on the possible dynamics of a Pacific war with Japan. Over the course of the 1920s and 1930s, logistics and basing figured prominently in many of these games, as chronicled by Edwin Miller in his book *War Plan Orange*. Eventually, the constraints of logistics and the need for expeditionary basing convinced the Navy to abandon a strategy of sailing directly to the Philippines from Pearl Harbor in the event of war with Japan and to adopt instead a sequential campaign via the Mandated Islands so that progressively farther-forward support bases could be established, these being necessary even after refueling and replenishment at sea became an embedded institutional skill.

Since the onset of the Cold War, the study of basing has been more or less episodic and sporadic at the College because one of the legacies of the Allied victory in World War II was a globe-girdling network of bases the Navy could use almost as it saw fit. The end of the Cold War resulted in a gradual drawdown of U.S. military basing, including such once-key bases as Roosevelt Roads in Puerto Rico. However, the residual global logistic infrastructure was sufficient to support the Navy's strategic pattern of operations. The next surge in the study of basing at the College came after the publication in 2002 of "Sea Power 21," of which one pillar was "sea basing." Sea basing became a frustrating concept to study because the Navy shied away from settling on a precise definition. Part of this reluctance was due to the fact that the U.S. Army, in the period preceding the drawn-out insurgency in Iraq, seized on the notion of sea basing as a way for it to maintain "strategic relevance"—that is, to become more like the Marine Corps. Seeing a potential budgetary Armageddon as a result of having to build the massive platforms the Army envisioned, as well as a potential mission threat to the Marines, the Navy staff retreated into silence about the concept, rebuffing several Naval War College initiatives to conduct games on the subject.

Basing became an auxiliary subject of Naval War College study as its student-advanced directed-research groups studied the implications of growing arsenals of Chinese, North Korean, and Iranian ballistic missiles. The increased range and accuracy of these missiles put at risk a number of the remaining key air and sea bases in both the Middle East and Far East. This fact becomes salient today as the United States rebalances once again to the Asia-Pacific. The confluence of technical, strategic, and political circumstances warrants a robust new focus at the College on matters of forward naval basing, especially in the Asia-Pacific—to include sea basing. This volume represents a running start on that process. The chapters contained herein reveal a much more complex environment with many more impinging factors than Mahan had to take into account when he advocated the establishment of a U.S. naval base in the Caribbean. However, now as then, the Navy has at its disposal an institution where incisive and objective analysis of the subject can take place.

Robert C. Rubel
Dean of Naval Warfare Studies
Naval War College

Introduction

Carnes Lord and Andrew S. Erickson

In an address to the Australian Parliament on 17 November 2011, President Barack Obama announced that the United States, as part of a general upgrade of its security cooperation with Australia, would deploy up to 2,500 U.S. Marines at Darwin in northern Australia. Although the United States has long enjoyed a close military (and intelligence) relationship with Australia, not since World War II has any significant American military force been stationed permanently on the continent. This move, the president explained, reflected "a deliberate and strategic decision—as a Pacific nation, the United States will play a larger and long-term role in shaping this region and its future."[1] Together with former secretary of state Hillary Clinton's late 2011 visit to Myanmar (Burma), the first by an American secretary of state in more than half a century, this is the most striking manifestation of what appears to be a new determination on the part of the Obama administration to reassert the United States' traditional interests in the Asia-Pacific region, to reassure the United States' friends and allies there of the long-term nature of its commitment to them, and to send an unmistakable signal to the People's Republic of China that the United States is and intends to remain a "Pacific power" fully prepared to meet the challenge of China's rise and its regional ambitions.[2]

It is striking that this very significant upgrade to the U.S.-Australian security relationship (which extends to other measures, such as increased joint exercises and greater access for U.S. aircraft to Australian air bases) passed without a great deal of comment in the United States; yet it is hardly surprising. While they have identified Asia as the most important region to the United States since 2011,

Americans have long taken for granted the global network of military bases and facilities of all kinds that the United States acquired following World War II and has largely if not completely retained ever since.[3] The "forward basing" or "forward presence" of American military forces around the world has become accepted by them as a natural and legitimate expression of America's geographical situation as well as its long-established role as the world's chief security provider. Yet the fact remains that America's global military presence is without parallel in the contemporary world, especially after the collapse of the Soviet Union led to a retraction of its military presence in Eastern Europe and other far-flung corners of the Soviet empire.[4] Only Britain and France also regularly maintain military bases and forces abroad, a legacy of their own imperial pasts.[5] But what Americans ignore or take for granted is neither ignored nor taken for granted by many foreigners, including friends and allies of the United States. For the latter, an American military presence on their soil raises inevitable questions of national sovereignty, often leads to frictions of various kinds with the host populations and political complications for their governments, and, not least, threatens to embroil them in unwanted military conflicts. Much skepticism or outright opposition to bases by allied and adversary populations, however, is shaped by the fact that the bases are indeed perceived to be militarily effective. Thus, skeptics or outright opponents in allied nations may emphasize bases' negative side effects or portray them as targets or obstacles to peace, but allied populations overall, over time and in times of crisis, tend to appreciate their utility. Potential adversaries, moreover, are keenly aware of the presence of American troops and warships on their doorstep and highly sensitive to their activities (exercises, notably) as well as to any alteration in their numbers or makeup. While they may vehemently oppose American bases on the territory of their neighbors, they are deterred by them all the more. In the minds of many, American bases abroad are one of the clearest manifestations of the United States' own brand of imperialism, deny or disguise it though we will. Particularly in this regard, in addition to the other aforementioned reasons, it is puzzling that serious students of American national security policy have paid so little attention to the subject of overseas basing over the years.[6]

After the end of the Cold War, the United States substantially reduced the number of American troops stationed abroad, particularly those intended for the defense of West Germany against a massive invasion by the Soviet-led Warsaw Pact. During the first half of the 1990s the United States withdrew nearly 300,000 military personnel from abroad and closed or turned over to host governments some 60 percent of its overseas military installations. Major bases closed included Subic Bay Naval Base and Clark Air Base in the Philippines and Torrejón Air Base in Spain as well as a complex of bases in Panama.[7] Still, much of the American base infrastructure of the Cold War era remained largely as it had been until after the turn of this century. In the first term of President George W. Bush, then secretary of defense Donald M.

Rumsfeld, as part of a larger project to "transform" America's armed forces for a new strategic and technological environment, launched a major review of the entire American military presence abroad. This initiative, which became known as the Global Posture Review (GPR), was spearheaded by the Office of the Secretary of Defense and involved intensive collaboration with the uniformed military and the Department of State as well as consultation with the affected host countries. In September 2004 the Pentagon released a report titled "Strengthening U.S. Global Defense Posture," which provided a summary of the overall effort—by then well under way—as well as a region-by-region survey of the projected changes.[8]

In a foreword to this document, Under Secretary of Defense for Policy Douglas J. Feith made the following comment:

> Since the United States became a global power at the turn of the 20th century, it has changed its forward posture as strategic circumstances have evolved: from bases for administering new overseas territories, to post–World War II occupation duties, and then to a Cold War containment posture. Today, fifteen years after the fall of the Berlin Wall, it is again time to change our posture to fit the strategic realities of our era: an uncertain strategic environment dominated by the nexus of terrorism, state sponsors of terrorism, and the proliferation of weapons of mass destruction.

Of the "strategic realities of our era," the global threat of radical extremist militant Islamist-inspired terrorism of course holds center stage. This threat in particular suggests a global basing or presence infrastructure quite different from that of the Cold War era—one more highly distributed and emphasizing new capabilities such as remotely piloted drones and special operations forces, and one extending to parts of the world not previously active theaters of American military operations.[9] In other respects, however, the transformation Feith alludes to should not be overstated. A substantial presence of U.S. ground forces in Europe as well as East Asia would continue to be required to give credibility to the U.S. commitment to its traditional allies in those theaters and to undergird regional stability. Under the new plan, some 70,000 U.S. troops were slated to redeploy to the United States over a period of ten years. Among these, some 15,000 would initially be drawn from Asia (South Korea and Japan) while the rest were to be taken from Europe. At the same time, in a number of places the U.S. military presence was actually to be augmented, notably in Eastern Europe (Romania and Bulgaria).

In the years following the release of the GPR, of course, there has been a massive increase in the American military presence abroad owing to the conflicts in Iraq and Afghanistan, which only now is beginning to be reversed. This has included the construction of numerous semipermanent as well as transient military facilities of all kinds in support of these wars, not only in Iraq and

Afghanistan themselves but in neighboring countries such as Kuwait, Qatar, and the United Arab Emirates, as well as Uzbekistan and Kyrgyzstan in Central Asia. The United States has also established a substantial facility in Djibouti in the Horn of Africa dedicated to the prosecution of the fight against radical extremist militant Islamist-inspired terrorism in Somalia and across northern sub-Saharan Africa. It remains unclear at this juncture what the future will hold regarding a permanent U.S. presence in this vital region.

Central to the reconceptualization of America's overseas military presence offered in the GPR report is its threefold categorization of types of bases or facilities. Most important are what the document calls "main operating bases," where American combat troops (and typically their families as well) are permanently stationed in significant numbers in facilities essentially controlled by the United States military, such as Ramstein Air Base in Germany or Kadena Air Base on Okinawa. Then there are "forward operating sites" that are normally maintained by a relatively small U.S. support presence and are used for temporary deployments or training purposes; an example is the Sembawang port facility in Singapore. Finally, "cooperative security locations" are austere facilities shared by the United States and host countries that may have little or no permanent U.S. presence and are designed essentially for contingency use. Clearly, the preferred option for the future is the latter two categories. They are less expensive, less visible, and less vulnerable, and they offer greater strategic and operational flexibility; just as important, they are less likely to create political problems for the host government and in fact serve to promote bilateral security cooperation.[10] Indeed, bases that do not have a foreign host government at all (as in overseas U.S. territories, which offer the additional benefit of spending tax dollars domestically, particularly in an era of fiscal austerity[11]) or at least have no local domestic population (as in the British Indian Ocean Territory that includes Diego Garcia) may be seen to have particular advantages in this regard. As of 2010, according to Defense Department figures, the United States had some 750 overseas bases or facilities of these types, of which 88 are in overseas U.S. territories and the rest in 38 foreign countries.[12]

It is customary in discussions of the U.S. military presence overseas to focus on its most visible manifestations, U.S. military personnel and the bases and facilities they occupy in a particular country and region. The U.S. global posture, properly speaking, is something much broader than this, however. It includes America's political or diplomatic relationships with host nations, the legal arrangements supporting the American presence in (or access to) those nations, prepositioned military equipment, capacity to surge forces overseas, and global logistics capabilities to transport and sustain forward-deployed forces.[13] Moreover, it is critical to understand bases and facilities not merely in the context of their host nation or the region where they are located but rather as part of a global system with complex interdependencies and interactions.[14]

This having been said, the present study takes a largely traditional approach to its subject, restricting itself to one region and organized by individual countries or territories rather than thematically. Practical considerations, however, make such an approach virtually unavoidable. A global survey of the U.S. overseas military posture would inevitably be unwieldy or else superficial. We have preferred to provide detailed data and analysis on the countries or territories hosting American bases in one particular region of increasing strategic salience today: the Asia-Pacific. The principal rationale for doing so is the need to rethink fundamentally the American forward presence in Asia in the light of the rapid growth in very recent years in the "anti-access/area denial" (A2/AD) capabilities of the armed forces of the People's Republic of China.

In the first chapter, "Guam and American Security in the Pacific," Andrew S. Erickson and Justin D. Mikolay examine Guam's role as a strategically central sovereign basing location. They document its great potential as a well-placed and politically reliable location wherein investment supports local Americans. At the same time, however, they explain that Guam requires significant additional resources to fully realize that potential, suffers from local challenges, and is entangled in larger regional dynamics, such as Japan's political difficulty in hosting U.S. forces in Okinawa and China's determination to hold the bases of potential opponents at risk with increasingly sophisticated long-range precision weapons, including ballistic and cruise missiles. As such, they contend, Guam represents an important microcosm and indicator of the wide spectrum of basing investments and efforts necessary if Washington is to retain its Asia-Pacific leadership in the future.

Toshi Yoshihara discusses the extensive and long-standing American military infrastructure in Japan, by far the most important element of the United States' Asia-Pacific basing network. The particular focus of this analysis is the People's Republic of China's (PRC) military buildup of recent years, especially the growing Chinese arsenal of conventional ballistic missiles, and its ramifications for the American forward presence in Japan and U.S.-Japanese defense cooperation generally. Using contemporary Chinese sources, which frequently offer surprisingly detailed and frank treatments of what is obviously a sensitive issue, Yoshihara notes the growing evidence of Chinese interest in the American military presence in Japan and the ways in which the PRC can leverage its missile arsenal as an instrument of coercive diplomacy against it. He pays particular attention to U.S. naval bases in Japan, given the relative scarcity of discussions of this subject (compared to the major U.S. air bases there) as well as the Chinese fixation on American aircraft carriers, one of which is permanently homeported in Japan. Beginning with a discussion of the enduring value of U.S. bases in Japan, something too easily taken for granted by Americans today, Yoshihara explores the Chinese doctrinal literature for insights into the way Beijing views the U.S. military presence in Japan and Asia generally, and how Chinese defense planners might employ conventional ballistic missiles in an attack on U.S. facilities in Japan. He then provides a critique of some of the assumptions such planners make about the anticipated effects of missile coercion and cautions as to the potential dangers they pose. Finally, Yoshihara identifies some key strategic and operational dilemmas facing the United States and Japan in such an eventuality.

In "South Korea: An Alliance in Transition," Terence Roehrig discusses the American base structure in the Republic of Korea (ROK) in relation to the current status of the U.S.-ROK alliance, formalized at the end of the Korean War. The last decade has seen a major evolution in this alliance, centering on a shift from U.S. dominance to a greater reliance on the South Koreans themselves. According to Roehrig, much of the impetus for this came from the United States in connection with the GPR of the Rumsfeld Pentagon. Modest reductions in U.S. combat troops were accompanied by substantial reduction and consolidation of the American basing infrastructure on the peninsula. Of some 110 separate bases or facilities at the beginning of the decade, 60 had been returned to the ROK government by its end, including some extremely valuable real estate in central Seoul. American forces were relocated in two major ground and air base complexes to the south and east of the capital, while ROK forces assumed responsibility for forward defense at the Korean Demilitarized Zone. This relocation also served to provide these forces greater flexibility for possible use in regional scenarios other than a North Korean invasion. From a U.S. perspective, gaining such flexibility while at the same time reassuring the South Koreans of its continuing strong commitment to ROK security was perhaps the most important outcome of these recent changes.

The following chapter, "The U.S. Strategic Relationship with Australia," by Australian defense analysts Jack McCaffrie and Chris Rahman, explores a topic that has recently attracted widespread interest, as noted earlier, in the context of the joint decision to enhance substantially the American military presence in northern Australia. As the authors note, the history of this relationship has differed greatly in its three phases, World War II, the Cold War, and the post–Cold War era. During World War II, Australia welcomed U.S. combat forces beginning in 1942, and the continent served as a secure rear base and staging area for allied operations in New Guinea and the Central Pacific; at its peak, the United States maintained some 250,000 troops at various bases throughout the continent. During the Cold War, by contrast, in spite of the signing of the ANZUS (Australia–New Zealand–United States) Treaty in 1951, Australia was regarded by the United States as something of a strategic backwater. The U.S. presence there consisted of a handful of facilities (the best known being Pine Gap) dedicated to technical functions such as ballistic-missile early warning, submarine communications, monitoring of Soviet nuclear testing, and communications intelligence. The authors emphasize the political complications surrounding some of these activities, most of them of a high level of secrecy and imperfectly known even to major elements of the Australian government of the day. At present, however, with the rise of China as a regional military (and especially naval) power, Australia has gained increasing strategic salience for the United States both as a regional ally and as a staging point for air and maritime operations in proximity to the vital Strait of Malacca and the increasingly volatile South China Sea. The authors foresee a growing collaboration between the Australian and American militaries as well as a greater acceptance of such collaboration by the Australian public and a general deepening of an already solid alliance relationship.

Perhaps the link most neglected by observers and analysts of the American military presence in Asia is the Republic of Singapore. In "Singapore: Forward Operating Site," Chris Rahman traces the development of the U.S.-Singaporean strategic relationship over the last several decades. A key moment was the closing of American bases in the Philippines in 1991. Since that time, Singapore has effectively replaced the Philippines as the key logistics hub of American military forces in and in transit through Southeast Asia, although the facilities they use there are operated and shared by the Singaporeans themselves. In 2001 Singapore completed construction of a new naval base at Changi at its own expense (reportedly $60 million) primarily to accommodate and service American warships, including aircraft carriers and submarines. In 2011 the Department of Defense revealed that it plans to permanently station at least two of its new littoral combat ships (LCS) in Singapore. Moreover, Singapore has become a favored venue for security cooperation, training, and exercising with other friendly nations throughout the region, for air as well as naval forces. Though Singapore is not a formal American ally, Rahman suggests that its partnership with the United States now exceeds in strategic significance America's long-standing alliance relationships with the Philippines and Thailand. At the same time, this collaboration remains low-key and politically uncontroversial among the Singaporeans, whose government has long looked to ensure continued U.S. strategic engagement in the region as a key guarantor of its own security.

In the next chapter, "Diego Garcia and American Security in the Indian Ocean," Walter C. Ladwig III, Andrew S. Erickson, and Justin D. Mikolay provide a comprehensive overview of the history, geopolitics, and strategic and operational military functions of the joint U.S.-British base on the remote island of Diego Garcia in the Indian Ocean. The largest, and virtually only, American military footprint in the Indian Ocean at the present time (though that is changing with the hosting of U.S. military forces in northern Australia), Diego Garcia has gradually assumed considerable strategic significance for the United States, primarily as a staging base for a disparate range of capabilities such as submarine replenishment, afloat prepositioning of U.S. Army and Marine Corps equipment and munitions, long-range bomber support, and the like. The authors emphasize that while this base is too distant to directly support the projection of U.S. military power ashore throughout the region (with certain exceptions such as B-52 missions) and is too small to house combat or other forces in great numbers, it also has important advantages. Notable among them is its status as a sovereign British territory with virtually no indigenous population and none currently resident, its relative invulnerability to attack, and its presence at the seam of the two American combatant commands that have responsibility for the Indian Ocean. The authors also discuss in some detail the roles and interests of other powers in the Indian Ocean, notably India and China, and how they perceive the U.S. presence there.

The massive U.S. military presence in Iraq, the Persian Gulf, and Afghanistan over the past decade is beyond the scope of this study, but it is highly instructive to look at the experience the United States has had in establishing new bases in Central Asia in support of its operations in Afghanistan. In "U.S. Bases and Domestic Politics in Central Asia," Alexander Cooley argues that domestic politics rather than Russian or Chinese pressure explains the difficulties the United States has encountered with the governments of Uzbekistan and Kyrgyzstan over the bases it gained access to in these countries beginning in 2001. U.S. forces were in fact expelled from Uzbekistan in 2005 in response to growing criticism by the U.S. government of the human rights abuses of the Karimov regime. Kyrgyzstan threatened to follow suit in the same year, though primarily as a ploy to extort financial aid from Moscow; the agreement over U.S. use of the base at Manas was subsequently renegotiated on more favorable terms. In spite of the fact that in both of these cases the bases in question were relatively modest in scale and used primarily as transit hubs for resupply of U.S. forces in Afghanistan, they proved susceptible to manipulation by their host governments for internal political purposes, demonstrating the extent to which U.S. bases are politically vulnerable in nations with whom the United States lacks established diplomatic or economic relations.

Finally, Sam J. Tangredi addresses the role of sea basing in the overall architecture of the United States' overseas military presence. Among military concepts that never quite seem to come into focus, so-called sea basing surely ranks high. Tangredi revisits the doctrinal and bureaucratic state of play on this issue, which for reasons he lays out has largely disappeared from public discussion over the last several years. Sea basing continues to be viewed and evaluated in very different ways by the different services, in spite of its formal status as a "joint" concept. Tangredi offers a cautious defense of the continuing relevance of sea basing, with reference less to the most commonly cited rationale—the potential political vulnerability of bases located in allied or neutral territory—than to the potential physical vulnerability of fixed land bases to long-range ballistic-missile attack. Among other concrete suggestions, he argues that Aegis-equipped ballistic-missile defense platforms need to be an integral part of any notional sea base designed to counter the A2/AD capabilities of our adversaries.

While these chapters together offer insights into many key dynamics of forward-based and forward-deployed American military forces in the Pacific, any fully adequate study would have to take account of a number of factors or options not discussed in this volume.

Although Alaska and Hawaii are integral parts of the United States, their geographical proximity to Asia gives them unique importance in any discussion of military bases on American soil. Both today are home to a significant military presence: Honolulu is the headquarters of the U.S. Pacific Command and Pacific Fleet, and Alaska has taken on new significance in recent years as one of two locations for the deployment of America's first-generation ground-based ballistic-missile defense system. Both, furthermore, are likely candidates for an enhanced military presence in the coming years as part of the Obama administration's strategic reorientation toward Asia: Hawaii thanks to its central location, and Alaska thanks to its nearly unparalleled strategic depth. It should also be remembered that the United States retains other sovereign or associated territories scattered across the Pacific that currently serve some military functions (notably, the missile-testing facility at Kwajalein) or could serve such functions in the future—as of course many of them did during World War II. It is not difficult to envision the United States reactivating a network of austere sites for contingency use at places like Midway or Wake Island that could provide the nation greater strategic depth in the western and central Pacific than it enjoys today.[15]

In addition, it has not been possible here to provide anything approaching a net assessment of the military capabilities of the United States (or its allies) and China as they bear on the present and future of the U.S. base infrastructure in Asia and the Pacific. Clearly, for example, it makes a great deal of difference whether or not U.S. ballistic-missile defense technologies and fielded systems will be capable at some future point (as they currently are not) of providing serious protection against a conventional missile strike by the Chinese on its forward bases in the western Pacific.[16] Not only fixed land bases, however, but also American naval vessels on the high seas are becoming increasingly vulnerable to attack by the burgeoning arsenal of conventionally armed, precision-guided Chinese ballistic missiles; and the Chinese are also becoming increasingly competitive in air as well as undersea, space, and cyber warfare.[17] All of this raises serious questions as to whether the United States can continue to rely on major surface combatants and, above all, its formidable nuclear-powered aircraft carriers to sustain a forward American presence in the Asia-Pacific region in the coming years.

Notes

1. Jackie Calmes, "Obama Says U.S. to Base Marines Inside Australia," *New York Times*, November 17, 2011.
2. See Brian McCartan, "U.S. Muscle Manifesto for Asia," *Asia Times*, November 24, 2011; and Michèle Flournoy and Janine Davidson, "Obama's New Global Posture," *Foreign Affairs*, July–August 2012, 54–63. Very recently the United States and the Philippines have expressed interest in enhancing the U.S. military presence in that country as well as helping to build up its long-neglected naval capabilities; the United States has been in discussions with Thailand about reestablishing a modest American military presence at U-Tapao airport, a major staging hub for American B-52 bombers during the Vietnam War; and Defense Secretary Leon Panetta became the first high-ranking U.S. official since the end of that war to visit the former U.S. naval base at Cam Ranh Bay, which he declared has "tremendous potential" for use by the U.S. Navy in the future. Craig Whitlock, "U.S. Seeks to Expand Presence in Philippines," *Washington Post*, January 26, 2012; and Craig Whitlock, "U.S. Seeks Return to SE Asian Bases," *Washington Post*, June 23, 2012.
3. On Asia as the most important region, see David J. Berteau, Michael J. Green, Gregory Kiley, and Nicholas Szechenyi, *U.S. Force Posture Strategy in the Asia Pacific Region: An Independent Assessment* (Washington, D.C.: Center for Strategic and International Studies, 15 August 2012), 13, http://csis.org/publication/pacom-force-posture-review. For the little-known yet fascinating story of American planning for the acquisition of permanent bases after the war, see Elliott V. Converse III, *Circling the Earth: United States Plans for a Postwar Overseas Military Base System, 1942–1948* (Maxwell Air Force Base, AL: Air University Press, 2005).
4. The exception is a minor ship-repair and replenishment facility in the Syrian port of Tartus. Russia does, however, retain (or has regained) bases throughout much of the former Soviet space. The largest is the naval base at Sevastopol in Ukrainian Crimea; bases or facilities of varying significance also exist in Azerbaijan, Armenia, Belarus, Georgia, Kazakhstan, Kyrgyzstan, Moldova, and Tajikistan. See Zdzislaw Lachowski, *Foreign Military Bases in Eurasia* (Stockholm: Stockholm International Peace Research Institute, June 2007), especially the table on p. 46. Recently, the head of the Russian navy expressed interest in reestablishing a naval facility in Cuba: Juan O. Tamayo, "Russian Navy Chief Says His Country Is Studying a Base in Cuba," *Miami Herald*, July 28, 2012.
5. Moreover, the overseas claims and force postures of London and Paris have diminished over time. See Robert E. Harkavy, *Strategic Basing and the Great Powers, 1200–2000* (New York: Routledge, 2007), 149–50.
6. The major exception during the Cold War era was the political scientist Robert E. Harkavy; see his *Great Power Competition for Overseas Bases: The Geopolitics of Access Diplomacy* (New York: Pergamon, 1982); and *Bases Abroad: The Global Foreign Military Presence* (Oxford: Oxford University Press, 1989). More recently, see especially Kent E. Calder, *Embattled Garrisons:*

Comparative Base Politics and American Globalism (Princeton, N.J.: Princeton University Press, 2007); Michael O'Hanlon, *Unfinished Business: U.S. Overseas Military Presence in the 21st Century* (Washington, D.C.: Center for a New American Security, June 2008); Michael O'Hanlon, *The Science of War: Defense Budgeting, Military Technology, Logistics, and Combat Outcomes* (Princeton, N.J.: Princeton University Press, 2009), ch. 3; and Alexander Cooley, *Base Politics: Democratic Change and the U.S. Military Overseas* (Ithaca, N.Y.: Cornell University Press, 2008). Andrew F. Krepinevich and Robert O. Work, *A New U.S. Global Defense Posture for the Second Transoceanic Era* (Washington, D.C.: Center for Strategic and Budgetary Assessments, 2007) is the best and most comprehensive recent treatment. It may be added that the subject has been a special target of (ideological) critics of American "empire" such as Chalmers Johnson; see his *The Sorrows of Empire: Militarism, Secrecy, and the End of the Republic* (New York: Henry Holt, 2004), esp. ch. 6 ("The Empire of Bases").

7. The military basing agreement between the United States and the Philippines following its independence, due to expire in 1991, drew increasing opposition in the 1980s from Filipino elites. In June 1991 Clark Air Base was for all practical purposes destroyed in the eruption of nearby Mt. Pinatubo. U.S. and Filipino negotiators could not agree on a formula for the Subic Bay Naval Base; all U.S. forces were therefore removed from the Philippines by the end of 1992. Under the terms of the Panama Canal Treaty of 1979, the Panama Canal Zone and its complex of military bases were returned to the Panamanians by the end of twentieth century. See, for example, William E. Berry Jr., *U.S. Bases in the Philippines: The Evolution of the Special Relationship* (Boulder, Colo.: Westview, 1989); and Anni P. Baker, *American Soldiers Overseas: The Global Military Presence* (Westport, Conn.: Praeger, 2004), chs. 6–7. In retrospect, while political opposition and hosting fees had risen to formidable levels, it is difficult to understand why the United States did not make a more concerted effort to retain the incomparable Subic Bay facilities, then its largest overseas naval base.

8. Flournoy and Davidson are incorrect in stating that the "guiding principle" or "cornerstone" of the Rumsfeld effort was simply to bring troops home and save money; Flournoy and Davidson, "Obama's New Global Posture," 55–56. For authoritative accounts of the GPR, see Ryan Henry, "Transforming the U.S. Global Defense Posture," in *Reposturing the Force: U.S. Overseas Presence in the Twenty-first Century*, Newport Paper 26, ed. Carnes Lord, 33–48 (Newport, RI: U.S. Naval War College Press, February 2006); and Lincoln P. Bloomfield Jr., "Politics and Diplomacy of the Global Defense Posture Review," in *Reposturing the Force: U.S. Overseas Presence in the Twenty-first Century*, Newport Paper 26, ed. Carnes Lord, 49–64 (Newport, RI: U.S. Naval War College Press, February 2006). The authors were the lead senior officials for the GPR in the departments of Defense and State, respectively. For the link between the GPR and "transformation," consider especially Henry, "Transforming the U.S. Global Defense Posture," 34–36.

9. See Krepinevich and Work, *New U.S. Global Defense Posture*, 275–84. It should also be noted, if only in passing, that the clandestine nature of many of these operations as well as the sensitivities of hosting nations (particularly Muslim ones) make it correspondingly more difficult than in the past to develop a full understanding of this new basing network or the political arrangements supporting it.

10. "Changes to our global posture aim to help our allies and friends modernize their own forces, strategies, and doctrines. We are exploring ways in which we can enhance our collective defense capabilities, ensuring that our future alliances and partnerships are capable, affordable, sustainable, and relevant. At the same time, we seek to tailor our military's overseas 'footprint' to suit local conditions, reduce friction with host nations, and respect local sensitivities. A critical precept in our global posture planning is that the United States will place forces only where those forces are wanted and welcomed by the host government and populace." Henry, "Transforming the U.S. Global Defense Posture," 40.

11. For detailed analysis of relevant financial and strategic choices confronting Washington, as commisioned per the 2012 Defense Strategic Guidance via the National Defense Authorization Act for Fiscal Year (FY) 2012, see Michael J. Lostumbo, Michael J. McNerney, Eric Peltz, Derek Eaton, David R. Frelinger, Victoria A. Greenfield, John Halliday et al., *Overseas Basing of U.S. Military Forces: An Assessment of Relative Costs and Strategic Benefits* (Santa Monica, Calif.: Rand Corporation, 2013), RR-201, http://www.rand.org/pubs/research_reports/RR201.html.

12. *Department of Defense Base Structure Report FY 2010 Baseline* (Washington, D.C.: Department of Defense, 2010). The majority of these, however, are in only three countries: Germany (218), Japan (115), and the Republic of Korea (86). (These figures do not include Iraq and Afghanistan.)

13. See especially Henry, "Transforming the U.S. Global Defense Posture," 40–42. One might also include in this mix global strike forces (including those based in the United States) and global reconnaissance and communications capabilities. See the discussion in Krepinevich and Work, who define global military posture in the following terms: "The deliberate apportionment and global positioning of forward-based and forward-deployed forces, and the development of supporting global attack, global mobility and logistics, forcible entry, global command, control, communications and intelligence forces, and supporting security relationships and legal agreements, in order to facilitate the rapid concentration of forces it time and space across transoceanic distances, to support and sustain US military presence and operations in distant theaters, and to establish a favorable global strategic balance"; Krepinevich and Work, *New U.S. Global Defense Posture*, 4.

14. See the discussion of this issue in the very valuable study of James R. Blaker, S. John Tsagronis, and Katherine T. Walter, *U.S. Global Basing (Task 4 Report): U.S. Basing Options* (Washington, D.C.: Hudson Institute, October 1987).

15. Consider the remarks of Krepinevich and Work, *New U.S. Global Defense Posture*, 294–95.
16. For recent analysis of the significant and growing Chinese and North Korean missile threats to U.S. bases in East Asia, see Lostumbo et al., *Overseas Basing of U.S. Military Forces*, 395–402; and Brad Hicks, George Galdorisi, and Scott C. Truver, "The Aegis BMD Global Enterprise: A 'High-End' Maritime Partnership," *Naval War College Review* 65 (Summer 2012): 65–80.
17. For recent details, see Office of the Secretary of Defense, *Military and Security Developments Involving the People's Republic of China 2013*, Annual Report to Congress (Arlington, VA: Department of Defense, 2013), http://www.defense .gov/pubs/2013_China_Report_FINAL.pdf.

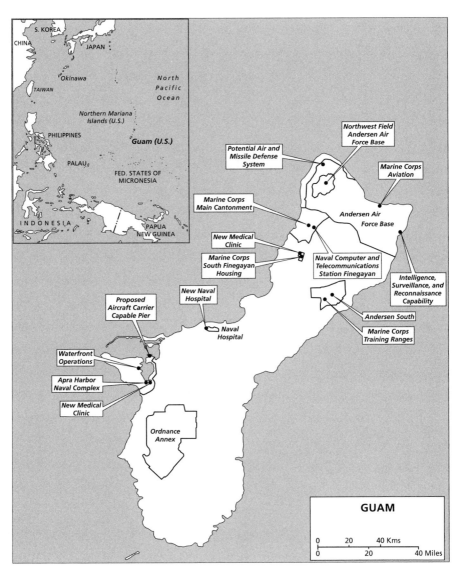

Map 1. Military Facilities in Guam

1

Guam and American Security in the Pacific

Andrew S. Erickson and Justin D. Mikolay

The United States' plans to enhance Guam's military capabilities represent an important part of its larger strategy to sustain U.S. strength across the Asia-Pacific region in the twenty-first century.[1] The island of Guam is the nearest sovereign U.S. territory to Asia-Pacific nations. It is a concrete element, and in many respects a microcosm, of the American rebalancing effort to the Asia-Pacific region. Long-term budget constraints and rising security challenges in the Asia-Pacific have driven the United States to emphasize the Asia-Pacific in its defense strategy and to "rebalance" its forces to that region. Continued U.S. military presence across the Asia-Pacific, and on Guam in particular, is challenged by infrastructure costs, local politics, and larger regional dynamics. Among these regional dynamics are Japan's political challenges in hosting U.S. forces in Okinawa and China's determination to hold the bases of potential opponents at risk with increasingly sophisticated long-range precision weapons, including ballistic and cruise missiles. The balance that the United States strikes in further developing Guam's military capabilities will be an important indicator of how Washington plans to retain its Asia-Pacific leadership in the future. See map 1 for a graphic depiction of Guam's position and military facilities.

A Sovereign Base for American Force Projection

Rising threats to international security in East Asia coincide with growing uncertainty concerning U.S. basing access in that strategically vital region. China's growing comprehensive national strength, coupled with political changes in host countries Japan and South Korea, calls into question the long-term utility of local American bases. Meanwhile, the United States has vital national-security interests in East Asia, including the ongoing North Korean nuclear crisis, periodic Taiwan Strait tension, and potential disruption of strategic sea-lanes by terrorism or conflict in the East Sea and the South China Sea. But as People's Republic of China (PRC) military assessments emphasize, "dependence on foreign-hosted bases and extended lines of logistical support for sustained combat operations in the West Pacific" represent a major American vulnerability.[2]

The U.S. Navy has a critical role to play in East Asia, given the region's extensive coastlines, islands, land barriers, and consequent susceptibility to maritime force projection. As a great air and sea power, the United States does not need the capacity to win land wars in East Asia in order to maintain strong military influence there. The key to America's power projection in the region is control of the air and sea. To exercise that control, the United States must maintain a global forward naval presence without succumbing to the Pacific's "tyranny of distance." The area of operations of the U.S. Pacific Command (PACOM) covers half the globe, or about 169 million square kilometers, over sixteen time zones. The Asia-Pacific region encompasses more than 50 percent of the world's population, contains the world's six largest armed forces and the three largest economies, and accounts for 35 percent of U.S. trade (over $550 billion), slightly more than the potential $500 billion in potential cuts to U.S. defense spending. It includes thirty-six of the world's most diverse and powerful nations, including five of the United States' seven treaty allies—Australia, Japan, South Korea, the Philippines, and Thailand. The United States maintains significant capabilities in this area, including 330,000 civilian and military personnel (one-fifth of U.S. forces overall); 5 aircraft carrier strike groups, containing 180 ships and 1,500 aircraft; two-thirds of the Marine Corps' combat strength, including 2 Marine expeditionary forces; and 5 U.S. Army Stryker brigades. The U.S. Coast Guard has 27,000 personnel in the region.[3] Excluding expenditures on equipment or U.S. Navy fleet operations, the Department of Defense has spent $36 billion on U.S. military presence in PACOM during fiscal years 2010 and 2013.[4]

Maintaining strong alliances is imperative for the United States to respond to security and humanitarian challenges in the region. PACOM's response to the 2011 earthquake, tsunami, and nuclear meltdown in Japan demonstrated the capabilities of its interoperable military systems to react to large-scale catastrophe and crisis. Guam, as America's closest major sovereign territory to these critical allies—and to the major flashpoints that helped to catalyze the treaties with them in the first place—is central to the support of its military presence in the region.

As part of a strategic rebalancing toward Asia-Pacific, the U.S. Navy is shifting its proportion of assets in that theater from 50 to 60 percent. As part of that shift, the United States is seeking to develop Guam as a sovereign anchor of American force posture in East Asia to protect the common security of the international community. The U.S. military is developing Guam as a forward logistics hub to support a complex constellation of both allied cooperation and access rights, on one hand, and American sea basing and crew rotation, on the other. Guam is positioned to play a key supporting role in military operations across the region. It lies between Northeast Asia, where the majority of existing American basing infrastructure is located, and Southeast Asia, where the majority of new security challenges are unfolding.

As the United States' only sovereign overseas base as well as its nearest port to East Asia, South Asia, and the Middle East, Guam combines foreign proximity—with attendant savings in time, fuel, and operational budgets—with domestic reliability and flexibility. It is closer by fourteen hours' flight time and five to seven days' sea-transit time to East Asia than is any other U.S.-based facility. It offers the region's only live-fire bombing range; an excellent deepwater port with significant room for wharf expansion; ample facilities for the U.S. Air Force, including its largest aviation fuel storage depots (66 million gallons) and its largest Pacific weaponry storage (100,000 bombs); and a naval magazine capable of holding considerable amounts of conventional and nuclear munitions. Guam's population produces more military recruits per capita than any other American jurisdiction, and 80 percent of registered voters support the future homeporting of an aircraft carrier battle group. Clearly, the U.S. military can depend on Guam.[5]

Enhancing U.S. naval presence in the Pacific Rim requires more time on station without a proportionate increase in operational tempo for an already strained Pacific Fleet. Therefore, Guam will be used to decrease transit times to strategic areas of operation. Routine deployments of U.S. bombers initiated in 2004 will "thoroughly integrate bombers into [the] Pacific Command's joint and coalition exercises from a forward operating base."[6] Adm. Thomas Fargo, a previous commander of the U.S. PACOM, emphasizes that Guam is "key to our military operations across the full spectrum of our capability."[7] As a forward logistics hub, Guam can also be used in innovative ways—the island was used, for example, to screen Kurdish refugees during Operation Iraqi Freedom.[8]

Crossroads of the Pacific

Guam is set to reclaim its historical position as a strategic American naval hub in the western Pacific. Acquired following the Spanish-American War of 1898, Guam served as a coaling stop on the great circle route to the west until World War I. Undefended at the outset of World War II, Guam was invaded by Japanese forces in 1941 and recaptured only in 1944. The Guam Organic Act of 1950 established Guam as an unincorporated organized territory and its people as citizens of the United States. Guam has hosted substantial U.S. military facilities ever since.

Guam's situation is not without its problems. It is farther from all strategic areas in Northeast Asia than are Japan, Korea, Vietnam, or the Philippines. Guam is three times farther from the Taiwan Strait than Okinawa; ships cruising at twenty-five knots from Guam would take a good two and a half days to reach the strait, as opposed to one day from the Philippines. (However, by the same token, the island is slightly less vulnerable than other points to Chinese missiles, several hundred of which are positioned in Fujian Province opposite Taiwan, or, especially, to North Korean missiles, including the Taepodong 2.) The island is often affected by adverse weather, including typhoons, which sometimes disrupt operations and damage infrastructure. (Korea and Japan are equally—if not more—vulnerable in this regard.)

Situation and Advantages

Vice Adm. Al Konetzni Jr., while commander, Submarine Force Pacific (1998–2001), reversed the decline of U.S. military capability on Guam. To reduce the strain of long deployments on both personnel and submarines, Vice Admiral Konetzni reestablished Submarine Squadron 15, which had been disbanded two decades before.[9] In September 2002 his lobbying succeeded: the *Los Angeles*–class attack submarines USS *City of Corpus Christi* (SSN 705), then homeported in Portsmouth, New Hampshire, and USS *San Francisco* (SSN 711), then based in Norfolk, Virginia, left for their new home port in Guam, the sovereign American territory 1,200 nautical miles east of the Taiwan Strait—to which it is more than 6,000 miles closer than Norfolk. USS *Houston* (SSN 713) joined them in January 2004.

The overriding goal of this change was to increase the total number of mission days for each U.S. naval platform in-theater and to improve response times. Submarines operating at twenty knots would take 5 days to reach the East Asian littoral from Guam, as opposed to 15.4 days from San Diego.[10] A Guam-based Stryker brigade combat team could deploy by air or sea to key PACOM areas in between 5 and 14 days.[11]

Stationing more submarines in Guam minimizes effective utilization hours for naval nuclear reactors and other sensitive and expensive components. A major reason for Guam deployment, thereby reducing transit times, is to keep submarine reactors from burning out their cores in Pacific transits.[12] In recent congressional testimony, Adm. Vern Clark, then chief of naval operations, cited forward-basing of ships in Guam as a key factor in maximizing use of naval assets.[13]

In addition, basing ships in Guam reduces "personnel tempo," or the frequency and duration of military deployments. A larger, better-supported Navy community on Guam would encourage more personnel to bring their dependents along and to stay on the island or in the region during periods of leave. Navy officials contend that submarines based in Guam will be in the theater 88 to 123 days per year, the latter figure being three times the 36-day average of submarines based in the continental United States (CONUS).[14]

Guam is also a major global support and logistics hub. The Military Sealift Command maintains afloat stocks for PACOM forces forward deployed out of Diego Garcia and Guam/Saipan, with the latter hosting Maritime Prepositioned Stock Squadron 3. Army Prepositioning Stock 3 likewise stations unit equipment, port-opening capabilities, and sustainment stocks in Guam/Saipan.[15]

To allow for flexible deployment of critical assets, however, Guam needs infrastructure modernization to improve the condition of schools, barracks, hangars, dry docks, ports, and maintenance activities. The expense of improving Guam's deteriorating infrastructure would be offset by the resulting decreased personnel tempo, reduced deployment time, and more persistent presence. Total infrastructure improvement costs to homeport additional ships at the island would probably come to around $200 million, far below expected procurement costs for U.S.-based ships with less access to this critical operating theater.

Together with Hawaii, Guam has been under consideration as a potential alternative base for a carrier battle group and its 5,500 personnel.[16] An aircraft carrier nuclear reactor requires large and expensive maintenance infrastructure and a shore facility to store low-level nuclear waste. For that reason, forward-basing a carrier in Guam seems unlikely at present because of both the additional "human footprint" burden and the estimated $6.5 billion cost of establishing the relevant nuclear-capable facilities (vice $1 billion for Mayport, Florida).[17]

Apart from that consideration, preparation for antisubmarine warfare would not necessarily require a full battle group. Additionally, Washington could station ships capable of theater missile defense (TMD) there as a politically acceptable means of protecting American interests in the region. Ongoing U.S. troop reductions in South Korea may facilitate the long-term goal of moving U.S. assets from more vulnerable foreign bases to Guam.

The most important U.S. capabilities to allow rapid response to regional contingencies would be at-sea prepositioning and air defense. Military commanders need airlift capabilities and tankers ready and in sufficient numbers to deploy into a theater quickly from Guam. For these missions, the United States needs a secure airfield from which it cannot be denied access; political area denial could allow China to push American forces out of the region before or during a crisis. Guam has a promilitary population, and its people suffer from a nearly 8 percent unemployment rate—and those economic challenges may reduce the political difficulty of building and operating assets on the island.[18] Support for additional military presence on Guam is increasing among residents, and 80 percent of registered voters support troop increases.[19] Guam is capable of significant physical expansion in addition to its deepwater port, revitalized repair dry dock, and proximity to the region's only live-fire bombing range. U.S. aircraft carriers are capable of entering and docking at Apra Harbor without encountering bridges over harbor entrances that might elsewhere block two-hundred-foot island and mast structures. Extra pier space could be engineered if necessary.

Like the Navy, the U.S. Air Force has a potentially important role to play in Guam's future. The Air Force envisions using Guam, with three-thousand-meter runways capable of accommodating any of its planes, as a "main operating base for tactical missions into the region."[20] Robert Kaplan has argued that "Andersen Air Force Base, on Guam's northern tip, represents the future of U.S. strategy in the Pacific. It is the most potent platform anywhere in the world for the projection of American military power."[21]

A contingent of B-52s could be retained at Andersen, perhaps rotated in small groups from CONUS. In addition to operational assets, Guam needs increased support resources. Existing Air Force infrastructure and support personnel would require upgrading to sustain newer-generation bombers and strike aircraft; stealth aircraft, for instance, require special hangars. Repair and maintenance shelters could be augmented the better to service carrier strike groups, and training centers would allow personnel to remain on station longer. As early as spring 2005, twelve F-15E fighter jets were rotated to Andersen from CONUS for training.[22] B-1, B-2, and B-52 bombers are also rotating through;[23] it was noted in 2005 that "Guam-based bombers have carried out missions against targets in Iraq."[24]

Andersen has become an intelligence, surveillance, reconnaissance (ISR) and strike Air Force hub—including two tactical aviation squadrons, bomber rotations, and a Global Hawk detachment—with "critical capabilities for most operations in the PACOM AOR [area of responsibility]" including "a China-Taiwan conflict."[25] Moving assets from CONUS to Guam "permits more persistent ISR coverage, peacetime intelligence gathering/tracking and prompt strike capability."[26] By contrast, crisis deployment of CONUS-based assets "would not only require scarce airlift sorties to deploy squadron support packages but could also be viewed as provocative and complicate crisis management."[27]

Additional Assets and Infrastructure: Developments and Challenges

Guam's new role will clearly require significant infrastructure and equipment upgrades.[28] Even as deliberations proceed, Guam is already preparing for a military buildup and attendant civilian-infrastructure enhancement. During his July 2012 trip across the Asia-Pacific, Deputy Secretary of Defense Ashton Carter declared that "Guam has become an important strategic hub for the U.S military in the Western Pacific."[29]

According to the Department of Defense, "the overarching purpose . . . is to locate U.S. military forces to meet international agreement and treaty obligations and to fulfill U.S. national security policy requirements to provide mutual defense, deter aggression, and dissuade coercion in the western Pacific region. . . . Guam [offers] the flexibility and proximity to the region to ensure the USMC capabilities [are] ready and effective, while contributing to regional deterrence, assurance, and crisis response."[30] Major new assets will include U.S. Marine Corps units previously based in Okinawa, such as a Marine air-ground task force (MAGTF) and part of the III Marine Expeditionary Force, an Army air missile defense task force, and the building of a wharf for a transient nuclear-powered aircraft carrier.

The Marine relocation hinges on United States–Japan negotiations. On 27 April 2012 the United States–Japan Security Consultative Committee, together with the American secretaries of state and defense and their respective Japanese counterparts, unveiled a new plan with several important components. Roughly 9,000 Marines and their dependents, or nearly half those currently stationed in Okinawa, will be transferred to Guam (to absorb approximately 4,700 Marines, based on current planning estimates), Hawaii, and Australia.[31] Some of this may be in the form of innovative "rotational unit deployments," as opposed to formal restationing. Of the estimated $8.6 billion required to fund the move, Japan will contribute $3.1 billion in cash, in a departure from its previous types of contributions (e.g., long-term, low-interest loans). The U.S. military and Japan Self-Defense Force (JSDF) will develop shared-use joint training ranges and facilities in Guam and in the Commonwealth of the Northern Mariana Islands (CNMI)—an approach that might facilitate joint access to a greater variety of JSDF and civilian facilities, airports, and ports in Japan in the future. This is part of a larger effort to enhance multilateral training and capabilities with other nations as well. To move beyond sensitive issues that have complicated bilateral efforts in the past, the relocation of Marines and the return of land from U.S. military use at Kadena Air Force Base have been formally delinked from resolution of the future of Marine Corps Air Station Futenma. On 27 December 2013, in a move that generated immediate protest, Okinawa Prefecture's governor Hirokazu Nakaima approved relocating the Futenma facility to reclaimed land off the coast of Henoko.[32]

Already, as noted, a squadron of three nuclear-powered attack submarines (SSN) has been stationed in Guam. In the future, between three and six additional submarines may join it, including "both SSNs and soon-to-be-converted nuclear-powered cruise missile boats."[33] A high-end approach would make Guam home to roughly one-fifth of the entire U.S. submarine fleet, giving it the platforms "required to track China's emerging SSBN capability."[34] Forward-deploying SSNs in Guam represents a particularly productive approach, as a recent study explains: "Given the increased size and operational reach of attack submarines from China's People's Liberation Army (PLA) Navy, the U.S. Navy faces an imbalance in its own submarine fleet in the Asia-Pacific region. This imbalance will grow rapidly in the mid-2020s as DoD [the Department of Defense] prepares to retire U.S. nuclear attack submarines at a rate twice that of new construction for replacements."[35]

The U.S. Air Force is considering the construction of a concrete hangar facility for two B-2 bombers, in addition to two ongoing construction projects: an $85 million air refueling facility and a $12.8 million effort to refurbish housing at Andersen Air Force Base.[36] In 1999 the U.S. Navy selected the Raytheon Corporation to upgrade and maintain support facilities, awarding it a $328.4 million contract over the following seven years.[37]

Further asset additions could prove advantageous, though they come with challenges. Andersen Air Base has room for assets in addition to the four B-52s or two B-2s currently deployable there, even an entire B-52 squadron. Global Hawk unmanned aerial systems have been deployed to Guam;[38] Andersen could also accommodate more of them as well as the MC-12W Liberty aircraft.[39] Options to increase operational survivability include stationing Terminal High-Altitude Area Defense (THAAD) and PAC-3 (upgraded Patriot) missile defenses in Guam, although they would likely not provide complete protection against a Chinese attack. Hardening facilities and building an improved fuel pipeline could provide further protection.[40] Increasing runway repair capability and dispersing tanker aircraft represent lower-cost approaches. The assets of Andersen's Contingency Response Group could be augmented as well.[41] Additional port capacity is available to host more vessels, although such an expansion would result in greater congestion.

Guam faces present problems in addition to these potential ones. The island suffers from susceptibility to typhoon damage, from high construction costs (more than twice the U.S. military average), obsolete infrastructure, limitations in the scope and utilization of existing training ranges, and bureaucratic delays in completing environmental impact assessments and approvals.[42]

Although numbers may be reduced slightly by a reduction of Marines headed to Guam from the full 9,000 originally envisioned, peak population growth on Guam may reach 41,000 during construction, later leveling off to 34,000 above today's level. Additional personnel include 4,700 permanent Marines and their dependents and as many as 2,000 transient individuals using training ranges on Guam, nearby Tinian, Saipan, Farallon de Medinilla, Pagan, and possibly other CNMI islands.[43] Construction may involve 21,000 workers by 2014, with roughly 18,400 from off-island.[44]

To help support a resident population that may be 20 to 25 percent larger than it is now, water and power infrastructures are being strengthened. Guam's port has been upgraded with $100 million in grant money. While the National Defense Authorization Act requires demonstration that Guam can support this buildup properly, section 2207 of that legislation limits federal loans for infrastructure; a supplemental bill in fiscal 2011 allowed the DoD to transfer $50 million for maritime administration, to be paired with an equivalent sum from the Department of Agriculture. Military construction money from the defense budget has funded improvements to defense access roads. For the past few years, despite its precarious budgetary and debt situation, the government of Guam has floated bonds for electrical and water improvements. Through a district court judge's ruling, the federal government has mandated legal changes, such as to mandate processing, as opposed to unregulated discharge, of raw sewage. Major water and sewer improvements remain aspirational, but Guam's only dump, once an Environmental Protection Agency Superfund site, has been shut down and replaced by a new one.[45]

Guam Buildup: Operational Considerations

In remarks at the Shangri-La Security Summit in June 2012, Secretary of Defense Leon Panetta said that plans to relocate Marines from Okinawa to Guam will "further develop Guam as a strategic hub for the United States military in the Western Pacific, improving our ability to respond to a wide range of contingencies in the Asia-Pacific region."[46]

For the United States, the use of sovereign American territory and submarines will assume greater importance in coming years. Owen R. Coté Jr., observes that "it is unlikely that access to [foreign] bases will become more predictable in the future because it is unlikely that the United States will establish new military alliances as formal as those it established to prosecute the Cold War."[47] He also notes that "unlike in air warfare, the technical trends in antisubmarine warfare will likely continue to favor stealth. Thus quiet submarines, especially those that deploy in littoral waters, will retain a significant advantage over submarine hunters. Together, these trends will make it more dangerous for U.S. surface combatants, amphibious ships, and sealift vessels to close hostile coastlines early in a conflict when opposing submarines are still extant." Coté foresees "an accompanying U.S. shift toward submarines deploying both overland sensor networks and fast standoff strike weapons," in part because "U.S. submarines will be the most effective means of providing a persistent source of fast standoff weapons close to opposing targets early in a conflict."[48]

Another critical factor is Guam's proximity to key commercial ports. American forces based in Guam are closer than any other U.S. troops to the deepwater ports known as "megahubs" in Southeast Asia. Those megahubs, which can accommodate the sixty-foot draft of the largest containerships, are central to the economic interests of America and its East Asian allies. With further investment, Guam could bring to life the current doctrinal focus on sea basing and its subcomponent known as "RSOI"—reception, staging, onward movement, and integration. Sea basing "replaces or augments [previous] fixed, in-theater airports and seaports . . . with . . . a mobile base of operations, command center, logistics node and transportation hub" operating from a surface vessel.[49]

The concept of RSOI is to transport troops rapidly into a crisis theater or area of operations and unite them with their equipment. First, in-theater ships would deploy equipment at sea or in Japan, or stage the equipment in Guam. Marines would then be flown in to assume control of the equipment. Finally, "the assembled units will either move over land to the operational area or be transported by sea to the [area of operations] or selected components of the force could move by air."[50] The process of assembling combat organizations in-theater depends on further transportation developments, mainly the transport of heavy (e.g., tanks) and light (e.g., mechanized infantry) equipment. It makes sense to preposition stocks in Guam and marry these stocks with troops using the RSOI process, rather than use a costly yet less dependable prestaged maritime option. All U.S. military services already preposition equipment; it is simply preferable to consolidate and then fly troops in to meet the vessels carrying it.

Guam also supports U.S. Navy operations in the region. The Navy has a critical role to play in East Asia, given the region's extensive coastlines, islands, land barriers, and consequent susceptibility to maritime force projection. In East Asia, naval forces collectively play a preventive role that is of equal importance to their offensive function. These dual processes can be categorized as "shape" and "respond."[51] Forward presence enhances U.S. ability not only to respond to regional events but also to shape them before they occur. Ships on station are launch pads for counterterrorism operations, platforms for TMD, and barriers to the proliferation of weapons of mass destruction (WMD); they are in themselves stabilizing political forces. The Navy plays a special role in safeguarding American interests in that, unlike the basing and staging–dependent Air Force or Army, "the Navy can establish a long-term presence without infringing on anyone's borders. It can be sent at a pace that allows diplomacy to cool a crisis even as the ships proceed."[52] A further advantage of naval presence is that ships can remain indefinitely in international waters, as close as twelve miles to another nation's coastline, to conduct electronic surveillance and bathymetric surveying.

To maximize America's ability to gather information, deter hostility, and overcome aggression in East Asia, therefore, the U.S. Navy needs to arrange assets for highest availability in times of crisis. Such a strategy calls for forward presence of ships operating from bases that are not politically constrained.

Regional Developments

In the Asia-Pacific region, the United States has vital national security interests in three major developments: first, China's rising economic and military strength; second, the continued threat of terrorism; and third, North Korea's provocative posture.

China

The growing ambitions of the PRC depend on increasingly assertive naval power. As mainland China moves closer to developing blue-water naval capability, especially in relation to Taiwan's defensive capability, the U.S. Navy finds it necessary to be ready not only to respond quickly to a contingency in the Taiwan Strait but also to counterbalance Chinese regional military reach. China closely follows U.S. military deployments on its periphery and is observing with great interest, including at a tactical level, the American buildup of nuclear submarines and other assets on Guam.[53]

Beijing may increase its nuclear targeting of the island's military installations (while recognizing that actual attack would invite a devastating U.S. response). Guam's facilities will need to be protected from ballistic missiles, submarine- and air-launched cruise missiles, and even sabotage. Hardened submarine moorings provide protection but are expensive. Avoiding overconcentration of Guam's assets during crises, particularly its growing submarine force, is essential to the island's military effectiveness. America's best strategy may be to disperse assets at sea, along the lines of the Cold War model: concentration of assets leaves them vulnerable to a strike, but dispersal based on strategic warning and—in a worst case scenario—the threat of nuclear retaliation mitigates risk.

A strong U.S. presence has regional advantages. The United States–Japan alliance helps to prevent destabilizing competition in a region that is still recovering from the horrors of World War II. Also, by guaranteeing the security of East Asian sea-lanes—a public good that even China does not yet have the capability to provide—the United States facilitates the flow of energy and trade in a region that depends on both to maintain its impressive economic growth.

Tension in the Taiwan Strait deserves separate consideration because it drives American basing strategy in the near and middle terms. The transit time to the strait for a carrier strike group stationed on the West Coast is 16.3 days, a week from the Indian Ocean, and 12.2 days from Hawaii.[54] If an additional aircraft carrier were forward deployed to Yokosuka, Japan, or on station in the Pacific or in port at Guam, the transit time would be reduced to between 3 and 5 days.

America's ability to respond to a Taiwan Strait crisis is also constrained by political forces in the region. Although many American analysts believe that Taiwan could still defend itself in a military engagement against mainland China, calamitous economic damage to the island would be a virtual certainty; if the United States failed to respond early and effectively, Taipei might sue for peace.

Based on past Chinese practice, the warnings of military action against Taiwan would be ambiguous, and collecting more detailed information would require close forward monitoring and presence. That, in turn, would require more robust permanent American presence in the region. Washington would thus improve its capacity to stabilize the Taiwan Strait and surrounding area by improving its rapid-response capabilities, thereby deterring Chinese offensives in the first place. A strengthened U.S. position in Guam would also increase American leverage and be less provocative than selling additional armaments to Taiwan. A stronger American presence might even persuade Beijing to reduce the chance of naval incidents by signing a more effective military maritime agreement that specifies appropriate conduct for encounters in or near territorial waters or airspace.[55] In the longer term, the United States and China will have to reach an understanding concerning their respective roles in the region. As a step to that end, Secretary Panetta called for enhancing military-to-military contact between American and Chinese forces.[56]

Terrorism

Localized Southeast Asian terrorist organizations—Jemaah Islamiah in Indonesia, among others—have demonstrated their capacity for regional violence. These organizations have to be uncovered and pursued, particularly where they are actively collaborating with al-Qaeda or other terrorist groups with global reach. The 12 October 2002 terrorist attack that killed 168 civilians in Bali, Indonesia, awakened American observers to the danger of terror cells in Southeast Asia. As yet, terrorists based in the Philippines and Indonesia have not demonstrated truly global reach. But this does not lessen the importance to the United States of a center in the region to monitor more closely such groups as Jemaah Islamiah and Abu Sayyaf, in the southern Philippines, and to assist in the training of friendly antiterrorist forces.

The U.S. Navy has an important role to play here, from special operations to construction battalions. U.S. special operations forces are currently helping to coordinate attacks on Abu Sayyaf in the Philippines. Construction battalions can be used in strategic, joint goodwill initiatives, such as helping the Philippine air force build a small airstrip on Mindanao. Guam is well suited to host joint military exercises, including those emphasizing special operations. The island has already been used in the 1990s as the premier training ground for the 31st Marine Expeditionary Unit's Exercise TRUE (training in an urban environment). Guam has hosted three Valiant Shield joint exercises. During the May 2012 Geiger Fury exercise, nearly a thousand Air Force and Marine Corps personnel traveled from Iwakuni, Japan, to train on Guam and Tinian.[57]

North Korea

Pyongyang has revealed clandestine nuclear weapons production in spite of the 1994 Geneva Agreed Framework by which North Korea rejoined the nuclear Non-Proliferation Treaty (NPT) in exchange for American delivery of heavy fuel oil.[58] This violation further destabilized the fragile political situation in Northeast Asia. In cooperation with South Korea, Japan, and others, Washington has led diplomatic efforts to deal with the threat posed by North Korea and its nuclear weapons capability.

The most pressing threat is North Korean aggression, should détente with the South fail. The North, in a time of rising tensions, could preempt major troop deployments, threatening Seoul with artillery or Japan with missiles. The United States could be restricted in its options to base a potential response force in South Korea. Indeed, South Koreans might well oppose even a defensive American military buildup on the peninsula. North Korea also has a greater potential to inflict a "sea of fire"—unacceptable mass casualties among American troops and allied civilians—which would greatly constrain U.S. military options in such a scenario. Military buildup on Guam could help alleviate some of these problems, especially if the United States were restricted for political reasons in its use of bases on Japanese soil.

For all these reasons, Washington needs to lay the groundwork for a flexible buildup designed not to support a bombing campaign or even an "Osirak style" operation (i.e., one modeled on Israel's 1981 preemptive attack on Iraq's developing nuclear facility) but rather to support proliferation containment. Targeted sanctions, for example, could involve diplomatic agreements or even a naval quarantine to prevent Pyongyang from exporting missiles (in violation of the Missile Technology Control Regime), nuclear material (in violation of the NPT), or related military technologies. Building up Guam as a home port for maritime-interdiction ships could greatly strengthen these promising initiatives.

A large conventional conflict on the Korean Peninsula is a high-cost, low-probability prospect. For decades, the need for the United States to respond to a full-scale invasion kept a permanent land force near the demilitarized zone. But the Pentagon is now backing away from this "tripwire" approach, since U.S. forces stationed within range of North Korean artillery undermine the American threat of preemptive strike. Moreover, the more likely contingency of heightened tensions—as opposed to immediate, full-scale war—suggests the need for a rapid-response force. Here, as in much of East Asia, the bulk of American influence lies not on land but at sea.

Regional Threats to Guam and Asia-Pacific Bases

Guam itself faces a number of threats, including the risk of terrorist or missile attack. The risk of terrorist attacks against fixed bases has grown worldwide. That danger already applies to many existing land bases, particularly in the Middle East, for which—despite efforts to improve at-sea basing—there is no substitute.[59] Moreover, permanent land bases are important military tools during a conflict, and perhaps even more so for their political value.

Bases are also vulnerable to the growing danger of missile attack, a factor of special relevance in East Asia. Some analysts have cited a growing PRC missile threat as a reason *not* to establish new bases anywhere in East Asia. They argue that China's CSS-3 (DF-4) missiles were designed to destroy facilities on Guam with a nuclear payload, and they point out that China is continuing to develop a wide range of nuclear and conventional ballistic missiles. Submarine-launched cruise missiles—with their potential for small radar cross sections, low-altitude flight, continually adjustable trajectories, and potential avoidance of global positioning system constraints through reliance on terrestrial imaging—could emerge as particularly lethal threats.

Irrespective "of the degree and nature of American military superiority," Beijing might become "impossible to deter" in the event of a Taiwan declaration of independence.[60] In such a desperate situation, Beijing might view surprise attacks on U.S. forces in Okinawa or Guam as a credible means of disrupting and even restraining American operations.

China has made a concerted effort to acquire offensive capabilities that could be used against U.S. bases. But by this logic, American bases in Japan and Korea are even more vulnerable. Yet despite growing missile threats from North Korea and even China, Japan continues to value U.S. bases as key elements of its own defense. South Korean public opinion may be more easily manipulated by a North Korean aggressor, but U.S. forces are moving out of range of North Korean artillery, and Pyongyang's missiles are insufficiently accurate to avoid risk to Korean civilians in South Korea if targeted against American bases there. For both operational and political reasons, South Korean bases would not likely play a major role in a Taiwan crisis and hence would not be a target of PRC missile coercion. As will be explained further, U.S. bases in Japan are more relevant to a Taiwan conflict, and hence a more likely target of PRC pressure, making it imperative that the United States not rely on unrestricted access to them in such a scenario.

As for Guam, while its target value would rise with infrastructure and asset improvement, Beijing knows that attacking a U.S. base—especially on sovereign territory such as Guam—would invite a devastating American response. As one analyst points out, "Presidents would not encounter major domestic opposition in reacting to aggression against U.S. forces or civilians at home. The question is not whether, but what form the response would take."[61]

Several measures for reducing U.S. base vulnerabilities are particularly relevant to Guam, including dispersion and the use of missile defenses. Dispersion could entail a periodic rotation of such assets as nuclear submarines to sea, away from Guam, thereby exploiting the island's potential as a useful hub while preventing a "Pearl Harbor"–style surprise scenario. At-sea dispersion might be augmented with specific access arrangements with nearby islands, such as Palau, to be used in time of crisis. While American ballistic-missile-defense architecture may not be able to neutralize fully a PRC missile attack, it could at least introduce uncertainty and thereby alter Beijing's calculus. There are even cross-cutting factors, such as the potential for increased defensibility of concentrated assets under a TMD system: "Against a high level missile threat, concentration of assets at a few highly defended regional bases, such as Guam, may be a more survivable posture than dispersing capabilities to a larger number of bases."[62] SM-3 ships stationed in Guam could serve as both localized deterrents and, collectively, as prepositioned regional protection.

American "base structure is not merely a derivative of strategy," the Overseas Basing Commission has counseled; "it is a driver in its own right."[63] As the Military Facility Structure Report has acknowledged, while emerging threats are not fully predictable and may be addressed from out of area, they must be at least roughly anticipated in order to inform properly the architecture of the new U.S. global basing footprint.[64]

Guam: A Strategic Hub

The United States must diversify its presence in the Asia-Pacific region by enhancing a chain of overlapping bases and access rights. A first step in that effort would be to move resources to Guam in order to establish a presence for strike and deterrence not wholly dependent on outside support. The United States must thus increase its capability to use existing access points and bases. One vehicle for such independent presence, though by no means a panacea, is the strategically located island of Guam.

Current basing arrangements and operating patterns in the Pacific Fleet seem to reflect excessive optimism about getting "more from less." Such arrangements strain U.S.-based naval assets, slow response time to the region, and rely too heavily on access rights that could evaporate during a crisis. These problems are hardly unique to East Asia; forces everywhere are stretched thin. But it would be a mistake to underestimate the growing need for increased presence in-theater or to keep asking for more from a burdened Pacific Fleet. American policy makers rightly conceptualize U.S. force posture in East Asia as a chain of overlapping bases and access rights. Fortunately, American planners have already committed themselves to reducing long-term dependence on these foreign bases through a significant expansion of Guam's facilities.

Aside from cosmetic and structural improvements on Guam, the United States needs to expand its portfolio of military assets in East Asia. U.S. force posture should reflect a capability not only to respond without delay to the Korean Peninsula, the Taiwan Strait, and critical sea-lanes in Southeast Asia but also to check the scourge of terrorism and the proliferation of WMD. These distinct but related tasks require a layered military strategy. In the event of a crisis on the Korean Peninsula, for instance, such a strategy would involve the use of bases in Korea as the front line, bases in Japan as the ready reserve, and a base in Guam as the deep reserve.

The United States needs a reliable center of operations—including supply, repair, logistics, and training—to "walk onstage" prepared to act. Deteriorating port facilities and infrastructure in Guam need to be transformed into the furnishings of an ample and well-appointed "dressing room backstage." The recent homeporting of three *Los Angeles*–class attack submarines on the island is a good first step. Increasing power projection into this vital region, however, will require that the U.S. Navy continue to "move west," shifting operational and support assets from San Diego and Pearl Harbor closer to their main area of operations.

There are no new islands or new access points to be discovered in East Asia;[65] the U.S. capability to use existing access points and bases must be increased. Building up the American presence on Guam is the single most important step that can be taken to effect this crucial transition. To maximize its ability to deter hostility, gather information, and overcome aggression, the U.S. Navy should continue to develop Guam as a forward logistics hub. A diversified and expanded American military presence on Guam will offer maximum flexibility in times of crisis and help ensure that future scenarios—such as the rise of a belligerent China, a change in Japanese foreign policy, or a reunification of the Koreas—do not create "missing links" in the chain of U.S. capabilities. Moving assets westward across the Pacific and maintaining a flexible and growing constellation of facilities and access rights in East Asia would keep that chain strong—and even the most determined enemies would not be able to dislodge its anchor, Guam.

Clearly, the United States' national interests call for maintaining a strong East Asian presence. Both current conditions and emerging long-term trends underscore the importance of building up Guam as a sovereign forward logistics hub to ensure American regional influence. But this significant strategic move merits careful consideration because it has already triggered significant scrutiny by other regional powers such as China. As much as one-fifth of the U.S. submarine fleet could conceivably be stationed at Guam. What would this mean for the fleet? What level of forces on Guam would represent an overconcentration of assets? How defensible is Guam from surprise attack? How easy, for instance, would it be for the PRC to launch a surprise attack with cruise missiles? Could Chinese submarines hide to the west of Guam? Will the United States station P-3s in Guam to protect submarines? Given their responsibility to prepare for worst-case contingencies, American defense planners must address these challenging questions.

Guam's status as a strategic military hub is promising, but the prospect brings a wide range of challenges that could threaten the island's development and the U.S. military rebalancing to the Asia-Pacific region. That rebalancing, in turn, is a cornerstone of the U.S. strategy to sustain military strength across a region vital to America's future interests.

China, challenged strategically by U.S. military buildup in Guam, is preparing "counterintervention" capabilities to hold at risk both the island and military platforms based there in the event of conflict. These capabilities reportedly include a four-thousand-kilometer-range ballistic missile that may be "ready for service" by 2015 and able to strike Guam from land-based mobile launchers.[66] Meanwhile, near Guam, China is pursuing exploration of the Marianas Trench for minerals, scientific research, prestige, and possibly information collection, to include monitoring of underwater communications cables. On 15 June 2012 its *Jiaolong* submersible reached a depth of six kilometers, and there are plans to reach seven kilometers.[67]

Efforts are under way to disperse military facilities (for example, to nearby CNMI islands), reduce some of Guam's vulnerabilities, and increase the number of stakeholders in key decisions.[68] However, Guam's buildup is complicated by decision making in Japan and by local sensitivities in Okinawa. Additionally, dispersal of MAGTFs previously based in Okinawa not only to Guam but also to Hawaii and Australia introduces a more complex equation.

There is currently a risk that Congress may not appropriate funding for Guam's military buildup because of significant budget challenges, specific concerns about actual versus estimated costs, and beliefs that insufficient information has been made available (for example, concerning actual costs of construction of training ranges).[69] One way to break the logjam, as the Center for Strategic and International Studies recommends, is to use limited military construction funding to upgrade roads and other infrastructure that will be required regardless of how many Marines arrive or when.[70] American personnel and infrastructure plans involving Guam must weigh the island's strategic value against its political and military challenges—and must find ways to maximize the strategic role of the island known as "Destiny's Landfall."[71]

Notes

1. For detailed analysis of Guam's past, present, and future role in supporting U.S. military presence, see Andrew S. Erickson and Justin Mikolay, "A Place and a Base: Guam and the American Presence in East Asia," in *Reposturing the Force: U.S. Overseas Presence in the Twenty-First Century,* ed. Carnes Lord, Newport Paper 26 (Newport, R.I.: Naval War College Press, 2006), 65–93, http://www.usnwc .edu/Publications/Naval-War-College-Press/Newport-Papers/Documents/26-pdf.aspx; Andrew S. Erickson and Justin D. Mikolay, "Anchoring America's Asian Assets: Why Washington Must Strengthen Guam," *Comparative Strategy* 24, no. 2 (April–June 2005), 153–71, doi:10.1080/01495933590952324.

2. Paul H. B. Godwin, "China's Defense Establishment: The Hard Lessons of Incomplete Modernization," in *The Lessons of History: The Chinese People's Liberation Army at 75,* ed. Laurie Burkitt, Andrew Scobell, and Larry M. Wortzel, 15–58 (Carlisle, Pa.: Strategic Studies Institute, U.S. Army War College, 2002), 35.

3. "USPACOM Facts," *United States Pacific Command*, www.pacom.mil/about-uspacom/facts.shtml.
4. David J. Berteau, Michael J. Green, Gregory Kiley, and Nicholas Szechenyi, *U.S. Force Posture Strategy in the Asia Pacific Region: An Independent Assessment* (Washington, D.C.: Center for Strategic and International Studies, 15 August 2012), 49, available at http://csis.org/publication/pacom-force-posture-review.
5. Information for this paragraph was largely derived from *Guam & the CNMI* [Commonwealth of the Northern Mariana Islands]: *Projecting Sea Power 21*, jointly prepared by the Guam and Saipan Chambers of Commerce, August 2003, available at www.guamchamber.com.gu/.
6. U.S. Pacific Command Public Affairs Office, "PACOM Announces Bomber Deployment to Guam," 2 February 2004, www.pacom.mil/.
7. Quoted in Steve Limtiaco, "Admiral: Guam Key to Strategy," *Pacific Daily News* (Guam), 21 July 2004, available at www.guampdn.com/.
8. "Services Praise Successes; Set Priorities" (U.S. Navy Posture Statement, U.S. Senate Armed Services Committee testimony, 25 February 1997), *Defense Issues* 12, no. 26, http://www.defense.gov/speeches/speech.aspx?speechid=633.
9. "Rear Adm. Konetzni: Changing a Subculture from Inside Out," *Hawaii Navy News*, 20 April 2001, www.hnn.navy.mil/Archives/ 010420/konetzni_042001 .htm.
10. *Report to the President and the U.S. Congress* (Arlington, Va.: Commission on Review of Overseas Military Facility Structure of the United States, May 2005), http://www.fas.org/irp/agency/dod/obc.pdf [hereafter Military Facility Structure Report], J5.
11. Ibid., L4.
12. Nuclear submarines have to be recored every fifteen to twenty years, and now the Navy faces a costly decision concerning whether to recore some boats for the second time.
13. U.S. Senate, *Resource Implications of the Navy's Interim Report on Shipbuilding: Statement of Admiral Vern Clark before the Senate Armed Services Committee, February 10, 2005* (Washington, D.C.: Congressional Budget Office, April 25, 2005), http://www.cbo.gov/sites/default/files/cbofiles/ftpdocs/63xx/doc6305/04-25-greggletter.pdf.
14. See *Chairman of the Joint Chiefs of Staff Submarine Study* (Washington, D.C.: November 1999). Also, see U.S. General Accounting Office, *Force Structure: Options for Enhancing the Navy's Attack Submarine Force*, Report GAO-02–97 (Washington, D.C.: November 2001); and U.S. Congressional Budget Office, *Increasing the Mission Capability of the Attack Submarine Force* (Washington, D.C.: March 2002), table 6, p. 11, 33.
15. Berteau et al., *U.S. Force Posture Strategy*, 60.
16. "U.S. Carrier Still in Balance for Hawaii, Guam," *Pacific Daily News*, 1 June 2005, available at www.guampdn.com/.
17. Berteau et al., *U.S. Force Posture Strategy*, 75.
18. Concerning Guam's unemployment, see "U.S. Carrier Still in Balance for Hawaii, Guam."
19. Ibid.

20. Justin Bernier and Stuart Gold, "China's Closing Window of Opportunity," *Naval War College Review* 56, no. 3 (Summer 2003): 10.
21. Kaplan, "How We Would Fight China," *The Atlantic*, 1 June 2005, http://www.theatlantic.com/magazine/archive/2005/06/how-we-would-fight-china/303959.
22. Natalie J. Quinata, "Fighter Squadron Arrives on Guam: 12 Jets to Conduct Training Missions to Familiarize with Asia-Pacific Region," *Pacific Daily News*, 30 April 2005, available at www.guampdn.com/.
23. William Cole, "Air Force Shifts Unit to Bolster Response," *Honolulu Advertiser*, 23 March 2005.
24. Military Facility Structure Report, J4.
25. Ibid., J3.
26. Ibid., J4.
27. Ibid.
28. Praveen Swami, "U.S. to Build £8bn Super Base on Pacific Island of Guam," *Telegraph* (U.K.), 26 October 2010.
29. Karen Parrish, "Carter Arrives in Guam to Meet with Leaders—7/19," *American Forces Press Service*, July 19, 2012. Available on the Department of Defense Web site, http://www.defense.gov/news/newsarticle.aspx?id=117177.
30. "About the Project," U.S. Department of the Navy Web site, "Guam and CNMI Military Relocation—(2012 Roadmap Adjustments) Environmental Impact Statement," http://www.guambuildupeis.us/about/about-the-project.
31. Notably, Secretary of Defense Leon Panetta has written, "I disagree with CSIS's suggestion that the Department could consider moving fewer than approximately 5,000 Marines to Guam. Moving fewer than this number would undermine our plan to establish multiple, fully capable Marine Air-Ground Task Forces across the Asia-Pacific region." Letter to the Honorable Carl Levin, Chairman, Committee on Armed Services, United States Senate, "Comments from the Secretary of Defense on *U.S. Force Posture Strategy in the Asia Pacific Region: An Independent Assessment*, Center for Strategic and International Studies," 24 July 2012, https://www.google.com/url?sa=t&rct=j&q=&esrc=s&source=web&cd=1&ved=0CC4QFjAA&url=http%3A%2F%2Fwww.levin.senate.gov%2Fdownload%2F%3Fid%3D362f5324-bc5f-4d36-8ef5-31f1eaee9a46&ei=wVl4UoaIOoWgsQT49oDgBg&usg=AFQjCNG3j2kUfWPq8RbhRo26SAbB3N_5bA&sig2=0owCVq4CzPZB5YKPn2LCvw&bvm=bv.55819444,d.cWc.
32. Berteau et al., *U.S. Force Posture Strategy*, 24, 64–65; "Okinawa Governor Approves Plan to Reclaim Henoko for U.S. Base Transfer," *Asahi Shimbun*, 27 December 2013, http://ajw.asahi.com/article/behind_news/AJ201312270050.
33. Andrew Koch, "US Basing Plans Shape Up for Speed and Flexibility," *Jane's Defence Weekly*, 16 June 2004.
34. Military Facility Structure Report, J5.
35. Berteau et al., *U.S. Force Posture Strategy*, 21.
36. Gaynor Dumot-ol Daleno, "Bombers May Be Based at Andersen," *Pacific Daily News*, 27 September 2003, available at www.guampdn.com/.
37. "U.S. Navy and Raytheon Sign $328.4 million Guam Base Operations Support Contract," Media News Release, 10 January 2000, available at www.prnewswire.com/.

38. Thomas G. Mahnken, with Dan Blumenthal, Thomas Donnelly, Michael Mazza, Gary L. Schmitt, and Andrew Shearer, *Asia in the Balance: Transforming U.S. Military Strategy in Asia* (Washington, D.C.: American Enterprise Institute, 4 June 2012), 20, http://www.aei.org/files/2012/05/31/-asia-in-the-balance-transforming-us-military-strategy-in-asia_134736206767.pdf.

39. Berteau et al., *U.S. Force Posture Strategy*, 75.

40. Ibid., 78.

41. Ibid., 94.

42. Ibid., 56.

43. Ibid., 8.

44. "About the Project."

45. For further details, see Department of the Navy and Department of the Army, *Record of Decision for Guam and CNMI Military Relocation including Relocating Marines from Okinawa Transient Nuclear Aircraft Carrier Berth Air and Missile Defense Task Force* (Washington, D.C.: September 2010), http://www.guambuildupeis.us/documents/record_of_decision/Guam_Record_Of_Decision_FINAL.pdf; and Naval Facilities Engineering Command (NAVFAC), *Final Mitigation Monitoring and Tracking Program Plan for Guam and CNMI Military Relocation Program* (Pearl Harbor, Hawaii: June 2011), http://www.guambuildupeis.us/documents/record_of_decision/Final_Program_Mitigation_Monitoring_and_Tracking_Plan_15Jun2011.pdf.

46. Secretary of Defense Leon E. Panetta, "Shangri-La Security Dialog," 2 June 2012, http://www.defense.gov/speeches/speech.aspx?speechid=1681.

47. Owen R. Coté Jr., "The Look of the Battlefield," *Aviation Week & Space Technology*, 15 December 2003, 72.

48. Ibid., 73.

49. Military Facility Structure Report, J20.

50. Ibid., J21.

51. See Edward Rhodes, Jonathan Di Cicco, Sarah Milburn Moore, and Tom Walker, "Forward Presence and Engagement: Historical Insights into the P Problem of 'Shaping,'" *Naval War College Review* 53, no. 1 (Winter 2000): 25–61.

52. Philip Shenon, "Gunboat Diplomacy, '96 Model," *New York Times*, 17 March 1996, http://www.nytimes.com/1996/03/17/weekinreview/the-world-gunboat-diplomacy-96-model.html.

53. See, for example, "美国重兵屯关岛" [U.S. Stations Massive Forces on Guam], 人民日报 [People's Daily], 19 February 2001, available at www.xinhuanet.com.cn/; and 黄明君 [Huang Mingjun], "关岛将成美霸权的筹码" [Guam Is Becoming America's Hegemonic Bargaining Chip], 军事展望 [Military Prospect], June 2002, 58–59.

54. Military Facility Structure Report, J5.

55. See Andrew Erickson, "Why America and China Need a New Military Maritime Agreement," National Committee on U.S.-China Relations *Notes from the National Committee* 31, no. 1 (Spring/Summer 2002), http://www.ncuscr.org/files/AE_honmenam2002.doc.

56. Leon E. Panetta, U.S. Naval Academy commencement address, 29 May 2012, http://www.defense.gov/speeches/speech.aspx?speechid=1679.

57. Berteau et al., *U.S. Force Posture Strategy*, 55.

58. Scott Snyder, *Negotiating on the Edge: North Korean Negotiating Behavior* (Washington, D.C.: U.S. Institute of Peace Press, 1998), 117. See also Jonathan D. Pollack, "The United States, North Korea, and the End of the Agreed Framework," *Naval War College Review* 56, no. 3 (Summer 2003): 11–49.

59. The USS *Cole* tragedy is reason for caution and careful planning but not for rejecting the idea of bases outright.

60. Thomas J. Christensen, "Posing Problems without Catching Up," *International Security* 25, no. 4 (Spring 2001): 34.

61. Joel Wuthnow, *The Impact of Missile Threats on the Reliability of U.S. Overseas Bases: A Framework for Analysis* (Carlisle, Pa.: U.S. Army War College Strategic Studies Institute, January 2005), 35, http://www.strategicstudiesinstitute.army.mil/pdffiles/PUB594.pdf.

62. Military Facility Structure Report, J4.

63. Ibid., 6.

64. Ibid., J11.

65. It might someday be possible to acquire rights to a small island or to create a man-made structure that would be the functional equivalent.

66. Song Shengxia, Zhang Han, and Huang Jingjing, "New Missile 'Ready by 2015': Global Times," *People's Daily Online*, 18 February 2011, http://english.people.com.cn/90001/90776/90786/7292006.html.

67. "Submersible Sets New China Dive Record," Agence France-Presse, 15 June 2012, http://www.defencetalk.com/submersible-sets-new-china-dive-record-43191/.

68. Berteau et al., *U.S. Force Posture Strategy*, 19.

69. Ibid., 9.

70. Ibid., 92.

71. Robert F. Rogers, *Destiny's Landfall: A History of Guam* (Honolulu: University of Hawaii Press, 1995).

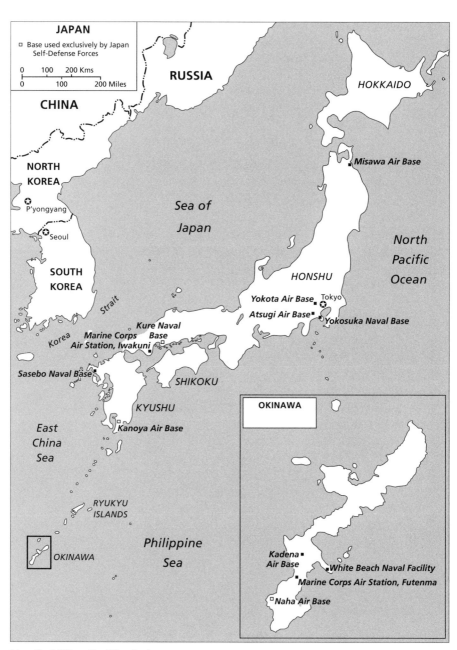

RUSSIA

CHINA

HOKKAIDO

NORTH
KOREA

◉ P'yongyang

◉ Seoul

SOUTH
KOREA

Sea of

Japan

North
Pacific
Ocean

■ Misawa Air Base

HONSHU

Yokota Air Base ■ ● Tokyo

Atsugi Air Base ■

● Yokosuka Naval Base

Strait

Kure Naval   Base

Korea

Marine Corps   Base
Air Station, Iwakuni

Sasebo Naval Base ■

SHIKOKU

KYUSHU

Kanoya Air Base

East
China
Sea

OKINAWA

Kadena ■
Air Base

■ White Beach Naval Facility

Marine Corps Air Station, Futenma
■

◻ Naha Air Base

RYUKYU
ISLANDS

OKINAWA

Philippine

Sea

Map 2. Military Facilities in Japan

2

Japanese Bases and Chinese Missiles

Toshi Yoshihara

In recent years defense analysts in the United States have substantially revised their estimates of China's missile prowess. A decade ago most observers rated Beijing's ballistic missiles as inaccurate, blunt weapons limited to terrorizing civilian populations. Today the emerging consensus within the U.S. strategic community is that China's arsenal can inflict lethal harm with precision on a wide range of military targets, including ports and airfields. As a consequence, many observers have jettisoned previously sanguine net assessments that conferred decisive, qualitative advantages to Taiwan in the cross-strait military balance. Indeed, the debates on China's coercive power and Taiwan's apparent inability to resist such pressure have taken on a palpably fatalistic tone.

A 2009 Rand monograph warns that China's large, modern missile and air forces are likely to pose a virtually insurmountable challenge to Taiwanese and American efforts to command the air over the strait and the island. The authors of the report believe that massive ballistic-missile salvos launched against Taiwan's air bases would severely hamper Taipei's ability to generate enough fighter sorties to contest air superiority. They state: "As China's ability to deliver accurate fire across the strait grows, it is becoming increasingly difficult and soon may be impossible for the United States and Taiwan to protect the island's military and civilian infrastructures from serious damage."[1] As a result, the authors observe, "China's ability to suppress Taiwan and local U.S. air bases with ballistic and cruise missiles seriously threatens the defense's ability to maintain control of the air over the strait."[2] They further assert, "The United States can no longer be confident of winning the battle for the air in the air. This represents a dramatic change from the first five-plus decades of the China-Taiwan confrontation."[3]

An unclassified Defense Intelligence Agency report assessing the state of Taiwan's air defenses raises similar concerns. The study notes that Taiwanese fighter aircraft would be unable to take to the air in the absence of well-protected airfield runways, which suggests a major vulnerability to the island's airpower. The agency further maintains that Taiwan's capacity to endure missile attacks on runways and to repair them rapidly will determine the integrity of the island's air-defense system.[4] While the report withholds judgment on whether Taipei can maintain air superiority following Chinese missile strikes in a conflict scenario, a key constituent of the U.S. intelligence community clearly recognizes a growing danger to Taiwan's defense.

China's missiles also threaten Taiwan's ability to defend itself at sea. William Murray contends that China could sink or severely damage many of Taiwan's warships docked at naval piers with salvos of ballistic missiles. He argues that "the Second Artillery's [China's strategic missile command's] expanding inventory of increasingly accurate SRBMs probably allows Beijing to incapacitate much of Taiwan's navy and to ground or destroy large portions of the air force in a surprise missile assault and follow-on barrages."[5] These are stark, sobering conclusions.

Combined with China's increasingly sophisticated aerospace capabilities, the potential effectiveness and lethality of the missile force of the People's Liberation Army (PLA) could extend well beyond Taiwan. Forecasting China's emergence as an Asia-wide challenge, Mark Stokes and Ian Eaton assert, "Largely driven by a Taiwan scenario, China's capacity to conduct a successful aerospace campaign for decisive air advantage is surpassing the defenses fielded by Taiwan, Japan, perhaps India, and even U.S. forces operating in the Western Pacific. . . . Over time, an expansion of its theater missile infrastructure, conventional airpower, and sensor systems could give China a decisive edge in securing the skies around its periphery should territorial disputes erupt into conflict."[6]

Indeed, there is growing evidence that China has turned its attention to Japan, home to some of the largest naval and air bases in the world. Beijing has long worried about Tokyo's potential role in a cross-strait conflagration. In particular, Chinese analysts chafe at the apparent American freedom to use the Japanese archipelago as a springboard to intervene in a Taiwan contingency. In the past China kept silent on what the PLA would do in response to Japanese logistical support of U.S. military operations. Recent PLA publications, in contrast, suggest that the logic of missile coercion against Taiwan could be readily applied to U.S. forward presence in Japan. The writings convey a high degree of confidence that China's missile forces could compel Tokyo to limit American use of naval bases while selectively destroying key facilities on those bases. These doctrinal developments demand close attention from Washington and Tokyo, lest the transpacific alliance be caught flat-footed in a future crisis with Beijing. This chapter is a first step toward better understanding how the Chinese evaluate the efficacy of missile coercion against American military targets in Japan.

This chapter focuses narrowly on Chinese assessments of U.S. naval bases in Japan. It excludes the literature on such other key locations as the Kadena and Misawa air bases in recognition of the extant U.S. analysis on post–Cold War air-base vulnerabilities to missile attacks.[7] By contrast, Western writings on the potential threat of long-range precision-strike systems against naval bases are rather sparse. This study adds analytical value by exploiting the abundant, but largely untapped, Chinese open-source literature on naval affairs. This maritime perspective demands attention not least because the dispatch of two carrier battle groups to Taiwan's vicinity during the 1996 cross-strait crisis stimulated Beijing's reevaluation of its military strategy toward the island. Not surprisingly, the Chinese are obsessed with the U.S. aircraft carrier, including the facilities and bases that support its operations. It is against this rich milieu that this study explores how the Chinese conceive their missile strategy to complicate American use of military bases along the Japanese archipelago, as depicted in map 2.

This chapter first revisits the enduring value of U.S. bases in Japan to both Washington and Tokyo. It then explores the reasons behind Beijing's interest in regional bases and surveys the Chinese literature on the U.S. naval presence in Japan to illustrate the amount of attention being devoted to the structure of American military power in Asia. Chinese analysts see U.S. dependence on a few locations for power projection as a major vulnerability. Second, it turns to Chinese doctrinal publications, which furnish astonishing details as to how the PLA might employ ballistic missiles to complicate or deny U.S. use of Japanese port facilities. Chinese defense planners place substantial faith in the coercive value of missile tactics. Third, the chapter assesses China's conventional theater ballistic missiles that would be employed against U.S. regional bases. Fourth, it critiques the Chinese writings, highlighting some faulty assumptions about the anticipated effects of missile coercion. Finally, the study identifies some key operational dilemmas that the U.S.-Japanese alliance would likely encounter in a PLA missile campaign.

Why U.S. Bases in Japan Matter

After enjoying sixty years of stable basing arrangements with Japan, it is easy for policy makers and planners to take for granted the enduring value of U.S. military facilities on the Japanese islands. Indeed, until recently, the assumption that the United States will enjoy indefinitely unfettered use of forward bases—a condition essential for American grand strategy and global primacy—was widely accepted as an article of faith. However, as China directs its gaze at U.S. bases in Japan, understanding the potential consequences of disrupted or even denied access to those bases has gained policy urgency.

Japanese bases are nothing short of essential to U.S. strategy in Asia. That has been the consensus among American strategic elites for decades. Indeed, various analysts and officials have unstintingly praised Japan as "the indispensable linchpin of our forward military and diplomatic presence in Asia and the foundation of a stable strategic equilibrium in the region," "the cornerstone of peace and stability in the region," and "a platform for U.S. military readiness in Asia."[8] These evocative depictions bespeak Tokyo's importance to the United States. According to a study by the Center for a New American Security, "In Asia, the [U.S.-Japanese] alliance constitutes an unrivaled platform for maintaining the United States as a 'resident power.' Because Japan hosts American bases, Washington can quickly deploy military assets throughout the region, as epitomized by the dispatch of U.S. ships to Indonesia following the 2004 tsunami. Moreover, bases in Japan enhance America's capacity to respond to sudden change on the Korean Peninsula and any contingency in the Taiwan Strait."[9]

Japan's proximity to potential flashpoints in Asia enhances allied deterrence while maximizing early warning, rapid crisis response, and wartime mobilization, should deterrence fail. Without Japan, the United States would lose a critical, irreplaceable foothold from which to radiate combat power along the East Asian littoral. At the same time, allied interoperability benefits enormously from regular interactions, training, and exercises that a substantial U.S. military presence affords. In the eyes of some American strategists, potential adversaries must take into account the emergence of a "joint command relationship" that increasingly characterizes the maturing U.S.-Japan alliance, dissuading adventurism and aggression. To them, "this deterrent effect would not be possible without forward deployed U.S. forces in Japan."[10] Presence, upon which allied cohesion rests, ultimately shores up deterrence.

Beyond these traditional security functions, U.S. forward presence provides intangible, though no less important, politico-psychological benefits to Japan. Japan confronts daunting challenges that have magnified its fears of marginalization in the region. Following decades of economic stagnation and relative decline, Tokyo has become increasingly unsure of itself and of its place in Asia. China's surge past Japan in 2010 as the second-largest economy in the world threw into sharp relief Tokyo's sluggish economic performance. The massive national reconstruction effort following the March 2011 earthquake, tsunami, and nuclear disaster added another onerous financial burden on an economy struggling to contain its public debt, which exceeds 200 percent of gross domestic product.

To compound this economic predicament, Japan's rapidly aging society is pushing the nation toward an unprecedented demographic crisis that could have dire implications for its defense posture. Some forecasts estimate that Japan's population may shrink to 90 million by midcentury from its peak of 127 million in 2005, representing an astounding 30 percent decrease.[11] Population decline inevitably reduces the pool of manpower available for military service. The cost of fielding troops for combat will rise correspondingly. In the coming years, maintaining satisfactory levels of recruitment and retention will likely tax Tokyo's resources. All of these socioeconomic pressures have increased temptations to turn inward even as Japan's external security environment grows more uncertain and contentious.

While North Korea's nuclear weapons deeply worry Tokyo, the rise of China and the unremitting Chinese military buildup pose collectively the most serious strategic challenge to Japan. Territorial disputes over the Senkaku/Diaoyu Islands, competing claims over exclusive economic zones in the East China Sea, and increased Chinese naval activism near the Ryukyu Islands have further heightened anxiety about Beijing's intentions. Repeated Chinese violations of Japanese airspace and territorial waters have already compelled the Japan Self-Defense Force (JSDF) to shore up its military position near the southwestern offshore islands.[12] One Japanese strategist evocatively describes such Chinese probing as "opportunistic creeping expansion," a strategy that continually seeks to exploit cracks and vulnerabilities in Japan's defensive posture.[13] China's retaliatory embargo on rare earths following the arrest of a Chinese captain who had rammed his fishing boat into a Japanese coast guard vessel near the Senkakus in September 2010 proved to be a rude awakening for Tokyo.

A stable maritime order, including free access to the seas, is vital to Japan's economic well-being and even survival. The intensely nautical nature of Sino-Japanese tensions is thus especially unsettling for a nation as dependent on seaborne transportation as Japan is. Beijing's undeclared economic sanctions against Tokyo and the sudden, though relatively short-term, downturn in manufacturing after the 11 March 2011 triple disaster further underscored Japan's acute vulnerabilities to supply-chain disruptions.

To complicate matters further, local opposition to U.S. military presence in Japan has bedeviled the alliance for decades. The contentious debate over bases in Okinawa, a political battleground throughout the history of the security partnership, has proven by far the most intractable. Given that Okinawa constitutes less than 1 percent of Japan's total landmass and yet hosts about 75 percent of military facilities used exclusively by U.S. forces, it is widely acknowledged that the island carries a disproportionate share of the burden.[14] Two major disputes— centered on the relocation of the Marine Corps Air Station Futenma, a facility situated in the heart of a dense urban area, and on the transfer of U.S. Marines from Okinawa to Guam—have been constant irritants for the alliance. As mentioned in chapter 1, in December 2013 the governor of Okinawa Prefecture made an initial decision to facilitate Futenma's relocation to landfill off the coast, but tremendous opposition remains. In both controversies the political imperatives to remove the intrusive presence of U.S. forces on Japanese soil run directly counter to strategic concerns that an American withdrawal of any kind might undermine the alliance's deterrent posture. It is against these worrying and often contradictory strategic trends that U.S. presence in Japan reassures an increasingly jittery

Tokyo as much as it deters regional threats. The U.S. bases are thus a symbol of American security commitments to Japan and a barometer of Japanese confidence in Washington's credibility.

The value of U.S. bases can also be measured in concrete operational terms. The Japanese archipelago hosts an unmatched share of U.S. forces in the Asia-Pacific region. Japan is home to roughly 50,000 American military personnel (about 38,000 ashore and 11,000 afloat), over eighty facilities under exclusive American control, a carrier strike group, the Fifth Air Force, and the III Marine Expeditionary Force.[15] Notably, Kadena Air Force Base in Okinawa is the largest of its kind overseas, Yokosuka Naval Base supports the U.S. Navy's only permanently forward-deployed aircraft carrier, and III Marine Expeditionary Force is the only division-sized fighting unit based outside of the United States. Given this array of combat power assembled in Japan, a U.S. think-tank report asserts, "Current U.S. force presence in Japan and particularly on Okinawa is strategically well placed to respond to any potential contingency in Northeast Asia."[16] Less well known, the United Nations Command in Japan, often derided as a relic of the Korean War, remains in place to manage surges in reinforcements and to lend legitimacy to U.S. military action should conflict break out again on the Korean Peninsula.[17]

Measured by monetary value, the United States' investment in Japan's basing infrastructure is unrivaled. The replacement value of U.S. bases in Japan exceeds $45 billion, constituting nearly a third of the total value of all overseas facilities. Of the twenty-one large overseas bases with replacement values of over $1.7 billion, Japan plays host to eight, and four of the eight are worth at least double the minimum cost of replacing a large site. In descending order, Kadena Air Base, Yokosuka Naval Base, Misawa Air Base, and Yokota Air Base are priced at $5.8 billion, $4.8 billion, $4 billion, and $3.9 billion, respectively. Only Ramstein Air Base in Germany, worth $3.7 billion, rivals these figures. As a percentage of the total value of overseas real estate, 35 percent of the U.S. Air Force, 46 percent of the Navy, and more than 99 percent of the Marine Corps are located in Japan.[18] Such concentrations of high-value military power attest to the importance of Japan as a hub for force projection.

In light of the strategic value, the operational dividends, intangible benefits, and sunk costs of U.S. bases in Japan, China's turn to U.S. regional bases should come as no surprise. Beijing's ability to put at risk U.S. use of facilities and forward-deployed assets could unhinge U.S. strategy in Asia, which rests on unimpeded access to a network of regional air and naval bases. Understanding how Chinese planners perceive the importance of U.S. regional bases and how they assess the efficacy of anti-access measures against those bases is thus an analytical task of considerable policy import.

Explaining China's Interest in Regional Bases

Taiwan remains the animating force behind China's strategic calculus with respect to regional bases in Asia. Beijing's inability to respond to the display of U.S. naval power at the height of the 1996 Taiwan Strait crisis proved highly embarrassing. There is evidence that the PLA had difficulty monitoring the movement of the two carrier battle groups, much less in offering its civilian leaders credible military options in response to the carrier presence. This galling experience steeled Beijing's resolve to preclude U.S. naval deployments near Taiwan in a future crisis. Notably, the Yokosuka-based USS *Independence* (CV 62) was the first carrier to arrive at the scene in March 1996, cementing Chinese expectations that Washington would dispatch a carrier from Japan in a contingency over Taiwan.

Beyond Taiwan, other territorial disputes along China's nautical periphery could involve U.S. naval intervention. A military crisis arising from conflicting Sino-Japanese claims over the Senkaku/Diaoyu Islands northeast of Taiwan could compel an American reaction. While doubts linger in some Japanese policy circles whether foreign aggression against the islands would trigger Washington's defense commitments as stipulated by the U.S.-Japanese security treaty, joint allied exercises and war games since 2004 suggest that the U.S. military is closely watching events in the East China Sea. Farther south, Chinese territorial claims over large swathes of the South China Sea could also be sources of regional tensions. If a local tussle there escalated into a larger conflagration that threatened international shipping, the U.S. Navy might be ordered to maintain freedom of navigation. In both scenarios, the U.S. carrier based in Japan and other strike groups operating near Asian waters would be called upon as first responders.

Concrete territorial disputes that have roiled Asian stability are not the only reasons that American naval power would sortie from regional bases to the detriment of Chinese interests. More abstract and esoteric dynamics may be at work. For example, Chinese leaders fret about the so-called Malacca dilemma. China's heavy dependence on seaborne energy supplies that transit the Malacca Strait has set off Chinese speculation that the United States might seek to blockade that maritime chokepoint to coerce Beijing.[19] This insecurity stems less from judgments about the possibility or feasibility of such a naval blockade than from the belief that a great power like China should not entrust its energy security to the fickle goodwill of the United States. As Ye Hailin, a researcher at the prestigious Chinese Academy of Social Sciences, bluntly asserts, "No matter how much China desires a harmonious world and harmonious oceans, it cannot possibly rely on other countries' naval forces to safeguard the safety of its SLOCs [sea lines of communication]. A big country that builds its prosperity on foreign trade cannot put the safety of its ocean fleet in the hands of other countries. Doing so would be the equivalent of placing its throat under another's dagger and marking its blood vessels in red ink."[20]

In Ye's view, U.S. naval power is a double-edged sword. While the U.S. fleet has been essential to Beijing's free access to and use of the seas, underwriting the nation's prosperity, it could just as easily be employed to strangle China's economy. If the U.S. Navy were ever called upon to fulfill an undertaking of such magnitude, forward basing in Asia would undoubtedly play a pivotal role in sustaining what could deteriorate into a protracted blockade operation.

Chinese analysts have also expressed a broader dissatisfaction with the United States' self-appointed role as the guardian of the seas. Sea-power advocates have vigorously pushed for a more expansive view of China's prerogatives along the maritime periphery of the mainland. They bristle at the U.S. Navy's apparent presumption of the right to command any parcel of the ocean on earth outside coastal states' territorial waters, including areas that China considers its own nautical preserves. Some take issue with the 2007 U.S. maritime strategy, a policy document that baldly states, "We will be able to impose local sea control wherever necessary, ideally in concert with friends and allies, but by ourselves if we must."[21] Lu Rude, a former professor at Dalian Naval Academy, cites this passage as evidence of U.S. "hegemonic thinking." He concludes, "Clearly, what is behind 'cooperation' is America's interests, having 'partners or the participation of allies' likewise serves America's global interests."[22] Some Chinese, then, object to the very purpose of U.S. sea power in Asia, which relies on a constellation of regional bases for its effects to be felt.

Long-standing regional flash points and domestic expectations of a more assertive China as it goes to sea suggest that Beijing's grudging acceptance of U.S. forward presence could be eroding even more quickly than once thought. Against this backdrop of increasing Chinese ambivalence toward American naval power, U.S. basing arrangements in Japan have come into sharper focus.

Chinese Views of U.S. Naval Bases in Japan

Chinese analysts have carefully studied the extent to which U.S. global strategy rests on uninterrupted access to overseas bases. Indeed, they are well acquainted with the centrality of foreign naval bases to seagoing forces, especially those forces that must operate far from the homeland for extended periods of time. In a comprehensive survey of strategic deployment, Senior Colonel Ou Yangwei underscores the nexus between expeditionary naval power and shore support: "Maritime power, whether it is a surface combatant or a submarine operating at sea and undersea respectively, must still depend on shore bases and island bases. As such, the various bases of a navy constitute the basic form and system of maritime power deployment." This interdependence extends to carrier operations. Colonel Ou argues, "The duration of maritime mobile deployments is a function of the endurance and survivability of the carrier strike group and the replenishment fleet. Endurance and survivability in turn are inseparable from fixed naval bases. Shore bases will always be the foundation upon which maritime power rests."[23]

Chinese strategists recognize that rear-area support from shore bases is indispensable to sustained combat operations of a modern carrier strike group. Senior Captain Li Jie, an analyst at the Naval Military Studies Research Institute, catalogues the enormous logistical needs of a carrier and its accompanying fleet.[24] A flotilla consumes massive quantities of fuel, food, ammunition, and spare parts while placing nearly continuous demands on maintenance and repair facilities. In an in-depth analysis of carrier operations, Senior Colonel Liu Yonghui of the Navy Arms Command College estimates that during high-intensity combat operations, naval aviation units require resupply of munitions every seven days while the carrier and other surface combatants need to be rearmed every five days. The replenishment fleet must shuttle between the carrier strike group and a network of bases that store these supplies to sustain continuous cruises at sea. Structural repairs and the replacement of military components, such as aircraft engines, require the direct support of major bases.[25] The Chinese clearly appreciate the dynamic and complex interaction between frontline formations and the shore-based infrastructure that supports their operations. It is this keen awareness that has informed Chinese thinking about U.S. naval bases in Japan.

Some Chinese strategists appraise Washington's military posture in the Asia-Pacific region in stark geopolitical terms. Applying the "defense perimeter of the Pacific" logic elaborated by Secretary of State Dean Acheson in the early Cold War, they see their nation enclosed by concentric, layered "island chains." The United States and its allies, they argue, can encircle China or blockade the Chinese mainland from island strongholds, where powerful naval expeditionary forces are based. Analysts who take such a view conceive of the island chains in various ways.

Yu Yang and Qi Xiaodong, for example, describe U.S. basing architecture in Asia as a "three line configuration [三线配置]."[26] The first line stretches in a sweeping arc from Japan and South Korea to Diego Garcia in the Indian Ocean, forming a "zone of forward bases [前沿基地带]." This broad notion that the U.S. presence in the western Pacific and the Indian Ocean constitutes a seamless, interlocking set of bases is widely shared in Chinese strategic circles.[27] The second line connects Guam and Australia. The last line of bases runs north from Hawaii through Midway to the Aleutians, terminating at Alaska. While these island chains may bear little resemblance to actual U.S. thinking and planning, that the Chinese pay such attention to the geographic structure of American power in Asia is quite notable. These observers discern a cluster of mutually supporting bases, ports, and access points along these island chains. Among the networks of bases in the western Pacific, those located on the Japanese archipelago—the northern anchor of the first island chain—stand out, for the Chinese. *Modern Navy*, a monthly journal published by the Political Department of the PLA Navy, produced a seven-part series on Japan's Maritime Self-Defense Forces in 2004 and 2005. Notably, it devoted an entire article on Japan's main naval bases, including Yokosuka, Sasebo, Kure, and Maizuru.[28] The depth of the coverage of these bases is rather remarkable, especially when compared to the sparse reporting on similar topics in the United States and in Japan.

Perhaps no other place captures the Chinese imagination as much as Yokosuka, which analysts portray as the centerpiece of U.S. basing in Asia.[29] One analyst depicts a "Northeast Asian base group [东北亚基地群]" radiating outward from Yokosuka to Sasebo, Pusan, and Chinhae.[30] Writers provide a wide range of details about the Yokosuka naval base, including its precise location, the surrounding geography, the number of piers (particularly those suitable for aircraft carriers), the types and number of maintenance facilities, and the storage capacity of munitions, fuel, and other supply depots.[31] Wu Jian, for instance, finds the geographic features of Yokosuka comparable to Dalian, a major base of the Chinese navy's North Sea Fleet.[32]

Beyond physical similarities, Yokosuka evokes unpleasant memories for the Chinese. One commentator recalls the U.S. transfer of 203-mm heavy artillery from Yokosuka to Nationalist forces on Jinmen during the 1958 Taiwan Strait crisis.[33] Tracking more recent events, another observer notes that the *Kitty Hawk* Strike Group's deployments from Yokosuka to waters near Taiwan invariably coincided with the presidential elections on the island, in 2000, 2004, and 2008.[34] As Pei Huai opines, "Yokosuka has all along irritated the nerves of the Chinese people."[35] Moreover, Chinese analysts are keenly aware of Yokosuka's strategic position. Du Chaoping asserts: "Yokosuka is the U.S. Navy's main strategic point of concentration and deployment in the Far East and is the ideal American stronghold for employing maritime forces in the Western Pacific and the Indian Ocean regions. A carrier deployed there is akin to the sharpest dagger sheathed in the Western Pacific by the U.S. Navy. It can control the East Asian mainland to the west and it can enter the Indian Ocean to the southwest to secure Malacca, Hormuz, and other important thoroughfares."[36] Ma Haiyang concurs: "The Yokosuka base controls the three straits of Soya, Tsugaru, Tsushima and the sea and air transit routes in the Indian Ocean. As the key link in the 'island chain,' it can support ground operations on the Korean Peninsula and naval operations in the Western Pacific. It can support combat in the Middle East and Persian Gulf regions while monitoring and controlling the wide sea areas of the Indian Ocean. Its strategic position is extremely important."[37] It is notable that both Du and Ma conceive of Yokosuka as a central hub that tightly links the Pacific and Indian oceans into an integrated theater of operations.

Intriguingly, some Chinese commentators view Yokosuka as the front line of the U.S.-Japanese defense cooperation on missile defense. They worry that Aegis-equipped destroyers armed with ballistic-missile-defense (BMD) systems based in Yokosuka could erode China's nuclear deterrent. Indeed, analysts see concentrations of sea-based BMD capabilities falling roughly along the three island chains described earlier. Ren Dexin describes Yokosuka as the first line of defense against ballistic missiles, while Pearl Harbor and San Diego provide additional layers.[38] Yokosuka is evocatively portrayed as the "forward battlefield position [前沿阵地]," the indispensable vanguard for the sea-based BMD architecture.[39] For some Chinese, these concentric rings or picket lines of sea power appear tailored specifically to bring down ballistic missiles fired across the Pacific from locations as diverse as the Korean Peninsula, mainland China, India, or even Iran.[40] Specifically, Aegis ships in Yokosuka, Pearl Harbor, and San Diego would be positioned to shoot down missiles in their boost, midcourse, and terminal phases, respectively.[41]

Chinese observers pay special attention to Aegis deployments along the first island chain. Some believe that Aegis ships operating in the Yellow, East, and South China seas would be able to monitor the launch of any long-range ballistic missile deployed in China's interior and perhaps to intercept the vehicle in its boost phase. Dai Yanli warns, "Clearly, if Aegis systems are successfully deployed around China's periphery, then there is the possibility that China's ballistic missiles would be destroyed over their launch points."[42] Ji Yanli, of the Beijing Aerospace Long March Scientific and Technical Information Institute, concurs: "If such [sea-based BMD] systems begin deployment in areas such as Japan or Taiwan, the effectiveness of China's strategic power and theater ballistic-missile capabilities would weaken tremendously, severely threatening national security."[43] Somewhat problematically, the authors seemingly assume that Beijing would risk its strategic forces by deploying them closer to shore, and they forecast a far more capable Aegis fleet than is technically possible in the near term.

The indispensability of the ship-repair and maintenance facilities at Yokosuka emerges as another common theme in the Chinese literature. Analysts in China often note that Yokosuka is the only base west of Hawaii that possesses the wherewithal to handle major carrier repairs. Some have concluded that Yokosuka is irreplaceable as long as alternative sites for a large repair station remain unavailable. Li Daguang, a professor at China's National Defense University and a frequent commentator on naval affairs, casts doubt on Guam as a potential candidate, observing that the island lacks the basic infrastructure and economies of scale to service carriers.[44] China's *Jianchuan Zhishi* (Naval and Merchant Ships) published a translated article from a Japanese military journal, *Gunji Kenkyu* (Japan Military Review), to illustrate the physical limits of Guam as a permanent home port for carriers.[45]

Chinese analysts also closely examine Sasebo, the second-largest naval base in Japan. Various commentators call attention to its strategic position near key sea-lanes and its proximity to China.[46] As Yu Fan notes, "This base is a large-scale naval base closest to our country. Positioned at the intersection of the Yellow Sea, the East China Sea, and the Sea of Japan, it guards the southern mouth of the Korea Strait. This has very important implications for controlling the nexus of the Yellow Sea, the East China Sea, and the Sea of Japan and for blockading the Korea Strait."[47]

It is clear, then, that Chinese strategists recognize the importance of U.S. naval bases in Japan for fulfilling a range of regional and extraregional responsibilities. Indeed, some believe that the American strategic position in Asia hinges entirely on ready military access to bases on the Japanese islands. Tian Wu argues that without bases in Japan, U.S. forces would have to fall back to Guam or Hawaii. Tian bluntly asserts: "If the U.S. military was ever forced to withdraw from Okinawa and Japan, then it would be compelled to retreat thousands of kilometers to set up defenses on the second island chain. Not only would it lose tremendous strategic defensive depth, but it would also lose the advantageous conditions for conducting littoral operations along the East Asian mainland while losing an important strategic relay station to support operations in the Indian Ocean and the Middle East through the South China Sea."[48]

This emerging discourse offers several clues about Beijing's calculus regarding U.S. naval basing arrangements in Japan. Chinese strategists see these bases as collectively representing both a threat to Chinese interests and a critical vulnerability for the United States. Bases in Japan are the most likely locations from which the United States would sortie sea power in response to a contingency over Taiwan. At the same time, the Chinese are acutely aware of the apparent American dependence on a few bases to project power. Should access to and use of these bases be denied for political or military reasons, they infer, Washington's regional strategy could quickly unravel. While the commentaries documented here are by no means authoritative in the official sense, they are clearly designed to underscore the strategic value and the precariousness of U.S. forward presence in Japan.

U.S. Bases in Japan and Chinese Missile Strategy

Authoritative PLA documents correlate with this emerging consensus that U.S. bases on the Japanese home islands merit close attention in strategic and operational terms. Indeed, Chinese doctrinal writings clearly indicate that the American presence in Japan would likely be the subject of attack if the United States were to intervene in a cross-strait conflict. The unprecedented public availability of primary sources in China in recent years has opened a window onto Chinese strategic thought, revealing a genuinely competitive intellectual environment that has substantially advanced Chinese debates on military affairs. This growing literature has also improved the West's understanding of the PLA.

In an effort to maximize this new openness in China, this chapter draws upon publications closely affiliated with the PLA, including the prestigious Academy of Military Science and the National Defense University, that address coercive campaigns against regional bases in Asia.[49] Some are widely cited among Western military analysts as authoritative works that reflect current PLA thinking. Some likely enjoy official sanction as doctrinal guidance or educational material for senior military commanders. The authors of the studies are high-ranking PLA officers who are either leading thinkers in strategic affairs and military operations or boast substantial operational and command experience. These works, then, collectively provide a sound basis for examining how regional bases in Asia might fit into Chinese war planning.

Among this literature, *The Science of Military Strategy* stands out in Western strategic circles as an authoritative PLA publication. The authors, Peng Guangqian and Yao Youzhi, advocate an indirect approach to fighting and prevailing against a superior adversary in "future local wars under high-technology conditions."[50] To win, the PLA must seek to avoid or bypass the powerful fielded forces of the enemy while attacking directly the vulnerable rear echelons and command structures that support frontline units. Using the human body as an evocative metaphor for the adversary, Peng and Yao argue, "As compared with dismembering the enemy's body step by step, destroying his brain and central nerve system is more meaningful for speeding up the course of the war."[51] To them, the brain and the central nervous system of a war machine are those principal directing and coordinating elements without which the fighting forces wither or collapse.

The aim, then, is to conduct offensive operations against the primary sources of the enemy's military power, what the authors term the "operational system." They declare, "After launching the war, we should try our best to fight against the enemy as far away as possible, to lead the war to enemy's operational base, even to his source of war, and to actively strike all the effective strength forming the enemy's war system."[52] In their view, operational systems that manage command and control and logistics (satellites, bases, etc.), are the primary targets; they relegate tactical platforms that deliver firepower (warships, fighters, etc.) to a secondary status. To illustrate the effects of striking the source of the enemy's fighting power, Peng and Yao further argue: "To shake the stability of the enemy's war system so as to paralyze his war capabilities has already become the core of the contest between the two sides in the modern high-tech local war. So, more attention should be paid to striking crushing blows against the enemy's structure of the operational system . . . especially those vulnerable points which are not easy to be replaced or revived, so as to make the enemy's operational system seriously unbalanced and lose initiative in uncontrollable disorder."[53] The authors are remarkably candid about what constitutes the enemy's operational system. Particularly relevant to this study is their assertion that the supply system emerges as a primary target: "The future operational center of gravity should not be placed on the direct confrontation with the enemy's assault systems. We should persist in taking the information system and support system as the targets of first choice throughout. . . . In regard to the supply system, we should try our best to strike the enemy on the ground, cut the material flow of his efficacy sources so as to achieve the effect of taking away the firewood from the caldron."[54]

Destruction of the supply system in effect asphyxiates the adversary. In order to choke off the enemy's capacity to wage war, Peng and Yao contend, a "large part of the supply systems must be destroyed."[55] Their prescriptions for winning local high-tech wars suggest that the horizontal escalation of a conflict to U.S. regional bases in Asia is entirely thinkable. Even more troubling, some Chinese appear to envision the application of substantial firepower to pummel the U.S. forward presence. While *The Science of Military Strategy* should not be treated as official strategic guidance to the PLA, its conceptions of future conflict with a technologically superior adversary provide a useful framework for thinking about what a Chinese missile campaign against regional bases might entail.

There is substantial evidence in Chinese doctrinal writings that PLA defense planners anticipate the possibility of a sizable geographic expansion of the target set, to include U.S. forward presence in East Asia. Although the documents do not explicitly refer to naval bases in Japan, they depict scenarios strongly suggesting that Yokosuka could be a major target. In the hypothetical contingencies posited in these writings, U.S. intervention is a critical premise, if not a given. In an important PLA study on joint campaigns involving "firepower strikes," the authors foresee external intervention by a "powerful enemy"—code for the United States—that would impact Chinese military operations. They contend: "In future joint firepower strike campaigns, the military intervention by the powerful enemy power is inevitable. The powerful enemy's main military intervention actions include: assisting the enemy's contest against us for information dominance, air superiority, and sea control; attacking our important coastal and strategic in-depth targets; assaulting our firepower forces, etc. The powerful enemy's military intervention greatly influences our joint firepower strike campaigns, severely complicates and adds to the difficulty of joint firepower strike campaigns, and increases the difficulty of joint firepower strike campaigns."[56]

In particular, Chinese planners expect Washington to order the deployment of carrier strike groups near China's coast, a prospect that deeply vexes Beijing. It is in this context of a highly stressful (though by no means inconceivable) scenario that U.S. military bases come into play in Chinese operational thinking.

For PLA planners, the primary aims are to deter, disrupt, or disable the employment of carriers at the point of origin—namely, the bases from which carriers would sortie. Given the limited capability, range, and survivability of China's air and sea power, most studies foresee the extensive use of long-range conventional ballistic missiles to achieve key operational objectives against U.S. forward presence. In *Intimidation Warfare*, Zhao Xijun proposes several novel missile tactics that could be employed to deter the use of naval bases in times of crisis or war.[57] Zhao proposes demonstration shots into sea areas near the enemy state to compel the opponent to back down. Zhao explains, "Close-in (near border) intimidation strikes involve firing ballistic missiles near enemy vessels or enemy states (or in areas and sea areas of enemy-occupied islands). It is a method designed to induce the enemy to feel that it would suffer an unbearable setback if it stubbornly pursues an objective, and thus abandons certain actions."[58]

One tactic that Zhao calls a "pincer, close-in intimidation strike" is particularly relevant to missile options against U.S. military bases. Zhao elaborates: "Pincer close-in intimidation strikes entail the firing of ballistic missiles into the sea areas (or land areas) near at least two important targets on enemy-occupied islands (or in enemy states). This enveloping attack, striking the enemy's head and tail such that the enemy's attention is pulled in both directions, would generate tremendous psychological shock."[59] Zhao also proposes an "island overflight attack" as a variation of the pincer strike. He states: "For high-intensity intimidation against an entrenched enemy on an island, an island over-flight attack employs conventional ballistic missiles with longer range and superior penetration capabilities to pass over the enemy's important cities and other strategic targets to induce the enemy to sense psychologically that a calamity will descend from the sky. This method could produce unexpected effects."[60]

While these missile tactics are primarily aimed at coercing Taiwan, they could in theory be applied to any major island or archipelago. Reminiscent of the 1996 cross-strait crisis, the PLA could splash single or multiple ballistic missiles into waters near Yokosuka (shot across Honshu Island, over major metropolitan cities) in the hopes that an intimidated leadership in Tokyo would stay out of a contingency over Taiwan, deny American access to military facilities, or restrict U.S. use of naval bases in Japan.

Should deterrence through intimidation fail, the Chinese may seek to complicate U.S. naval operations originating from bases located in the Japanese home islands. The authors of *The Science of Joint Campaign Command* believe that countries aligned with the United States could join actively in an anti-China coalition, significantly widening the scope of a Sino-U.S. confrontation. They state, "Allies of the powerful enemy along China's periphery could provide military bases; some countries that have territorial and maritime rights disputes with us could take advantage of the opportunity to make unreasonable demands or perhaps provoke an incident, trapping us in a disadvantageous position of confronting two lines of operations."[61] Japan certainly fits the description of a regional power that not only could furnish bases to U.S. military forces but could also escalate tension with China over the Senkaku/Diaoyu Islands and the exclusive economic zone in the East China Sea.

The Science of Second Artillery Campaigns, the most authoritative work on the PLA's strategic rocket forces, furnishes astonishingly vivid details on the conditions under which China might seek to conduct conventional missile operations against outside intervention.[62] Notably, the document explores "firepower harassment" as a potentially effective tactic to resist external interference. Given its explicit references to the U.S. use of military bases on foreign soil, a passage on harassment strikes is worth quoting in its entirety:

> When the powerful enemy uses allied military bases in our periphery and aircraft carriers as aircraft launch platforms to implement various forms of military intervention; and when the powerful enemy's allied military bases around our periphery are beyond our air arm's firing range, and when the carrier battle groups are far away from our shores, thus making it difficult to carry out the overall operational advantages associated with firepower coordination among the armed services and service arms, conventional missiles can be used to implement harassment strikes against the military bases of the enemy's allies around our periphery as well as the carrier battle groups.[63]

In other words, PLA planners intend to assign long-range strike missions to the ballistic-missile force if warships, bombers, and submarines prove unable to reach enemy bases. Since U.S. bases in South Korea are well within reach of China's short-range ballistic missiles, shore-based aircraft, surface combatants, and undersea fleet, the "allied military bases" to which the study refers can only be those located in Japan. For the authors, harassment strikes might involve periodic missile launches into "no go" zones erected near the naval bases in order to "block the points of entry and exit to important enemy ports," or they might entail direct attacks against "key targets within the enemy ports, such as fueling and fuel loading facilities, and logistical supply facilities."[64] Such operations would be intended to disrupt seriously the resupply and movement of U.S. naval forces.

Beyond selective attacks, some Chinese analysts advocate highly destructive operations against U.S. military bases. In a study on the PLA's blockade operations against Taiwan, Chinese defense planners entertain the possibility of significant vertical and horizontal escalation to defeat U.S. intervention. The authors call for "opportune counterattacks" to defeat a carrier strike group engaged in combat operations against Chinese targets at sea, in the air, or on the mainland coast. In such a scenario, the PLA would do everything it could successively to weaken, isolate, and ultimately sink the carrier. In addition to lethal strikes against aircraft carriers, the authors envision concerted efforts to inflict massive damage on the military bases supporting carrier operations. According to Zhu Aihua and Sun Longhai, "To punish the external enemy and to accommodate world opinion, it is not enough to sink the external enemy's aircraft carrier. . . . It is necessary to destroy the springboard of combat operations, to pulverize the operational bases, to cut off the enemy's retreat . . . in order to render obsolete hegemonism and power politics."[65]

It is clear, then, that Chinese strategists have systematically examined the strategies, doctrines, and operational concepts for dissuading, disrupting, and denying the use of U.S. military bases along China's periphery. These studies suggest that the PLA is prepared to calibrate the scale and magnitude of its military exertions against American forward bases across a spectrum that includes deterrence, compellence, and high-intensity conflict. It is equally evident that an extension of missile operations to the Japanese homeland is well within the bounds of Chinese planning. Should circumstances warrant, the PLA may not hesitate to escalate a crisis or conflict radically with missile salvos directed at Japan in order to demonstrate political resolve, preclude Japanese involvement, or unhinge U.S. intervention.

Critical Analysis of Chinese Missile Doctrine

There are compelling reasons for the Chinese to consider vertical and horizontal escalation in coercive campaigns against regional bases in Asia. At the same time, the PLA's missile force appears poised to extend its reach far beyond China's immediate periphery. Notably, the PLA's conventional theater-strike system, the DF-21, can hit all military facilities along the entire Japanese archipelago. Between 2005 and 2012, according to the Pentagon's annual report on the PLA, DF-21 airframes grew nearly fourfold while the number of DF-21 launchers more than doubled.[66] The alignment of Chinese aspirations and capabilities will complicate crisis management and stability, escalation control, and war termination in the event of conflict. The gaps in Chinese doctrinal writings offer reasons to worry about these complications.

First, Chinese analysts seldom consider the mechanisms or chain of events that link the use of precision fire with the intended operational effects the PLA hopes to achieve. Most discussions assume or assert with certitude that the employment of certain missile tactics would induce a predictable set of American responses. But closer examination suggests that strategists may have underrated the ability of U.S. naval forces to sustain operations under severe duress, thus oversimplifying the action/reaction dynamic. For example, the wholesale destruction of fuel depots and logistical facilities would not likely have a direct or immediate impact on a carrier strike group either en route to or actively operating in a combat zone. The U.S. Navy could surge additional carriers into the theater of operations and rush at-sea-replenishment vessels from Guam, Hawaii, and San Diego to the scene. Such work-arounds would cushion a devastating blow against logistical facilities in Japan, enabling U.S. operations to continue unimpeded. Indeed, many frontline units would not feel the effects of infrastructure damage in Yokosuka or Sasebo for many weeks. In this scenario, China would likely have to settle in for a more protracted struggle. This potential outcome runs directly counter to the PLA's long-standing preference for quick, decisive victories at the operational level of war.

Second, doctrinal publications exhort PLA commanders to maintain an offensive spirit and to seize the initiative in the opening stages of a military campaign. Indeed, Chinese analysts insist that China should make the first move in any conflict. A crushing initial blow would throw the enemy off balance, enabling the PLA to dictate the tempo of the war. The *Science of the Second Artillery Campaigns* asserts:

> To "strike the enemy at the first opportunity" mainly refers to the need for the Second Artillery conventional missile force to act before the enemy, take the enemy by surprise, and attack the enemy when it is unprepared during its operational activities. It should be used first during the initial phase or at a certain stage of the campaign. . . . Therefore, in terms of campaign planning, it is necessary to launch an attack before the enemy, strike first, and maintain the offensive intensity until the victorious conclusion of the campaign.[67]

More troubling, Chinese strategists foresee the preemptive use of conventional ballistic missiles against the enemy's rear areas:

> Using its advantages of concealment and surprise, active and intelligent response, and powerful penetration capability the missile force implements preemptive strike(s) against the enemy's important in-depth targets. . . . Therefore, speedily striking the enemy, striving to seize the initiative, and avoiding losses are issues with which the campaign commander must first be concerned. It is necessary to strike the enemy at the first opportunity, before the enemy has discovered our campaign intentions and actions, surprise the enemy, act before the enemy, strike rapidly, catch the enemy by surprise.[68]

Given these operational parameters, the Chinese might conduct a bolt-from-the-blue missile strike against vulnerable carriers and warships anchored and at pierside to knock out the U.S. Navy.[69] An attack on a fleet in port would be akin to strikes against fixed targets. The impact—in terms of vessels sunk or damaged—would be direct, immediate, and relatively easy to measure. The Imperial Japanese Navy's surprise attacks against the Russian fleet at Port Arthur and the U.S. Pacific Fleet at Pearl Harbor illustrate the logic of such a bold move.

From a strictly operational perspective, preemption is highly efficacious. At the same time, Chinese planners acknowledge the need to balance tactical advantages against the potential international backlash arising from foreign perceptions that China had launched an unprovoked attack. PLA writings are acutely attuned to such moral and reputational considerations. Yet they offer no concrete guidance as to how to reconcile the emphasis on striking first with the broader strategic factors that would likely hold back policy makers in Beijing, the final arbiters of the weighty decision to order a surprise attack. This tension between operational expediency and political imperatives is left unresolved. A policy/strategy mismatch looms.

It is entirely conceivable that even at the height of a major crisis Chinese decision makers might recoil from the missile options presented to them. They could very well reject preemption out of hand as overly incendiary and politically counterproductive. A precedent in Sino-U.S. Cold War history is illustrative. During the 1958 Taiwan Strait crisis, American civilian leaders rejected the military's planned nuclear riposte to Chinese provocations on the grounds that massive retaliation was out of proportion to the confrontation at hand. President Dwight Eisenhower firmly declined to consider recommendations by the Pacific Air Force to order tactical nuclear strikes against Chinese troops massed near Xiamen.[70] Whether PLA commanders are sufficiently attuned to national policy to anticipate similar civilian pushback or to appreciate the political rationales for restraint is unclear.

Third, escalation control will be a severe challenge for Beijing.[71] Chinese writings exhibit an awareness of escalation problems associated with missile coercion. Analysts worry that misapplication of missile tactics could dramatically reshape the dynamics of the war, provoking greater exertions by the intervening power while widening the conflict and drawing in additional third parties. Capturing such volatility in war, *The Science of Joint Campaign Command* observes, "Especially under circumstances when a powerful enemy's military has intervened—and because the method, the scale, and intensity of the powerful enemy's intervention are highly uncertain—the potential for unexpected events on the battlefield increases significantly, making the battlefield situation ever more mutable."[72]

As Zhao Xijun warns, "In conducting close-in intimidation strikes, one must maintain a certain distance from the enemy's border (sea area) line and select highly accurate missiles to prevent them from falling into enemy territory (or enemy-occupied islands) or directly hitting the enemy's aircraft carrier owing to imprecision or loss of flight control."[73] Zhao acknowledges that accidents or miscalculations that cross the bounds of intimidation could transform the nature of the conflict, to China's detriment. Suffering direct harm could harden an enemy's resolve substantially, immunizing him against subsequent attempts at intimidation. Concurring, *The Science of Second Artillery Campaigns* cautions, "Commanders should cautiously make decisions, choose the appropriate opportunities, select high-precision missiles for precision strikes against key targets, and prevent missile firepower from deviating from the targets and giving others the excuse to permit the third country's participation in the military intervention."[74]

The Science of Joint Campaign Command is even more explicit about concerns over collateral damage. The authors counsel, "We must strictly discriminate between military targets and civilian targets as well as between armed forces and civilians. When we have no choice but to strike military targets near civilian targets, we should use highly precise or specialized high-technology weapons and munitions, avoiding to the extent possible harm to civilian targets and reducing associated casualties."[75] An errant ballistic missile destined for the Yokosuka naval base could very well plummet into densely populated civilian areas surrounding the base or a major city along its flight path. It is conceivable that an aggrieved Japan would punish China by refusing to limit (or even agreeing to expand) U.S. access to military bases on the home islands. Indeed, continued Japanese acquiescence to American use of military facilities might be enough to foil China's strategy.

But Beijing faces even more daunting challenges than the writings let on. Chinese defense planners seem to assume that the Japanese leadership and the public would make a clear, objective distinction between targeted attacks against strictly military installations and wanton strikes against civilian population centers. Missile launches against Yokosuka would be an act of foreign aggression against the homeland unprecedented since the Second World War. It is hard to imagine the Japanese quibbling about the nature and intent of Chinese missile strikes under such circumstances; the strident Japanese response to North Korea's Taepodong missile launch over the home islands in 1998 is instructive. In other words, the escalatory pressures are far stronger than the Chinese writings assume. Intimidation warfare will be neither clean nor straightforward. Indeed, it could unleash the forces of passion intrinsic to any war far beyond China's control.

More broadly, PLA planners seem excessively confident that certain missile tactics would accurately telegraph Beijing's intentions. They assume that the precise application of firepower could send clear, discrete signals to the adversary in times of crisis or war. A small dose of well-placed missiles, they seem to believe, might persuade the enemy to back down or to cease and desist. This line of reasoning in part explains the counterintuitive logic that China could engage in escalation in order to compel its opponent to de-escalate. The logic is as beguiling as it is potentially misleading. Missiles are not finely tuned weapons for those on the receiving end. The adversary may perceive what is intended as a warning shot or demonstration of resolve as a prelude to an all-out attack and then overreact rather than pausing or acting with caution. The result for the Chinese could be unanticipated vertical or horizontal escalation, or both.

Equally worrisome, operational interactions between Chinese and American forces could prove highly escalatory and destabilizing. As a team of RAND researchers astutely observe, the operational doctrines on both sides share a proclivity for seizing the initiative at the outset of a conflict through surprise, speed, and attacks against enemy rear echelons. They further argue: "Neither body of doctrine appears to consider how an adversary might react to such operations in a limited war—indeed, each seems to assume that it will suppress enemy escalation by dominating the conflict. Consequently a Sino-American confrontation would entail risks of inadvertent escalation if military forces were permitted to operate in keeping with their doctrinal tenets without regard for escalation thresholds."[76] It is clear, then, that an attack against regional bases is neither a trump card nor a substantially risk-free option. If plans go awry, as they always do in war, China could find itself in a protracted conflict against more than one implacable, well-resourced enemy as intent as the Chinese upon achieving escalation dominance. Whether Beijing would find the stakes over Taiwan or another dispute sufficiently high to run such a risk is unclear.

Disturbingly, however, Chinese writings suggest that some segments of the PLA are inclined to accept the repercussions of a coercive campaign against U.S. bases in Japan. What explains this cavalier attitude about escalation? It is possible to infer that these writings may be symptomatic of a broad underdevelopment in coercion and deterrence theory. Chinese strategic theoreticians may still be grappling with the power and options that long-range conventional missiles confer on China. Beijing's analytical efforts to harness new military capabilities hitherto unavailable to it may be analogous to the intellectual growing pains that U.S. strategic thought underwent in the early years of the nuclear revolution.

On a related point, the absence of hard-won experience from modern warfare and crisis could account for optimism about escalation control. The Chinese have not fought a war for more than thirty years, since the Sino-Vietnamese border conflict. Moreover, China has not yet confronted sobering incidents (comparable to the Cuban missile crisis) against which to reassess and radically revise prevailing assumptions. The U.S. development of airpower doctrine and theory during the interwar period is an apt historical parallel. In the absence of real-world combat experiences and sufficient empirical data, American airpower theorists were left to their own devices, and deeply flawed assumptions seeped into their thinking. An exaggerated sense of what strategic airpower could accomplish resulted. Indeed, airpower zealots of the period made extravagant claims about the promise of strategic bombardment, claims that failed to bear fruit in the crucible of the Second World War. In short, it is easy to succumb to logical fallacies when operating in a theoretical vacuum.

Institutional incentives may be at work as well. Those with vested bureaucratic and budgetary interests in promoting the Second Artillery's conventional strike mission at the expense of sister services may be inclined to oversell the surgical nature of missile warfare. By touting the unique capabilities of long-range precision-strike systems, missile advocates may be hoping to sharpen the Second Artillery's future war-fighting role, thereby enhancing its negotiating position in decisions over resource allocations. Again, this is not new. Following Operation Desert Storm, a bitter interservice debate erupted in the United States over the degree to which airpower had contributed to the lopsided American victory. Not surprisingly, U.S. Air Force leaders pushed a narrative that unabashedly credited airpower for delivering the decisive blows against Iraqi forces. It is conceivable that the Second Artillery too is attempting to carve out a larger institutional space for itself.

Alternatively, Chinese overconfidence in managing escalatory pressures could reflect the lessons that defense planners learned from the cross-strait confrontation in 1996. Some analysts in China have unequivocally concluded that the missile tests deterred the island from the road to independence while signaling clear red lines to the United States.[77] The notion that a limited number of missile launches could produce far-reaching success in coercive diplomacy is a seductive narrative likely to attract adherents within the Second Artillery Corps. Indeed, such an uncritical story line could reinforce preferences, biases, and faulty assumptions underlying the discourse within the missile community. Troublingly, *The Science of Second Artillery Campaigns* explicitly credits the missile tests in 1995 and 1996 for generating multiple studies that "have filled in a blank in conventional guided missile operation theories of the Second Artillery Corps."[78] A sample set comprising one case study is hardly a basis for universally applicable principles of war.

Another possible explanation is mirror-imaging. The assumption that missile strikes against forward logistics hubs could severely disrupt the functionality of U.S. carrier strike groups may be a reflection of China's own dependence on shore bases at home. As noted earlier, the United States boasts a very diverse and durable global basing infrastructure, one that would cushion, to some extent, Chinese blows against bases in Japan. By contrast, China's ability to sustain fleet operations—on scales larger than those of the modest task forces that it has dispatched thus far—at great distances from fixed shore facilities remains relatively limited. In other words, the Chinese literature may reveal more about the PLA's own vulnerabilities than about U.S. weaknesses. Nevertheless, mirror-imaging may exert a stubborn influence on Chinese thinking, reinforcing analytical biases and blind spots that are hard to shake off.

Finally, the writings themselves may be a form of peacetime signaling. The studies clearly communicate to foreign audiences China's willingness to gamble in a big way in high-stakes disputes. If the doctrinal works convince outside powers that China may just be reckless enough to carry out the implied threats, they will have effectively cast a shadow of deterrence over potential adversaries. Mao Zedong's cunning efforts to deprecate the power of nuclear weapons—by famously depicting atom bombs as "paper tigers"—in order to signal Chinese resolve are instructive.

Any combination of these reasons should give pause to those inclined to dismiss the strategic significance of the doctrinal writings.

Strategic and Operational Implications for the U.S.-Japanese Alliance

Washington and Tokyo will encounter a more complex geometry of deterrence with the emergence of a robust Chinese theater-strike capability. The action/reaction dynamic in the United States–Japan–China triangle will be far less straightforward than that of the alliance's deterrent posture toward North Korea. The existential threat that U.S. conventional and nuclear superiority poses to Pyongyang is often presumed to be sufficient to deter the North's adventurism. Such is not the case with China. Boasting an increasingly survivable retaliatory nuclear strike complex, including a growing road-mobile strategic missile force and a nascent undersea deterrent, Beijing may be confident enough to conduct theater-level conventional missile operations under its protective nuclear umbrella. The war scares in the South Asian subcontinent over the past decade suggest that nuclear-armed regional powers, less inhibited by fears of enemy nuclear coercion or punishment, may feel emboldened to escalate a conventional conflict.[79] Japan and its many lucrative basing targets could well become a conventional, theater-level battlefield trapped between two nuclear-armed powers.

Assuming that vertical escalation toward nuclear use can be contained, the alliance must still consider efforts at denying attempts to punish Japan. Allied missile defenses, as they are currently configured, will have great difficulty coping with theater ballistic missiles like the DF-21. In the context of a cross-strait scenario, retired rear admiral Eric McVadon observes, "Being an MRBM with a much higher reentry velocity than SRBMs, the DF-21C is virtually invulnerable to any missile defenses Taiwan might contemplate."[80] While the alliance possesses a far more sophisticated, multilayered missile defense architecture than does Taipei, longer-range missiles pose similar stresses to the defense of Japan. If the missiles were fired from launch sites in northeastern China, allied response times would be very compressed. Inexpensive techniques and countermeasures by the PLA, such as saturation tactics and decoys, could be employed to overwhelm or defeat missile defenses, which are designed for less sophisticated regional threats from North Korea and Iran. If the Second Artillery Corps launched successive missile salvos against the same strategic site, the alliance could quickly exhaust its ammunition, constraining its ability to defend other targets.

Escalation control would also bedevil the alliance. One critical escalation threshold pertains to the initiation of hostilities, were China to prepare for or launch its first missile strike. The allies would be very hard pressed to distinguish confidently conventional missiles from nuclear-tipped missiles. Indeed, finding the missiles at all would be hard enough, since the road-mobile DF-21s would almost certainly disperse to a variety of concealed launch sites to diminish the threat of a disarming preemptive strike by enemy forces. To compound matters, Chinese conventional missiles might share the basing facilities with their nuclear counterparts. Space-based surveillance and reconnaissance would provide at best an incomplete picture of China's wartime missile posture. In short, no one would know for sure whether a Chinese warhead hurtling toward Yokosuka was a nuclear or a conventional weapon. The fog and friction that accompanies any crisis or war would multiply this uncertainty.

Would the alliance be willing to discount the possibility that the launch could be a nuclear strike? Or would it assume the worst? In the event of Chinese conventional bombardment, what would be the appropriate military response from the United States? What might underlie and inform Japanese expectations of the U.S. reaction? Would the alliance be prepared to expand the war to the mainland? Would a besieged Japan demand more punitive strikes against China than the United States was willing to inflict? Would Tokyo lose confidence in Washington if the latter refrained from what it considered disproportionate escalation? What would be the consequences of such a breakdown in trust during and after the conflict? These troubling questions make it imperative that Tokyo and Washington clearly recognize the operational temptations to overreact and the political consequences of *under*reaction. Though prudence called for restraint, the stresses of crisis and war could radically skew rational calculations.

The foregoing analysis demonstrates that theater-level interactions involving conventional missile strikes against regional bases could be highly unstable and prone to miscalculation on all sides. The apparent underdevelopment of Chinese doctrine on missile coercion, littered as it is with questionable assumptions about the adversary, could exacerbate this latent instability. In the meantime, it seems that the U.S.-Japanese alliance has not moved far beyond rudimentary discussions of extended deterrence, a concept that does not fully capture the complexities of the emerging missile threat in Asia.[81] It thus behooves Washington and Tokyo to anticipate a far more ambiguous and stressful operational environment than has been the case over the past two decades. The alliance must come to grips with the advances in Chinese thinking about coercive campaigns while exploring options for hardening the partnership, both politically and militarily, against Beijing's emerging missile strategy.

Notes

1. David A. Shlapak, David T. Orletsky, Toy I. Reid, Murray Scot Tanner, and Barry Wilson, *A Question of Balance: Political Context and Military Aspects of the China-Taiwan Dispute* (Santa Monica, Calif.: Rand Corporation, 2009), 126.
2. Ibid., 139.
3. Ibid., 131.

4. Defense Intelligence Agency, *Taiwan Air Defense Status Assessment*, DIA-02-1001-028 (Washington, D.C.: DIA, 21 January 2010), 3.

5. William S. Murray, "Revisiting Taiwan's Defense Strategy," *Naval War College Review* 61, no. 3 (Summer 2008): 24.

6. Mark A. Stokes and Ian Easton, *Evolving Aerospace Trends in the Asia-Pacific Region: Implications for Stability in the Taiwan Strait and Beyond* (Washington, D.C.: Project 2049 Institute, May 2010), 34.

7. For a classic on this topic, see John Stillion and David T. Orlestky, *Airbase Vulnerability to Conventional Cruise-Missile and Ballistic-Missile Attacks: Technology, Scenarios, and U.S. Air Force Responses* (Santa Monica, Calif.: Rand Corporation, 1999).

8. On "indispensable linchpin," see Michael J. Green, Japan Chair of the Center for Strategic and International Studies, *Prepared Statement for Hearing on the Future of Japan*, Foreign Affairs Committee, Subcommittee on Asia and the Pacific, House of Representatives, 11th Cong., 1st sess., 24 May 2011, 2; On "cornerstone," see Hillary Clinton, "America's Pacific Century," *Foreign Policy*, November 2011, 58; on "platform," see Emma Chanlett-Avery, *The U.S.-Japan Alliance*, Report to Congress RL33740 (Washington, D.C.: Congressional Research Service, 18 January 2011), 1.

9. Patrick M. Cronin, Daniel M. Kilman, and Abraham M. Denmark, *Renewal: Revitalizing the U.S.-Japan Alliance* (Washington, D.C.: Center for a New American Security, October 2010), 9.

10. David J. Berteau, Michael J. Green, Gregory Kiley, and Nicholas Szechenyi, *U.S. Force Posture Strategy in the Asia Pacific Region: An Independent Assessment* (Washington, D.C.: Center for Strategic and International Studies, 15 August 2012), 26, available at http://csis.org/publication/pacom-force-posture-review.

11. United Nations, *World Population Prospects: The 2008 Revision*, vol. 1 (New York: United Nations, Department of Economic and Social Affairs, Population Division, 2008), 292–93.

12. "Defense Ministry to Set Up Radio Wave Measuring Device in Nagasaki in Response to PRC Military Threat," *Sankei Shimbun*, 7 March 2007; "Government to Deploy 20 F-15s to Naha Base," *Yomiuri Shimbun*, 31 August 2007; and "With Eye on China, Defense Ministry to Bolster Southwest Flank," *Nihon Keizai Shimbun*, 8 October 2007.

13. Sugio Takahashi, "Counter A2/AD in Japan-U.S. Defense Cooperation: Toward 'Allied Air-Sea Battle,'" *Futuregram*, no. 3 (18 April 2012): 5.

14. Yukie Yoshikawa, "Listen to Okinawa," *Nikkei Weekly*, 1 July 2012, 47.

15. The U.S. personnel numbers are based on figures provided by *U.S. Forces Japan: Official Military Website*, www.usfj.mil/.

16. Berteau et al., *U.S. Force Posture Strategy*, 51.

17. Robert Karniol, "A Cold War Relic Refuses to Die," *Straits Times*, 13 May 2008.

18. U.S. Defense Department, *Base Structure Report: Fiscal Year 2012 Baseline* (Washington, D.C.: Office of the Deputy Under Secretary of Defense for Installations and Environment, 2012).

19. For an assessment of how the U.S. sea power feeds the "Malacca dilemma," see 海洋战略 徐志良 [Li Lixin and Xu Zhiliang], "海洋开发与管理" [An Oceanic Strategy Is the Optimal National Policy for Constructing Long-Term Chinese Overseas Energy Security], 海洋开与管理 [Ocean Development and Management], no. 4 (2006): 7–8. The authors are officials representing China's State Oceanic Administration.

20. Ye Hailin, "Safe Seas," *Beijing Review*, 2 April 2009.

21. U.S. Navy, Marine Corps, and Coast Guard, "A Cooperative Strategy for 21st Century Seapower," October 2007, www.navy.mil/maritime/MaritimeStrategy.pdf.

22. Lu Rude, "The New U.S. Maritime Strategy Surfaces," trans. Andrew S. Erickson, *Naval War College Review* 61, no. 4 (Autumn 2008): 60.

23. 欧阳维 [Ou Yangwei], 战略部署论 [On Strategic Deployment] (Beijing: Liberation Army Press, 2011), 38. Senior Colonel Ou Yangwei holds a doctoral degree and serves as a professor in the Strategy Department of the National Defense University.

24. 李杰 [Li Jie], 航母之路—海上巨无霸的发展，争论及思考 [The Road to Carriers: The Debates and Reflections on the Development of a Behemoth at Sea] (Beijing: Haichao, 2009), 193.

25. 刘永辉 [Liu Yonghui], 国外航空母舰作战指挥 [Foreign Aircraft Carrier Operational Command] (Beijing: Military Science Press, 2007), 323–24.

26. 于洋 祁小东 [Yu Yang and Qi Xiaodong], "美海外基地大调整" [Reconfiguration of U.S. Overseas Bases], 当代海军 [Modern Navy], no. 8 (August 2005): 23. See also 潘远强 廖军俊 [Pan Yaunqiang and Liao Junjun], "美军亚太基地的最新扩展计划" [The Newest Expansion Plan of U.S. Bases in the Asia Pacific], 国际资料信息 [International Data Information], no. 9 (September 2006): 19–22.

27. 文选凯 [Wen Xuankai], "中国周边的美国航母基地" [U.S. Carrier Bases along China's Periphery], 国际展望 [International Outlook], September 2001, 66.

28. 赵宇 长永 [Zhao Yu and Chang Yong], "日本海上军事力量—日本海军军事基地港口部署" [Japanese Maritime Military Power: Japanese Naval Base Deployments], 当代海军 [Modern Navy], no. 10 (October 2005): 40–43.

29. 俞风流 危骏 [Yu Fengliu and Wei Jun], "美军要全面遏制西太平洋" [U.S. Military Seeks Comprehensive Containment of the Western Pacific], 当代海军 [Modern Navy], no. 3 (March 2006): 58.

30. 秦明李国强胡勇为李奂 [Qin Ming, Li Guoqiang, Hu Yongwei, and Li Huan], "美国海军太平洋基地" [Pacific Bases of the U.S. Navy], 国防科技 [National Defense Science and Technology], no. 2 (February 2006): 55.

31. See 静海 [Jin Hai], "美国太平洋舰队海军基地" [Naval Bases of the U.S. Pacific Fleet], 舰船知识 [Naval and Merchant Ships], no. 3 (March 2006): 28–29; "日本海军基地和军港" [Japan's Naval Bases and Ports], 当代海军 [Modern Navy], no. 7 (July 2003): 23; 钟海英 [Zhong Haiying], "美在中国当面海区驻军最多" [The U.S. Deploys Most Troops in Sea Areas Facing China], 当代海军 [Modern Navy], no. 4 (April 2003): 33; 孙立华 [Sun Lihua], "美军东亚基地" [U.S. Military Bases in East Asia], 环球军事 [Global Military], November 2001, 7; and 赵利 [Zhao Li], "美海军太平洋及远东基地扫描" [Survey of U.S. Naval Bases in the Western Pacific and Far East], 现代舰船 [Modern Ships], no. 8 (August 2000): 8.

32. 吴建 [Wu Jian], "全球最著名的海军基地" [The World's Most Famous Naval Bases], 当代军事文摘 [Contemporary Military Affairs], no. 4 (April 2007): 11.

33. 佩坏 [Pei Huai], "'全球著名海军基地'扫描" [Review of "The World's Most Famous Naval Bases"], 环球军事 [Global Military], no. 145 (March 2007): 10.

34. 杜朝平 [Du Chaoping], "美海外航母母港的由来，现况与展望" [The Origins, Present Situation, and Prospects of Overseas Homeports for U.S. Carriers], 现代舰船 [Modern Ships], no. 8A (August 2008): 14–15.

35. Pei Huai, "Review of 'The World's Most Famous Naval Bases,'" 9.

36. Du Chaoping, "Origins, Present Situation," 14.

37. 马海洋 [Ma Haiyang], "横须贺海军基地—美国在西太平洋的前进基地" [Yokosuka Naval Base: The Forward Base of the U.S. in the Western Pacific], 环球军事 [Global Military], no. 17 (2001): 40.

38. 任德新 [Ren Dexin], "太平洋的宙斯盾反导系统" [Aegis Anti–Ballistic Missile System in the Pacific], 当代军事文摘 [Modern Military Digest], October 2007, 18–19.

39. 海研 [Hai Yan], "军事重镇—横须贺军港" [Strategic Military Site: Yokosuka Naval Base], 当代海军 [Modern Navy], vol. 156, no. 9 (September 2006): 59.

40. 刘江平 [Liu Jiangping], "太平洋上的宙斯盾反导战舰群" [Aegis Anti–Ballistic Missile Fleet in the Pacific], 当代海军 [Modern Navy], vol. 177, no. 6 (June 2008): 29.

41. 任德新 程健良 [Ren Dexin and Cheng Jianliang], "宙斯盾反导系统在太平洋的部署及使用" [The Deployment and Use of the Aegis Anti–Ballistic Missile System in the Pacific], 舰船知识 [Naval and Merchant Ships], July 2007, 17.

42. 戴艳丽 [Dai Yanli], "我周边宙斯盾舰的运行及威胁" [The Functioning and Threat of Aegis Ships on Our Periphery], 舰船知识 [Naval and Merchant Ships], September 2007, 18.

43. 齐艳丽 [Ji Yanli], "美国海基中段防御系统" [The U.S. Sea-Based Midcourse Defense System], 导弹与航天运载技术 [Missiles and Space Vehicles], no. 3 (2005): 61.

44. 李大光 [Li Daguang], "美国在亚洲最大的海军基地：横须贺港" [America's Largest Naval Base in Asia: Yokosuka Port], 当代海军 [Modern Navy], no. 11 (2008): 48.

45. "核航母入驻日本解读" [Interpreting the Homeport of Nuclear Carrier in Japan], 舰船知识 [Merchant and Naval Ships], no. 2 (February 2006): 27.

46. 刘伟 赵艳杰 [Liu Wei and Zhao Yanjie], "美西太海军基地新体系" [The New Structure of U.S. Military Bases in the Western Pacific], 舰船知识 [Naval and Merchant Ships], no. 2 (February 2006): 21.

47. 于凡 [Yu Fan], "佐世保：美国在日第二大海军基地" [Sasebo: America's Second-Largest Naval Base in Japan], 当代海军 [Modern Navy], no. 12 (December 2008): 49.

48. 田武 [Tian Wu], "驻日美军海军基地扫描" [A Survey of U.S. Naval Bases in Japan], 舰载武器 [Shipborne Weapons], no. 1 (January 2004): 17.

49. To the extent possible, this chapter attempts to discern the weight and credibility of the works cited. As an aid to the reader, citations include, where appropriate, details of the identity and background of the author(s), the nature and purpose

of the publication, and the degree to which the writing enjoys official sanction or reflects PLA thinking.

50. Originally published in 2001, *The Science of Military Strategy* was published in English by the Academy of Military Science in 2005 to reach foreign audiences. Major generals Peng Guangqian and Yao Youzhi are members of the Department of Strategic Studies at the Academy of Military Science. Both have written widely on strategic and military affairs and appear regularly in Chinese media as authoritative figures on the PLA.

51. Peng Guangqian and Yao Youzhi, *The Science of Military Strategy* (Beijing: Military Science Publishing House, 2005).

52. Ibid., 461.

53. Ibid., 464.

54. Ibid., 465.

55. Ibid.

56. 张培高 [Zhang Peigao, ed.], 联合战役指挥学 [The Science of Joint Campaign Command] (Beijing: Military Science, 2005), 262. Members of the Operations Theory and Regulations Department at the Academy of Military Science contributed individual chapters to this volume. The research department has been responsible for producing a new generation of highest-level operational and training guides, including 司令部条例 [Regulations of Headquarters Department], 联合战役指挥纲要 [Essential Outline of Joint Campaign Command], and 联合战役协同纲要 [Essential Outline of Joint Campaign Coordination].

57. Lieutenant General Zhao Xijun served as deputy commander of the PLA Second Artillery Corps from 1996 to 2003. He was a PLA delegate to the Tenth National People's Congress in 2006.

58. 赵锡君 [Zhao Xijun], 摄战—导弹威慑纵横谈 [Intimidation Warfare: Comprehensive Survey of Missile Intimidation] (Beijing: National Defense University Press, 2003), 191.

59. Ibid., 191–92.

60. Ibid., 192.

61. Zhang Peigao, *Science of Joint Campaign Command*, 270.

62. 中国人民解放军第二炮兵 [China's People's Liberation Army Second Artillery Corps], 第二炮兵战役学 [The Science of Second Artillery Campaigns] (Beijing: Liberation Army Press, 2004). The Second Artillery Corps conducted the feasibility study and compiled the collective writing effort for this work. Members of the writing team, including faculty members at the Second Artillery Command Academy, completed the individual chapters. According to the postscript, the volume was "written under the unified organization of the General Staff Department." The authors "used the *Guidelines of Joint Campaigns* and the *Guidelines of Second Artillery Corps Campaigns* as the basis" for the study. The guidelines are analogous to the U.S. military's Joint Publication series, which provide the fundamental principles for the employment of military force. The intended audiences could include PLA officers attending the Second Artillery Command Academy and the National Defense University.

63. Ibid., 401.

64. Ibid., 400.

65. 朱艾华, 孙龙海 [Zhu Aihua and Sun Longhai], "近岸岛屿封锁作战" [Offshore Island Blockade Operations] (Beijing: Military Science Press, 2002), 132. Senior Colonel Zhu Aihua is a professor in the Military Training and Management Department at the PLA's Nanjing Army Command Academy. The textbook is based on Colonel Zhu's many years of studying and teaching offshore-island blockade operations. The materials are written for midgrade to senior military officers attending PLA command colleges.

66. See U.S. Defense Department, *Annual Report to Congress: Military Power of the People's Republic of China* (Washington, D.C.: Office of the Secretary of Defense, 2005); and U.S. Defense Department, *Annual Report to Congress: Military and Security Developments Involving the People's Republic of China* (Washington, D.C.: Office of the Secretary of Defense, 2012), 29.

67. PLA Second Artillery Corps, *Campaign Science of the Second Artillery*, 322.

68. Ibid., 326.

69. This is an admittedly implausible scenario. It is difficult to imagine real-world crisis situations or periods of high tension in which the U.S. Navy would not have acquired the early warning and lead time to sortie its surface fleet to safety at sea.

70. Bernard C. Nalty, *The Air Force Role in Five Crises 1958–1965: Lebanon, Taiwan, Congo, Cuba, Dominican Republic*, U.S. Air Force Historical Division Liaison Office, June 1968, excised copy, 20–21, National Security Archive, George Washington University, Washington, D.C., available at www.gwu.edu/~nsarchiv/nukevault/ebb249/doc10.pdf.

71. For an excellent analysis of the factors that could accelerate or dampen escalation pressures, see Ron Christman, "Conventional Missions for China's Second Artillery Corps," *Comparative Strategy* 30, no. 3 (2011): 216–18.

72. Zhang Peigao, *Science of Joint Campaign Command*, 272.

73. Zhao Xijun, *Intimidation Warfare*, 192.

74. PLA Second Artillery Corps, *Science of the Second Artillery Campaigns*, 400.

75. Zhang Peigao, *Science of Joint Campaign Command*, 264.

76. Forrest E. Morgan, Karl P. Mueller, Evan S. Medeiros, Kevin L. Pollpeter, and Roger Cliff, *Dangerous Thresholds: Managing Escalation in the 21st Century* (Santa Monica, Calif.: Rand Corporation, 2008), 169.

77. John Garver, *Face Off: China, the United States, and Taiwan's Democratization* (Seattle: University of Washington Press, 1997), 155–56.

78. PLA Second Artillery Corps, *Campaign Science of the Second Artillery*, 12–13.

79. See S. Paul Kapur, "Ten Years of Instability in a Nuclear South Asia," *International Security* 33, no. 2 (Fall 2008): 71–94.

80. Eric A. McVadon, "The Taiwan Problem: Beijing Arms for a Fight It Hopes to Avoid," *Armed Forces Journal*, no. 11 (2005), available at www.afji.com/.

81. For an excellent analysis of the current Japanese debate over U.S. extended deterrence, see Michael J. Green and Katsuhisa Furukawa, "Japan: New Nuclear Realism," in *The Long Shadow: Nuclear Weapons and Security in 21st Century Asia*, ed. Muthiah Alagappa (Stanford, Calif.: Stanford University Press, 2008), 347–72.

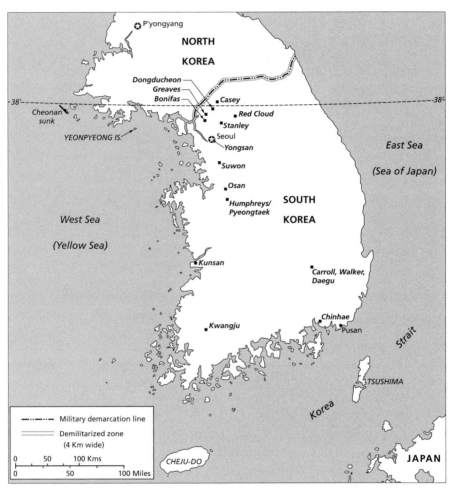

P'yongyang

NORTH

KOREA

Dongducheon
Greaves
Bonifas

Casey

38°   38°

Cheonan
sunk

Red Cloud

Stanley

YEONPYEONG IS.

Seoul

Yongsan

East Sea

(Sea of Japan)

Suwon

Osan

SOUTH

Humphreys/
Pyeongtaek

KOREA

West Sea

(Yellow Sea)

Kunsan

Carroll, Walker,
Daegu

Kwangju

Chinhae

Pusan

Strait

TSUSHIMA

- - - · - · - · Military demarcation line

Demilitarized zone
(4 Km wide)

Korea

0   50   100 Kms

0   50   100 Miles

CHEJU-DO

JAPAN

Map 3. Military Facilities in South Korea

3

South Korea: An Alliance in Transition

Terence Roehrig

For sixty years, the United States has maintained an extensive network of military bases on the Korean Peninsula to ensure South Korea's security. The U.S. presence is part of a commitment that was formalized in October 1953 with the signing of the U.S.–Republic of Korea Mutual Defense Treaty. At the end of the Korean War, American leaders believed that they needed to provide a more robust demonstration of their determination to protect the Republic of Korea (ROK). In addition to the security treaty, the United States provided South Korea with extensive amounts of economic and military aid, deployed tactical nuclear weapons to the peninsula, and stationed U.S. combat troops close to the demilitarized zone (DMZ). U.S. troops and military bases on Korean soil were a particularly important part of the commitment. The United States maintained over a hundred bases in South Korea as a visible sign of American resolve to protect its ally and as part of Washington's global containment strategy to halt the spread of communism. Map 3 depicts major current facilities in South Korea.

An alliance that lasts for over half a century is likely to evolve as power configurations and the security environment change; this has certainly been the case for the U.S.-ROK alliance. The location and number of U.S. troops in South Korea have been adjusted on several occasions, and the command relationships have changed as well. More modifications are currently in process for American bases and the U.S.-ROK command structure, with the relocation of U.S. forces to bases south of Seoul and the scheduling of the return of wartime operational control (OPCON) to South Korea in December 2015.

Although the U.S. force structure has changed, the central goal of the alliance and U.S. forces in South Korea remains the same: to deter, and if necessary defeat, another North Korean attack on the South. However, even the scope of the alliance is beginning to change, as the two alliance partners look at security in broader terms that go beyond what happens on the peninsula. In a summit meeting in June 2009, presidents Barack Obama and Lee Myung-bak outlined a "Joint Vision" of the alliance that seeks "to ensure a peaceful, secure and prosperous future for the Korean Peninsula, the Asia-Pacific region, and the world." The two nations will strive to maintain a "comprehensive alliance" to address a variety of global challenges such as terrorism, piracy, disease, and human rights, and "will work to achieve our common Alliance goals through strategic cooperation at every level."[1] In May 2013 South Korea's new president, Park Geun-hye, the first woman to hold the post, journeyed to Washington, D.C., for a summit on the occasion of the sixtieth anniversary of the alliance. Presidents Park and Obama reaffirmed the Joint Vision, noting that the United States and South Korea have made "significant progress" in advancing this "blueprint for the future development of our strategic alliance."[2] Thus, both Washington and Seoul are moving the alliance relationship toward a broader set of shared goals for regional and global security.

These changes to the structure and scope of the U.S.-ROK alliance are having important impacts on American bases in South Korea. As the scope and purpose of the alliance have changed, so have the basing arrangements. Some of the changes remain "works in progress," but it is likely that they will be accomplished at some point in the next decade. All of these elements are signs of an alliance that is evolving. The U.S.-ROK relationship is no longer the patron-client relationship of old, where South Korea was relatively weak and brought few assets to the alliance. The ROK is a dynamic powerhouse, with the world's twelfth-largest economy and ambitions to be an important regional and global player. Washington has a vision for the alliance to become more flexible, with U.S. forces there able to meet and be available for security concerns outside Korea. The alliance is likely to remain an important relationship because it is a useful tool to address common concerns, but the structure and basing arrangements of the alliance will continue evolving. This chapter will examine the key dimensions of this evolution as they alter the U.S. military presence in South Korea.

The History of U.S. Bases and Forces in South Korea

The U.S. military presence in South Korea began at the end of World War II with the need to devise an arrangement for accepting the Japanese surrender in Korea. In a hastily arranged proposal, American officials suggested to the Soviets that they accept the Japanese surrender north of the thirty-eighth parallel while Washington did so south of that line. Stalin accepted the offer, despite the fact that

Russian forces were already in Manchuria and there was little the United States could have done to prevent the Red Army from seizing the entire peninsula.

U.S. forces arrived in South Korea on 8 September 1945 to accept the Japanese surrender and administer the area after thirty-five years of occupation. American officials jumped into a difficult and complicated postwar political environment, with little experience or understanding of the complex factors at work.[3] American occupation authorities soon were caught up in the struggles between factions on the left, right, and center vying for power in postwar Korea. Washington had every intention of reuniting North and South Korea, but negotiations with Moscow stalled as Cold War hostility exacerbated an already complicated situation in Korea. In addition, there was pressure in the U.S. Congress and the American public to scale back U.S. commitments and forces abroad after the long, two-front war. Furthermore, many questioned the extent of American interests in Korea and whether these justified an extensive commitment to South Korea's security.[4]

In the fall of 1947, with little hope of progress with the Soviets, the Harry S. Truman administration turned the Korea problem over to the United Nations. In November the UN General Assembly approved a plan to reunite the two Koreas by holding elections throughout the peninsula and establishing a unified government. North Korea and the Soviet Union refused to abide by the UN decision and did not hold elections in the North. Nonetheless, separate elections were held in the South, and on 15 August 1948 the ROK came into being under its first leader, President Syngman Rhee. On 9 September 1948 the Soviet Union followed suit, creating a separate government, the Democratic People's Republic of Korea (DPRK) in the North, under Kim Il-sung. With a government in place in Seoul, the United States withdrew its last occupation forces in June 1949 and maintained only a small contingent of American military advisers, the Korea Military Advisory Group (KMAG), which helped train the young South Korean military. When the Korean War began on 25 June 1950, the United States sent large ground, air, and naval forces to South Korea's defense. After the numerous rapid advances and retreats of the first year of fighting, the war settled into a stalemate along a front that resembled the war's starting point at the thirty-eighth parallel. U.S. bases after the Korean War conformed largely to the positions held by U.S. forces in the last two years of the war.

At the time the armistice was signed in July 1953, the United States had eight combat divisions in Korea. These forces were spread throughout the peninsula, with many of their bases between Seoul and the DMZ. In the next two years, Washington reduced this strength to two combat divisions, the 2nd and 7th Infantry Divisions. These two divisions were deployed north of the Han River along the two major invasion corridors from the North. Among the Army bases north of Seoul were camps Casey, Red Cloud, Bonifas, and Greaves, to name a few.

The 2nd Division was the forwardmost deployed of the U.S. forces, defending an eighteen-mile-long sector of the west-central DMZ. The 7th Division was posted south of the 2nd as a reserve but along the chief invasion routes. In addition to these two infantry divisions, the U.S. Army also maintained the 38th Artillery Brigade (which included air-defense units), the 4th Army Missile Command, the 2nd Engineering Group, and other support units.[5] Other Army bases located south of Seoul included Camp Humphreys and U.S. Army Garrison (USAG) Daegu. The U.S. Air Force established five bases in South Korea—in Daegu, Kwangju, Kunsan, Osan, and Suwon—to address shortfalls in ROK airpower. Although the United States kept a naval command—U.S. Naval Forces Korea, with its headquarters in Seoul and a naval base at Chinhae—it did not actually base naval forces in Korea. Commander, Naval Forces Korea, a one-star admiral, has no ships assigned to the command but does have three hundred personnel to help in planning and executing operations. The commander also serves as a liaison to other U.S. commands in Korea, the U.S. Seventh Fleet (which operates in the Pacific), and the ROK Navy.[6] From 1954 to 1971, U.S. forces in Korea, including naval and air units, averaged approximately 63,000.

In 1971 President Richard Nixon altered the U.S. force structure by removing the 7th Infantry Division from Korea. Two years prior, with the United States deeply involved in the Vietnam War, the Nixon administration had conducted a reappraisal of American policy in Asia and concluded that the country was overextended, with too many commitments for the resources it had available. Under what became known as the Nixon Doctrine, the president announced that Washington would maintain its treaty commitments but would expect alliance partners to furnish greater shares of the manpower for their defense.[7] As a result, Nixon withdrew the 7th Division, approximately 20,000 troops, and moved the 2nd Division to positions farther south from the DMZ, though still between Seoul and the border. ROK units took their place along the DMZ. The 2nd Division's new positions were between the two likely invasion routes from the North, allowing U.S. forces to move in either direction to confront a DPRK assault.[8] Nixon originally intended to withdraw all but one combat brigade of the 2nd Division but decided not to do so.[9] South Korean leaders were very concerned with these developments, which portended the possibility of a complete withdrawal of U.S. forces and the slow deterioration of the alliance.

When Jimmy Carter entered the White House in January 1977, major changes to U.S. bases and force presence were again placed on the table. During the 1977 campaign, Carter had called for the removal of all U.S. ground forces from the peninsula and soon after his inauguration signed Presidential Review Memorandum/NSC 13, which directed a review of the American presence in Korea. From the start, President Carter made it clear that the purpose of the review was not to determine whether U.S. troops would be removed but rather how this removal could be best accomplished.[10] Carter confronted strong opposition from groups within the United States and South Korea. In the face of vociferous criticism, Carter eventually agreed to limit withdrawals to one brigade of the 2nd Division, approximately 6,000 soldiers, while retaining air, naval, intelligence, and support units. By 1978, however, evidence had begun to surface of an extensive North Korean conventional military buildup, and pressure to drop the troop withdrawal plan mounted. In February 1979 President Carter announced that there would be no further withdrawal of U.S. forces from Korea.[11] In the end, he removed only 800 combat troops and 2,600 support personnel, chiefly from air-defense battalions, much of whose equipment was outdated.[12]

During the Reagan years, the United States increased its troop strength in Korea to 43,000 and modernized force capabilities with new aircraft, antitank weapons, surface-to-surface missiles, and artillery. Reagan had been dismayed by the deterioration of the U.S.-ROK alliance during the Carter years and was determined to repair the damage he believed had been done. Reagan also received South Korean president Chun Doo-hwan as the first foreign leader to visit the White House—a controversial move since Chun had only recently led a military coup to seize control of the ROK government. However, the visit was also a quid pro quo for a stay of execution of longtime dissident Kim Dae-jung.[13]

When the Cold War ended many assumed that an opportunity had arrived to adjust U.S. troop levels in Korea, as was occurring in Europe. In April 1990 the Department of Defense released a report, *A Strategic Framework for the Asian Pacific Rim: Looking toward the 21st Century*, that stated that the United States would "begin to draw down ground presence and modify command structures so as to transition from a leading to a supporting role for U.S. forces."[14] In South Korea, U.S. troops were scheduled for a three-phase drawdown to an undetermined end strength. Phase I removed five thousand from the 2nd Infantry Division and close to two thousand support personnel, chiefly from Air Force units, and closed three of the five U.S. air bases in Korea—Kwangju, Daegu, and Suwon. (The Air Force bases at Kunsan and Osan remained in operation.) The reductions were made contingent on the actions of North Korea and the security situation on the peninsula. However, in fall 1991 Secretary of Defense Dick Cheney announced a moratorium on any further withdrawals due to growing concern over Pyongyang's nuclear program and its lack of cooperation with International Atomic Energy Agency inspection demands.[15] President Bill Clinton reaffirmed the pause, and U.S. troop levels remained at 37,500 for the remainder of the decade.

The Purpose of U.S. Bases in South Korea

U.S. bases in South Korea have fulfilled and continue to fulfill several important functions, though these have evolved over the years. First and foremost, the bases are part of the U.S.-ROK alliance that seeks to deter, and if necessary defeat, an attack on South Korea. Many American bases were, as noted, originally located close to the DMZ and along the major invasion routes leading into the South to act as a trip wire to enhance deterrence. The presence of U.S. troops signaled Washington's determination to come to South Korea's aid if attacked and that they were prepared to "fight tonight" should the alliance be tested. The American commitment and presence in Korea began largely as an effort to contain the spread of communism and reflected little intrinsic interest in the South. In fact, prior to the Korean War many doubted that American interests in the ROK were sufficient for a large-scale, formal commitment to its security. If the North attacked, however, which most American leaders assumed would be directed by Moscow or Beijing, the defense of South Korea would leap up the list of U.S. defense priorities because it would then be on the frontline of the Cold War.[16] Thus, the U.S. presence in South Korea was closely tied to broader strategic goals.

In addition, bases in South Korea provided the United States with a forward presence on the Asian mainland that helped contain Soviet and Chinese influence in the region. The U.S. presence addressed a security vacuum after the Second World War that could have been filled by Moscow, Beijing, or a resurgent Japan. The U.S.-ROK alliance and U.S. bases in South Korea became part of the regional security architecture that included alliances with Japan, the Philippines, Thailand, Australia, and, for a time, New Zealand that helped to bring peace and stability to the region. U.S. bases demonstrated Washington's determination to defend the region and the credibility of the American defense commitment, not only for South Korea but also for other U.S. allies, especially Japan. U.S. ties to Japan have often been described as the cornerstone of American security policy in the region. The U.S.-ROK alliance is linked to the defense of Japan by helping to bring stability to Japanese foreign and defense policy. U.S. forces in South Korea reduce the need for Japan to rearm, which in turn reassures others that Japan will not seek to dominate the region.

As East Asian economies flourished after the Korean War and U.S. economic ties with them grew, American interests in maintaining peace and stability also increased. Moreover, when South Korea transitioned to a democracy in 1987, Seoul and Washington shared the same political values, so defending South Korea was now defending a fellow democratic state. Thus, in 1992 President George H. W. Bush described U.S.-ROK ties as "more than a military alliance, our countries are moving toward a political, economic and security partnership."[17]

Today, while U.S. bases are focused on deterrence and defense of South Korea, they also provide a base for power projection in the region should that become necessary. This is particularly so for U.S. Air Force units stationed on the peninsula, which could be used in regional contingencies. The use of U.S. ground forces in that role is possible but more problematic. American soldiers are trained and configured primarily for one mission—defense of South Korea—and are not easily deployable on short notice for other contingencies. Matters became particularly difficult when U.S. forces were stretched thin as a result of extended operations in Iraq and Afghanistan. However, this issue was also part of a broader reassessment of U.S. military forces and their use for other purposes. As Patrick Morgan argues, "the USA now wants its alliances to operate with concern for security much more broadly defined, extending well beyond military operations. The alliances are supposed to contribute to the general welfare, to systemic security. Hence the USA has been seeking to make the alliances applicable over wide areas, ready for missions almost anywhere."[18]

Soon after the September 11 tragedy, the Pentagon began to reexamine the U.S. defense posture in South Korea and globally. Under the rubric of "transformation," the Pentagon began exploring ways to make the American military more agile, swift, and expeditionary and better suited to the challenges of a new threat environment.[19] Secretary of Defense Donald Rumsfeld maintained,

> If our goal is to arrange the Department and our forces so we are prepared for the challenges of this new century—the newer enemies and the more lethal weapons—it is clear that our existing arrangements are seriously obsolete. We have entered an era where enemies are in small cells scattered across the globe. Yet America's forces continue to be arranged essentially to fight large armies, navies, and air forces, and in support of an approach—static deterrence—that does not apply to enemies who have no territories to defend and no treaties to honor.[20]

Concerning South Korea, Secretary Rumsfeld argued, "Our troops were virtually frozen in place from where they were when the Korean War ended in 1953."[21] American troops and bases in South Korea were there to deter and defeat an invasion from the North, but the United States could no longer afford to have them there solely for that purpose. Deterring aggression on the peninsula remained their foremost priority, but these troops had to be prepared and available for other missions as well. In December 2009 Gen. Walter Sharp, then commander of U.S. Forces Korea (USFK), cited the need for strategic flexibility to address regional and global issues so that USFK troops could "regionally engage and globally deploy, but never forgetting that our No. 1 responsibility in Korea is to defend the Republic of Korea if we did go to war."[22] General Sharp indicated that USFK was not yet ready for this but that "sometime in the future we could have forces that could, with consultations between both nations, be able to deploy, either ourselves or together, in different places around the world"; but after the deployments, these forces would return to South Korea.[23] In addition, as the wars in Iraq and Afghanistan were consuming more American personnel and resources, there was significant pressure to shift troop strength from South Korea to these theaters. As a result, the United States began a multipart initiative to meet these transformation goals and restructure the U.S. military presence in South Korea.

Restructuring the U.S. Force Presence in South Korea

In 2003 the Pentagon took the first step announcing that it would be withdrawing 12,500 troops from South Korea. The initial target date for completion of the withdrawal was 2005, but after negotiations with the ROK Ministry of National Defense, the deadline was moved to 2008. American officials intended to complete the withdrawal in three phases. In 2004 the Pentagon completed the first phase, with the withdrawal of 5,000 troops. Of these, 3,700, from the Second Brigade of the 2nd Infantry Division, were subsequently sent to Iraq and did not return to South Korea; they are now based in Fort Lewis, Washington. Phase 2, completed in 2006, removed an additional 5,000 troops, largely combat-support units, from the peninsula. The planned third phase entailed the withdrawal of another 2,500 by 2008, again largely from support units. This would bring the total number of U.S. troops in South Korea to 25,000. However, due to events on the peninsula, particularly North Korea's detonation of a nuclear device in October 2006, Washington suspended the third withdrawal and settled on 28,500 troops, the current troop level in South Korea.

To compensate for these withdrawals, the Pentagon pledged to provide $11 billion in additional spending to modernize the U.S. forces that remained on the peninsula. The upgrades included improvements to their Apache helicopters and the delivery of PAC-3 Patriot missile batteries. Arguing in support of the move before the Senate Armed Services Committee, then-USFK commander Gen. Leon LaPorte maintained,

> Historically, the metric of readiness has been the number of troops on the ground. However, what is truly important is the complementary deterrent and combat capabilities that each nation contributes to the security of the peninsula. These capabilities allow us to focus overmatching combat power when and where we choose to defeat armed aggression. United States forces can now be sized to provide tailored capabilities that complement those of the Republic of Korea ally, providing overwhelming strategic deterrence. Our regional and strategic reinforcement capabilities allow us to defeat any potential North Korean aggression.[24]

In 2012 Gen. James Thurman, commander of USFK, sought a few modifications requesting that an additional squadron of AH-64 Apache attack helicopters be deployed to South Korea. Two of the three squadrons that had been in Korea were deployed to Iraq and did not return. He also requested increased PAC-3 Patriot missile batteries to improve U.S. capabilities.[25]

The second portion of the force planning initiative was the relocation of remaining U.S. forces from their forward positions north of Seoul to bases south of the Han River. Secretary Rumsfeld told the Senate Armed Services Committee in February 2003, "I'd like to see a number of our forces move away from the Seoul area and from the area near the . . . DMZ and be more oriented toward an air hub and a sea hub, with the ability to reinforce so there's still a strong deterrent, and possibly, with our improved capabilities of moving people, some of those forces come back home."[26] To accomplish this goal, Washington and Seoul announced in June 2004 their intention to move the bulk of U.S. forces to two "hub" locations south of Seoul. The first was a northwest hub, centered on Pyeongtaek and consisting of the U.S. Army base at Camp Humphreys and Osan Air Force Base. The second is the Daegu hub, in the southeast; it includes USAG Daegu and the naval base at Chinhae. According to Bobby Rakes Jr., deputy director of Installation Management Command Korea, Region Transformation Office, "Basically, after the Korean war, we just settled where we were. So we were all over the place, mainly along what were the former main supply routes. By closing all of these antiquated and inefficient installations, we gain a lot of efficiency in terms of improving the quality of life and achieving cost savings. We also get increased safety because we put less soldiers on the road moving back and forth."[27]

The relocation of U.S. forces has two components. One, the Yongsan Relocation Program (YRP), involves the removal of most U.S. forces from the Seoul metropolitan area, including USFK Headquarters from Yongsan to Camp Humphreys. The YRP will affect approximately five thousand service members and should be completed by 2016. The U.S. military will retain a small presence in Seoul around the Dragon Hill Lodge area.[28] General Thurman has also indicated that "under YRP, a forward Command element remains in Seoul to maintain necessary and habitual relationships with the ROK government, U.S. Embassy, and other key organizations and leaders in the capital area."[29] The return of Yongsan to the ROK is particularly significant. When the formal U.S. defense commitment began in 1953, the headquarters and garrison at Yongsan had been viewed by Koreans as a guarantee that American troops would not readily abandon Seoul if war broke out. Today many South Koreans have a different view of the U.S. presence in Yongsan. The base occupies valuable real estate in the heart of Seoul and is sensitive historically because of associations with periods of foreign occupation. In 1882 Chinese troops of the Qing dynasty were stationed at Yongsan during a revolt; Japan later placed a small garrison there, which grew in size when Tokyo annexed Korea in 1910. After World War II U.S. forces entering Seoul occupied the same headquarters as had the hated Japanese occupiers. Once Yongsan is turned over to South Korean authorities, the site may be rebuilt as a national park. Some of the land may be sold to developers to help cover the ROK government's costs in carrying out the YRP. The return of Yongsan will lessen a highly visible aspect of the U.S. footprint in South Korea.

The other element of the relocation plan is the Land Partnership Plan (LPP), which will relocate U.S. forces currently north of the Han River and elsewhere in South Korea to one of two hubs south of Seoul. General Thurman has maintained that relocation will help USFK improve its facilities, consolidate forces, improve force protection, and lower costs while also strengthening "mutual trust within the U.S.-ROK Alliance by signaling enduring American commitment."[30] The move will affect close to 7,000 personnel and is expected to be completed by 2016, though this target may be extended. As a result of the LPP and the YRP, American installations will decrease from 104 to 47, returning close to 60 military installations to South Korean authorities. Over 36,000 acres, valued at more a billion dollars, will be returned to South Korea. Nevertheless, the move to Camp Humphreys and Osan Air Base required the purchase of more than 2,800 acres for expansion of these facilities.[31] Resulting struggles with local residents and protesters caused construction delays. Much of the acreage was lowland rice paddies that needed large amounts of fill, adding another challenge to construction efforts. USFK will retain the Joint Training Facility close to the DMZ for "crew-served training and armored vehicle training."[32] USFK may also keep the 210th Fires Brigade of the 2nd Division in Dongducheon north of Seoul. The brigade has thirty multiple-rocket-launcher systems that have the mission of blunting a North Korean mechanized assault and suppressing its long-range artillery.[33] This unit, along with General Thurman's request to add an Apache squadron and PAC-3 missile batteries, was echoed in a report produced by the Center for Strategic and International Studies to review the U.S. Asia-Pacific rebalance.[34] In addition to reducing further the U.S. footprint, these base consolidations will help to lessen infrastructure and transportation costs while making U.S. operations more efficient.[35] According to the status of forces agreement (SOFA) that specifies guidelines for the U.S. troop presence in South Korea, the United States will not be compensated for any capital improvements, such as buildings or facilities, on land it returns to South Korea. Sixteen of forty-eight bases returned as of December 2011 required extensive environmental cleanup due to the discovery of toxic chemicals that had been dumped in the 1970s. The cleanup effort took two and a half years and cost approximately $148.7 billion, an expense covered by the ROK government.[36]

The relocation of U.S. forces on the peninsula will also allow the Pentagon to normalize the tours of American service personnel based in South Korea. In the past, most served one-year, unaccompanied tours—a relatively short time in comparison to the usual two- or three-year tours and without their families. With the expanded and improved facilities at Camp Humphreys and elsewhere, USFK will offer many more two-year tours for single service members and three-year tours for those with families. This arrangement would make assignment to South Korea similar to being sent to Europe or Japan, where approximately 75 percent of American personnel are accompanied by their family members. The number of families on accompanied tours to South Korea has increased from 1,700 to 4,645. The goal had been to make all tours to South Korea accompanied.[37] However, General Thurman indicated that tour normalization will remain at its current level for the time being, due to cost considerations.[38]

Normal tours provide several benefits, according to former USFK commander General Sharp. First, families and service members experience less stress. Many service members have deployed to Iraq and Afghanistan on unaccompanied tours; this modification in South Korea removes one more instance of separation and the accompanying strain on families. Second, tour normalization reduces turnover and the need for more frequent training of new personnel, making for a more effective force. Finally, longer accompanied tours help to show the U.S. commitment to South Korea and the region; with their families in South Korea, the determination of U.S. troops to defend the peninsula will be that much greater.[39]

In spring 2011, nevertheless, strong criticism surfaced in the Senate regarding tour normalization and the costs of the relocation plan. Following testimony by General Sharp, senators Carl Levin (D-Mich.), John McCain (R-Ariz.), and Jim Webb (D-Va.) of the Armed Services Committee released a letter that called for "placing the realignment of the basing of U.S. military forces in south Korea on hold pending further review, and reevaluate any proposal to increase the number of family members accompanying military personnel," citing the costs to American taxpayers.[40] A Government Accountability Office report released in May 2011 at the request of the Senate Appropriations Committee indicated that the Department of Defense (DoD) had not provided sufficient justification or fully considered other options for the tour-normalization plan. Although no funds had been requested for fiscal year 2012 for military construction related to tour normalization in South Korea, the Senate committees on appropriations and armed services made it clear that no further funding would be approved until further reviews and a complete "business case analysis" had been conducted by DoD.[41]

Changing the Command Structure: Return of Wartime Operational Control

The third and most controversial element of the restructuring of U.S. forces has been the return of wartime OPCON to South Korea. Soon after North Korea invaded the South on 25 June 1950, the UN Security Council created the United Nations Command (UNC) to coordinate the military contributions of the sixteen countries that provided aid to the ROK under the UN flag.[42] In July 1950 ROK president Syngman Rhee signed the "Pusan Letter," giving the UNC operational control of all South Korean forces. When the Korean War ended, OPCON of ROK troops shifted to the United States.

This arrangement continued until 1978, when Washington and Seoul altered the command structure to create the Combined Forces Command (CFC). Under this new arrangement, the United States remained in the lead, but South Korea increased its participation in an integrated command relationship. The new structure was composed of fourteen sections with a chief and a deputy in each. For eight of these sections a U.S. officer holds the position of chief, with the most important of these being the commander in chief. ROK officers hold the top positions in the remaining six sections. In each section, if an American officer is the chief, a ROK officer is the deputy, and vice versa. The eight sections led by an American officer include commander in chief, chief of staff, planning, operations, logistics, judge advocate, public affairs, and secretary of the combined staff. The six South Korean–led sections are personnel, intelligence, communications, engineer, operational analysis, and headquarters commandant.

The CFC is an integrated command structure that facilitates joint planning, training, exercises, and war fighting. Should hostilities break out, the CFC is prepared to assume OPCON over U.S. and ROK forces and to coordinate additional U.S. forces brought in from outside Korea through the various ground, air, and naval component commands. The American commanders of CFC have been four-star Army generals and serve simultaneously as commander of USFK and the UNC. The ROK deputy commander is also a four-star general. The CFC commander reports directly to the presidents of both South Korea and the United States, so the decision to go to war rests with the respective governments, not the CFC commander. Moreover, the CFC arrangement does not give the United States command over ROK forces. Former CFC and USFK commander Gen. Burwell Bell maintained, "The United States does not command ROK forces during wartime—it is a shared responsibility. [Under CFC arrangements], I direct combat operations . . . in full coordination and with the mutual consent and guidance of both nations."[43]

In addition to its war-fighting responsibilities, the CFC structure plays a role in deterring North Korea. Washington's lead in the command structure strengthens the credibility of the U.S. commitment to South Korea and demonstrates that in a crisis, it would be more difficult for the United States to abandon its commitment to the South. Despite CFC's contribution to deterrence, however, South Korean politics and sovereignty sensitivities made it likely that at some point these command relationships would be altered.[44]

Changes to the OPCON arrangement began soon after the end of the Cold War. In 1990 ROK president Roh Tae-woo began talks to change the OPCON arrangement at the same time that U.S. president George H. W. Bush started an earlier phased troop withdrawal from South Korea. After several years of discussions, Washington returned peacetime OPCON to South Korea in 1994, giving Seoul routine, daily management of ROK forces under the ranking South Korean commander. However, wartime OPCON of ROK forces remained with the United States.

In 2002 ROK and American officials began a dialogue concerning the transfer of wartime OPCON as well to South Korea. The ROK's new president, Roh Moo-hyun, was an enthusiastic proponent of the change, maintaining that it was a crucial issue for the country's sovereignty. Once South Korea expressed interest, the Pentagon was happy to move forward on transferring OPCON. The one obstacle was agreement on when the transfer should occur. South Korean officials wanted a 2012 transfer date, arguing they needed more time to accomplish all of the necessary preparations, while the Pentagon believed it could be completed by 2009. Eventually Washington complied with Seoul's wishes, and the OPCON transfer was set for 17 April 2012, but subsequent events would alter this deadline.

The transfer of OPCON had initially included the deactivation of the CFC, to be replaced by some type of parallel command structure with a separate U.S. Korea Command, or KORCOM, and an ROK command that will collaborate through a military cooperation center to coordinate joint operations in a crisis. South Korea would be in the lead and the United States in a supporting role, the reverse of the current command relationship. It is expected that both militaries will continue after the OPCON transfer to have high levels of integration, conduct joint exercises, and operate a joint intelligence center. However, in June 2012 General Thurman suggested that perhaps the CFC structure could be retained with the OPCON transfer but with a Korean general in the lead and the U.S. commander as the deputy. This could be problematic since it would violate the norm that American personnel serve only under U.S. command, and the American deputy might be reduced to a three-star billet, a move ROK officials would oppose.[45] In April 2013 officials announced that the CFC would be retained after the OPCON transfer, though details needed to be finalized.

Despite agreement on the 2012 date, the OPCON transfer and the relocation of U.S. forces remained controversial. Critics on the right in South Korea believed the OPCON change was a mistake. Conservatives and retired ROK flag officers went to great lengths to have the date postponed or even canceled. They argued the OPCON transfer would hurt South Korean security by eliminating the integrated command structure, which would weaken deterrence and the U.S.-ROK alliance. Some feared it might be a first step in a gradual termination of the alliance. Finally, the costs of assuming wartime OPCON were significant and would weaken the ROK economy. Thus, these opponents argued, it was absolutely necessary to maintain the CFC arrangements by delaying or reversing the OPCON transfer to ensure ROK security and preserve the U.S.-ROK alliance.

Others, particularly those on the left, feared that these changes to U.S. bases and the OPCON transfer were part of a "strategic flexibility" posture that could lead the United States to use its forces based in South Korea for other regional conflicts. For example, they feared that if the United States went to war with mainland China over Taiwan, U.S. aircraft at Osan Air Base might strike Chinese targets and drag Seoul into a fight with Beijing that it does not want. In a 2006 agreement, South Korea recognized the U.S. need for greater flexibility for its forces and strategy, while the United States acknowledged the South Korean position that "it shall not be involved in a regional conflict in Northeast Asia against the will of the Korean people."[46] Later President Roh Moo-hyun declared that

Seoul had the right to veto the use of American troops based in South Korea for operations outside the peninsula.⁴⁷

South Korean officials are also concerned that any deployment of USFK troops to other regional contingencies would reduce the number in Korea. In July 2010 Adm. Michael Mullen, chairman of the U.S. Joint Chiefs of Staff, provided reassurance that troop levels would remain at 28,500 but added that these forces might be used for deployments in other parts of Asia, though discussions with ROK officials on this issue were ongoing. Referring to U.S. ties with others in the region, Mullen noted, "We have longstanding relations not just with the ROK but also with Japan. We have emerging relationships with countries in the area—Vietnam, Cambodia—strong, long-lasting relationships with Singapore, et cetera. So the forces we have here are very much in support of all that, as well. We haven't worked any of the details out on how that might happen in the future, and whether it would include a deployment to Iraq or Afghanistan or somewhere else. So we're just not there, yet."⁴⁸

On 26 March 2010—ironically, the day ROKS *Cheonan* was sunk—General Sharp hinted that the door for revising the OPCON transfer date might have opened: "If the Republic of Korea comes and asks for a delay, I'm sure that will be a discussion at the highest levels of both governments, because both governments agree to this timeline of 17 April 2012. And to change that timeline, both governments will have to agree to change that."⁴⁹ Indeed, talks were already under way between American and ROK officials for an adjustment of the OPCON transfer date, and during the 2010 G-20 Summit in Toronto, presidents Lee and Obama announced postponement until December 2015. In a joint press conference, President Obama stated that the new target date "gives us appropriate time . . . to do this right, because this alliance is the lynchpin of not only security for the Republic of Korea and the United States but also for the Pacific as a whole. And South Korea is one of our closest friends—we want to make sure that we execute what's called the opcon transition in an effective way."⁵⁰ Although the revision had already been in the works, the attack on *Cheonan* provided further impetus for the postponement. Kim Sung-hwan, the ROK administration's senior secretary for foreign affairs and security, told reporters in South Korea that the administration was not abandoning the ultimate goal of reclaiming its "military sovereignty."⁵¹ However, Kim noted, "the situation surrounding the Korean Peninsula could become unstable in 2012, when presidential elections will be held in South Korea, the United States, and Russia, and the term of the Chinese president ends."⁵²

In June 2013 ROK authorities approached Washington about the possibility of delaying the transfer again beyond December 2015. Debate continues over the wisdom of another extension, and leaders are expected to make a decision sometime later in the year. However, uncertainty regarding the date and the details of the transfer remain.

The Cost of Maintaining U.S. Forces in Korea

Until the 1990s the United States bore most of the cost of the alliance. After the Korean War, South Korea was devastated; its economy struggled for the remainder of the decade, and per capita gross national income never rose above one hundred dollars. Consequently, Washington covered most of the cost of U.S. bases in South Korea and provided extensive amounts of military and economic aid, approximately $5.8 billion from 1955 to 1967. In the 1970s further support came through the Military Assistance Program and Foreign Military Sales to facilitate South Korea's purchase of American military equipment to modernize its forces. From 1970 to 1986 Washington provided $2.4 billion in loan guarantees or direct credits for acquiring military equipment. Excluding the International Military Education and Training program, South Korea no longer receives these types of security assistance.[53]

With the end of the Cold War, South Korea began to assume a greater share of its defense costs. In 1991 South Korea paid approximately $150 million to support the U.S. presence, and by 2004 the amount had grown to $623 million, a significant increase but less than the U.S. contribution to South Korea's defense. Seoul's direct contribution in 2007 was $770 million, approximately 41 percent of the total by U.S. calculations. In 2008 the total cost of the American presence for nonpersonnel stationing expenses in South Korea was just over $2 billion, and South Korea covered approximately $810 million of that amount. The United States has been trying to encourage South Korea to increase its contributions to 50 percent but so far has been unsuccessful; in comparison, Japan covers 75 percent of the cost of U.S. forces in Japan. South Korean officials disagree with the American calculation of burden sharing, noting that programs such as the Korean Augmentation Troops to the U.S. Army, or KATUSA, are not included in ROK contributions and that South Korea provides at no cost land for firing ranges and bases. In addition, Seoul exempts U.S. forces in Korea from taxes and reduces their electricity and telephone fees.[54] Thus, South Korea believes its contributions are more than the 41 percent Washington claims.

In January 2009 South Korea and the United States signed a new Special Measures Agreement (SMA) that laid out the cost-sharing provisions for the next five years. American officials were pleased that these arrangements were now on a more predictable long-term basis; previous agreements had been biennial. In the SMA, South Korea agreed to give $741 million for its annual contribution, paying for wages for the Korean workforce on U.S. bases, service contracts, maintenance, and construction. Each year under the agreement Seoul's contribution is adjusted based on the cost of living index. The SMA also allows South Korea to provide services on an "in kind" basis, especially for construction, where ROK firms build facilities to U.S. specifications.[55] Talks continue for renewal of the next SMA that begins in 2014, and, as expected, it has been difficult to reach an agreement.

The Future of U.S. Bases in South Korea

U.S. bases in South Korea are part of an alliance relationship that has been evolving. The alliance is slowly moving toward an arrangement that is more of a partnership than a patron-client relationship dominated by the United States. South Korea is in a stronger position within the alliance to steer the direction of the relationship rather than following the American lead. However, U.S. bases in South Korea will continue to be an important part of the security relationship between the two allies for the foreseeable future. The primary goal of the alliance and U.S. bases in South Korea will remain deterring an attack from the North, but increasingly the relationship is also addressing common global security concerns, such as piracy, peacekeeping, trafficking, and the spread of nuclear weapons and technology—issues that require a broader vision of the alliance, as expressed by presidents Lee and Obama at their June 2009 summit and reaffirmed by Obama and Park during the May 2013 meeting.

The relocation of U.S. bases in South Korea and the future of the OPCON transfer will continue to be a focus of alliance relations, though secondary to the chief concern of providing for South Korea's defense. Important issues connected with these changes will need to be settled, particularly disagreements over cost sharing. Despite these points of friction, which any long-term relationship will have, the alliance is strong and in its best shape in a number of years. Time will tell if these good years can endure beyond the close personal ties between presidents Obama, Lee, and now Park.

There is also potential for increased U.S.-ROK naval cooperation.[56] In the wake of the *Cheonan* attack, Washington and Seoul announced their intention to increase the number of naval exercises, with particular emphasis on antisubmarine warfare and the Proliferation Security Initiative. In addition, South Korea will likely play a greater role in maintaining security in the maritime commons, where both countries have a growing set of mutual interests. South Korea's participation in Combined Task Force 151, the international effort to curtail piracy off the Somali coast, is an important example.[57] With ROK naval capabilities increasing and its development of a blue-water navy maturing, Seoul will play a greater role in maintaining global peace and stability.

Much will depend on North Korea's future, particularly the country's direction under Kim Jong-un, and on the possibility of Korean reunification. Once the DMZ disappears, there may be pressure to remove U.S. bases from the peninsula. However, even a unified Korea under Seoul's authority might find the U.S.-ROK alliance and American bases helpful for its security, depending on China's future strategic direction. However, this will likely be a point of significant debate only if North and South become one.

The bases that support the U.S.-ROK alliance are an important part of the relationship between these two countries. Their numbers, size, and location have changed on several occasions since the mutual security agreement was signed in

1953 and are now in the process of further alterations. The U.S.-ROK alliance is likely to remain an important part of the security calculations of both countries and an important part of the regional security architecture. The specific form of the alliance may change, and the U.S. footprint may decrease further in the years ahead. Yet close U.S.-ROK ties and American bases in the region will continue to help maintain peace and stability in this uncertain regional security environment.

Notes

The views expressed in this report are the author's alone and do not represent the official position of the Department of the Navy, the Department of Defense, or the U.S. government.

1. *Joint Vision for the Alliance of the United States of America and the Republic of Korea* (Washington, D.C.: 16 June 2009), http://www.whitehouse.gov/the_ press_office/Joint-vision-for-the-alliance-of-the-United-States-of-America-and-the-Republic-of-Korea/.
2. "Joint Declaration in Commemoration of the 60th Anniversary of the Alliance between the Republic of Korea and the United States of America," 7 May 2013, http://www.whitehouse.gov/the-press-office/2013/05/07/joint-declaration-commemoration-60th-anniversary-alliance-between-republ.
3. For a more detailed discussion of this time, see Bruce Cumings, ed., *Child of Conflict: The Korean-American Relationship, 1943–1953* (Seattle: University of Washington Press, 1983); Bruce Cumings, *The Origins of the Korean War*, vol. 1, *Liberation and the Emergence of Separate Regimes, 1945–1947* (Princeton, N.J.: Princeton University Press, 1981); Bruce Cumings, *The Origins of the Korean War*, vol. 2, *The Roaring of the Cataract, 1947–1950* (Princeton, N.J.: Princeton University Press, 1990); and James I. Matray, *The Reluctant Crusade: American Foreign Policy in Korea, 1941–1950* (Honolulu: University of Hawaii Press, 1985).
4. See Terence Roehrig, *From Deterrence to Engagement: The U.S. Defense Commitment to South Korea* (Lanham, Md.: Lexington Books, 2006), 117–19.
5. U.S. Senate, *United States Security Agreements and Commitments Abroad: Republic of Korea*, hearings before the Subcommittee on U.S. Security Agreements and Commitments Abroad of the Committee on Foreign Relations, 91st Cong., 2nd sess., part 6, 24–26 February 1970 (Washington, D.C.: GPO, 1970), 1733–41.
6. See Terence Roehrig, "ROK–U.S. Maritime Cooperation: A Growing Dimension of the Alliance," *International Journal of Korean Studies* 14, no. 1 (Spring/Summer 2010): 108.
7. Richard Nixon, "American Policy in the Pacific: Informal Remarks of President Nixon with Newsmen at Guam," 25 July 1969, in *Public Papers of the Presidents of the United States, 1969* (Washington, D.C.: U.S. Government Printing Office [hereafter GPO], 1971), 544–49.

8. U.S. House of Representatives, *Review of the Policy Decision to Withdraw United States Ground Forces from Korea*, testimony of Maj. Gen. John K. Singlaub, hearings before the Investigations Subcommittee and Committee on Armed Services, 95th Cong., 1st and 2nd sess., 25 May, 13–14 July, 1 August, 3 September 1977, and 4–6, 9–14 January 1978 (Washington, D.C.: GPO, 1978), 30–31.

9. U.S. House of Representatives, *Review of the Policy Decision to Withdraw United States Ground Forces from Korea*, statement of Gen. Bernard W. Rogers, Chief of Staff of the U.S. Army, hearings before the Investigations Subcommittee and Committee on Armed Services, 95th Congress, 1st and 2nd Sessions (Washington, D.C.: GPO, 1978), 89.

10. William H. Gleysteen Jr., *Massive Entanglement, Marginal Influence: Carter and Korea in Crisis* (Washington, D.C.: Brookings Institution Press, 1999), 22–23.

11. Ibid., 28–29.

12. Peter Hayes, *Pacific Powderkeg: American Nuclear Dilemmas in Korea* (Lanham, Md.: Lexington Books, 1991), 85.

13. See Uk Heo and Terence Roehrig, *South Korea since 1980* (New York: Cambridge University Press, 2010), 36.

14. U.S. Defense Department, *A Strategic Framework for the Asian Pacific Rim: Looking toward the 21st Century* (Washington, D.C.: DoD, 1990), 7.

15. "Citing North Korean Atom Threat, U.S. to Delay Troop Cuts in South," *New York Times*, 21 November 1991.

16. See Roehrig, *From Deterrence to Engagement*, 124–29.

17. George H. W. Bush, "Text of Remarks at Camp Casey in Yongsan, South Korea," 6 January 1992, in *Public Papers of the Presidents of the United States, 1992–1993* (Washington, D.C.: GPO, n.d.), 1:43.

18. Patrick M. Morgan, "American Grand Strategy and the U.S.-ROK Alliance," *Pacific Focus* 24, no. 1 (April 2009): 30.

19. See U.S. Defense Department, *Quadrennial Defense Review Report* (Washington, D.C.: DoD, 30 September 2001); and U.S. Defense Department, *2004 Global Posture Review* (Washington, D.C.: DoD, 2004).

20. *Global Posture*, testimony as prepared for delivery by Secretary of Defense Donald H. Rumsfeld to the Senate Armed Services Committee, 23 September 2004, 108th Cong., 2nd sess., available at www.defense.gov/.

21. Ibid.

22. Gen. Walter Sharp, "The U.S.-ROK Alliance: The Future," remarks to the Military Strategy Forum, Center for International and Strategic Studies, Washington, D.C., 14 December 2009, available at csis.org/.

23. Ibid.

24. Quoted in Jim Garamone, "In Korea, Think Capabilities, Not Numbers, General Says," American Forces Information Service, 24 September 2004.

25. "USFK Wants More Attack Helicopters, Missiles," *Chosun Ilbo*, 13 June 2012, http://english.chosun.com/site/data/html_dir/2012/06/13/2012061301388.html.

26. Quoted in Sonmi Efron and Mark Magnier, "Rumsfeld May Reduce Forces in S. Korea," *Los Angeles Times*, 14 February 2003.

27. Quoted in R. Slade Walters, "U.S. Forces Korea Transformation Update," *Army.mil*, 12 January 2010, http://www.army.mil/media/102403/.

28. Ibid.

29. House Armed Services Committee, *Statement of General James D. Thurman, Commander, United Nations Command; Commander, United States–Republic of Korea Combined Forces Command; and Commander, United States Forces Korea*, 28 March 2012, 13–14.

30. Ibid., 13.

31. "U.S. Land Returns Continue," *United States Forces Korea*, 14 July 2006, http://www.usfk.mil/usfk/press-release.us.land.returns.continue.506.

32. Walters, "U.S. Forces Korea Transformation Update."

33. "USFK Wants to Keep Artillery Brigade North of Seoul," *Chosun Ilbo*, 15 June 2012, http://english.chosun.com/site/data/html_dir/2012/06/15/2012061 500652.html.

34. David J. Berteau, Michael J. Green, Gregory Kiley, and Nicholas Szechenyi, *U.S. Force Posture Strategy in the Asia Pacific Region: An Independent Assessment* (Washington, D.C.: Center for Strategic and International Studies, 15 August 2012), 92–94, http://csis.org/publication/pacom-force-posture-review.

35. Gen. Walter L. Sharp, "Transformation Conference Commander's Welcome," *United States Forces Korea*, 5 April 2010, 10, www.usfk.mil/. (General Sharp was commander, USFK.)

36. "Defense Ministry to Complete Cleanup of Former US Bases This Week," *Yonhap News*, 29 December 2011, available at english.yonhapnews.co.kr/.

37. Sharp, "Transformation Conference Commander's Welcome," 11.

38. House Armed Services Committee, *Statement of General James D. Thurman*, 14.

39. Sharp, "Transformation Conference Commander's Welcome," 12.

40. "Senators Levin, McCain, Webb Call for Re-examination of Military Basing Plans in East Asia," *Carl Levin: U.S. Senator Michigan*, 11 May 2011, http://www.levin.senate.gov/newsroom/press/release/senators-levin-mccain-webb-call-for-re-examination-of-military-basing-plans-in-east-asia/?section=alltypes.

41. See Mark E. Manyin, Emma Chanlett-Avery, and Mary Beth Nikitin, *U.S.–South Korea Relations*, Report R41481 (Washington, D.C.: Congressional Research Service [hereafter CRS], 28 November 2011), 5; and Daniel H. Else, *Military Construction: Analysis of the FY2012 Appropriation and Authorization*, Report R41885 (Washington, D.C.: CRS, 13 July 2011), 10–12.

42. United Nations Security Council Resolution 84, 7 July 1950, http://www.un.org/en/ga/search/view_doc.asp?symbol=S/RES/84%281950%29.

43. Gen. B. B. Bell, U.S. Forces Korea, speech to the Korean National Assembly–Security Forum, 13 July 2006, 2.

44. See Roehrig, *From Deterrence to Engagement*, 185–86.

45. "USFK Proposal Is Worth Considering," *Chosun Ilbo*, 15 June 2012, http://english.chosun.com/site/data/html_dir/2012/06/15/2012061501235.html.

46. U.S. State Department, "United States and the Republic of Korea Launch Strategic Consultation for Allied Partnership," 19 January 2006, http://seoul.usembassy .gov/rok20060119.html.

47. Larry A. Niksch, *Korea: U.S.–Korean Relations: Issues for Congress* (Washington, D.C.: CRS, 21 July 2006), 15.

48. Quoted in Hwang Doo-hyong, "U.S. Troops in Korea to Be Sent to Conflict Regions in Coming Years: Adm. Mullen," Yonhap News Agency, 22 July 2010, available at english.yonhapnews.co.kr/.

49. Ibid.

50. White House, "Remarks by President Obama and President Lee Myung-bak of the Republic of Korea after Bilateral Meetings," 26 June 2010, http://www .whitehouse.gov/the-press-office/remarks-president-obama-and-president-lee-myung-bak-republic-korea-after-bilateral-.

51. Quoted in Ser Myo-ja, "Troop Control Transfer Delayed," *JoongAng Daily*, 28 June 2010, available at joongangdaily.joins.com/.

52. Quoted in "U.S. to Delay Troop Control Handover to S. Korea," *Chosun Ilbo*, 28 June 2010, available at english.chosun.com/.

53. Roehrig, *From Deterrence to Engagement*, 173–75.

54. Jung Sung-ki, "Defense Cost-Sharing Talks to Test Korea-US Alliance," *Korea Times*, 29 April 2008, available at www.koreatimes.co.kr/.

55. "Special Measures Agreement Signed," *United States Forces Korea*, January 2009, www.usfk.mil/.

56. See Roehrig, "ROK–U.S. Maritime Cooperation," 91–124; and Yoji Koda, "The Emerging Republic of Korea Navy: A Japanese Perspective," *Naval War College Review* 63, no. 2 (Spring 2010): 13–34.

57. See Terence Roehrig, "South Korea's Counter-Piracy Operations in the Gulf of Aden," in Scott Bruce, John Hemmings, Balbina Y. Hwang, Terence Roehrig, and Scott A. Snyder, *Global Korea: South Korea's Contributions to International Security*, Report for the Council on Foreign Relations, October 2012.

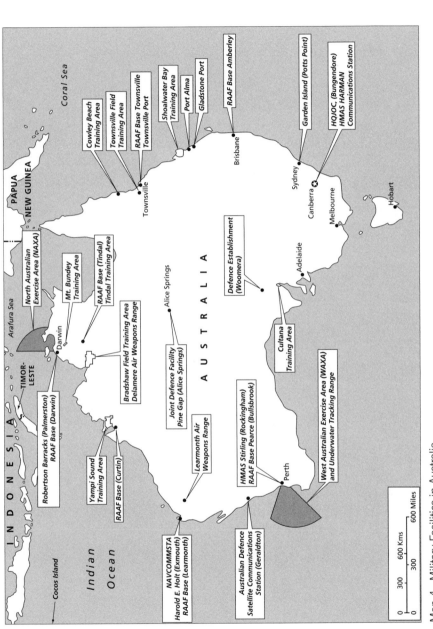

Map 4. Military Facilities in Australia

4

The U.S. Strategic Relationship with Australia

Jack McCaffrie and Chris Rahman

A ustralia has hosted U.S. bases or troops for most of the last seventy years, beginning in the early part of the Second World War in the Pacific. Ironically, the arrival of American troops in Australia was at least partly the result of the failure of the "Singapore strategy," whereby the Royal Navy's Singapore naval base was to support any British fleet sent to the Far East in the event of a war with Japan. Seventy years on, Australia still hosts U.S. defense facilities and U.S. forces continue to visit—primarily now for exercises. Map 4 depicts major facilities utilized at present.

U.S. basing in Australia has occurred in three distinct periods: the Second World War, the Cold War, and the post–Cold War era. The extent and nature of the American military presence have evolved significantly since the first American troops arrived in 1942. During the Cold War especially, there was considerable controversy in Australia as to the legitimacy of the substantial number of U.S. bases, many of which had deterrence or warning functions associated with U.S. nuclear forces. There was controversy also about their potential to make Australia a target in any nuclear exchange and about the manner in which the Australian government managed the entire issue.

The end of the Cold War, with the attendant changes in the characteristics of security threats, seems to have removed most of the controversy associated with the U.S. force posture in Australia. Agreement in late 2011 for the U.S. military to increase its presence in northern Australia, in the context of the Global Posture Review, thus far has elicited only limited negative comment. Australian reaction to a June 2012 think-tank report for the U.S. secretary of defense on American force-posture options in the Asia-Pacific region indicates, however, that there are limits to what is politically acceptable.[1] Consequently, the future of the American military presence in Australia may be different in kind and in scope from what it has been, but it may also be attended by less controversy than in the past.

As has been the case since at least 1945, Australia wants to ensure that the United States remains fully engaged in, and strategically committed to, the security and stability of the Asia-Pacific region. Perceptions that this may prove more difficult than in the past, as well as concerns relating to China's rise, may well make U.S. forces ever more welcome in Australia.

U.S. Military Basing in Australia during the Second World War

Britain's inability to send a fleet to Singapore early in the war against Japan and the consequent failure of the Singapore strategy led Australia to turn to the United States for assistance.[2] This resulted in Australia's becoming a major base for U.S. Navy and Army operations in the Pacific. The U.S. Army buildup began very early, in December 1941, when 4,500 soldiers who had been bound for the Philippines were diverted to Brisbane.[3] By the time Gen. Douglas MacArthur arrived in Darwin on 17 March 1942, the number of American troops in Australia had grown to 25,000—but, in MacArthur's view, they were poorly trained and equipped.[4]

This was just the beginning of a huge buildup that by mid-1943 had some 250,000 U.S. troops in Australia. They were camped in Brisbane, Sydney, and Melbourne as well as in several smaller towns.[5] Clearly, Australia proved to be a very suitable base from which to launch operations against the Japanese in the southwest Pacific. Nevertheless, the huge number of American servicemen did create some problems for both U.S. and Australian authorities. Although the American troops were very popular with the general public, who were grateful for the efforts being made for their defense, they were less popular with Australian military personnel.

Resentment grew because U.S. military wages and conditions of service were significantly better than those provided to Australians. Consequently, American servicemen had advantages over Australian military personnel and over members of the public in seeking access to goods and services.[6] More serious for the Australian government, there was growing resentment among the U.S. troops, who saw many Australian soldiers remaining in Australia while they embarked on operations in the South West Pacific theater, ostensibly to save Australia. This was because although Australia had a volunteer army that could serve abroad, its conscript militia was initially limited to service within Australia.[7]

Prime Minister John Curtin changed the rules for militia employment, enabling them to fight in the southwest Pacific. He did so because he recognized the inefficiency of having a good part of his armed forces hobbled by such restrictions and because the restrictions were becoming increasingly difficult to justify to Americans.[8] In doing so, Curtin was mindful of the Labor Party's long-standing opposition to conscription. As the war in the Pacific progressed, however, MacArthur made it plain that Australian troops were to take an increasingly secondary part in the fighting in any event.[9]

The U.S. Navy presence in Australia may not have been as numerically strong as that of the Army, but it was certainly widespread. Its presence also resulted in the development of many basing facilities around the Australian coast because the Royal Australian Navy (RAN) of the period was a very small force based primarily in Sydney. Its strength immediately before the outbreak of the war was 5,440 officers and enlisted and a combatant force of six cruisers, five destroyers, and four sloops (roughly, destroyer-escort equivalents), two of which were still being completed.[10] RAN exposure to the U.S. Navy and its ships left it shocked at the American materiel superiority over British ships, its better logistics support systems, and in some respects its crew facilities.[11]

Throughout the war in the Pacific, the RAN operated alongside the Americans, initially as part of Task Force 44, beginning in April 1942.[12] This pattern was maintained in the southwest Pacific and much farther afield, including the Leyte Gulf invasion in October 1944. These wartime operations established a pattern that remains in effect today.

U.S. Navy basing in Australia centered on a small number of major bases situated in Australia's Trust Territories and New Britain, New Caledonia, and the New Hebrides. Any controversy generated by this arrangement remained localized. American authorities apparently expected that sovereignty would be transferred to the United States on the grounds that it was the only entity in a position to protect these places.[13] Australian refusals did offend, and there were some "angry editorials in American newspapers." The *Chicago Tribune* expressed American sentiment in this way: "Britain and France jointly controlled the New Hebrides, yet the two together were unable to protect them. Neither can Australia. The United States is not likely to take permanent possession of New Britain, although she may want the permanent right to use any naval and air installation she has built there."[14]

There was considerable Australian unease at the American attitude, and it was most strongly expressed by External Affairs Minister H. V. Evatt, who felt growing irritation at American attempts to exclude Australia (and New Zealand) from the main counteroffensive drive toward Japan and at Australia's exclusion from the Cairo Conference of 1943, which discussed the future disposal of territories taken by Japan.[15] Evatt apparently suspected the United States of intending to retain any useful island bases captured during the war. Consequently, the

Australia–New Zealand (ANZAC) Agreement of January 1944 contained a clause asserting "as a recognised principle of international practice that the construction and use, in time of war, by any Power, of naval, military, or air installations in any territory or under the sovereignty or control of another Power, does not in itself afford any basis for territorial claims or rights of sovereignty or control after the conclusion of hostilities."[16] This did not prevent Evatt from suggesting that the United States could retain Manus Island if it accepted security responsibility for the area protected by it.[17] Nevertheless, Washington felt that Evatt was anti-American and his overall approach, together with the terms of the ANZAC Agreement, may well have contributed to the U.S. decision against focusing on Manus Island as a postwar base.[18]

One of the major U.S. Navy basing activities in Australia supported submarine operations. Albany, on the south coast of Western Australia, hosted American submarines from May 1942. Submarines also operated from Exmouth, on the northwest coast of Western Australia, from 1943 and from Fremantle, farther south, from March 1942. The great advantage of Exmouth, despite its remoteness and lack of prior development, was its relative nearness to South and Southeast Asia.[19] Significantly, in view of later developments, both the United States and Australia established communications stations in Exmouth.[20] The major west coast submarine base was Fremantle, which, inter alia, supported U.S. Navy submarine operations into the South China Sea. Brisbane, on the east coast, was the other submarine operating base and in fact the largest U.S. Navy base in Australia during the war, serving as the main base and chief supply point for the assault on eastern New Guinea.[21]

Darwin, on the north coast, was the only other major base, and it supported submarines, patrol boats, and various surface units at different times during the war. Several other lesser bases, such as Cairns in north Queensland and Thursday Island in the Torres Strait, supported patrol boats and other surface forces.

Most of the bases either shut down or became much less active as the naval war switched to the Central Pacific and beyond in 1944 and 1945. By mid-1944 Manus Island, off the northeast coast of New Guinea (Australian Trust Territory), had been retaken from the Japanese;[22] it quickly became one of the biggest U.S. bases in the Pacific.[23] It also became the first point of interest with respect to American basing in Australia in the Cold War period.

U.S. Military Basing in Australia during the Cold War

American military bases in Australia during the Second World War for the most part hosted operational units and supported them during operations in the Pacific. The nature of U.S. basing in Australia during the Cold War was quite different. Apart from the much-reduced scale, the focus became surveillance and early warning in relation to the Soviet nuclear threat as well as communications associated with the U.S. nuclear deterrent. In the immediate aftermath of the war, however, the United States took some time to identify its major strategic interests and needs in the Pacific.

Soon after the end of the Second World War, the United States indicated a strong desire to retain Manus Island, first as a major but ultimately as a secondary naval base.[24] Difficulties arose in negotiations with both Britain and Australia, with neither keen to see sovereignty relinquished without some reciprocal benefit. Even at this early point, Australia wanted any transfer to be in the context of a regional security agreement, which Washington was simply not interested in establishing.[25] Thus, there was a very real tension between Australia, which wanted the United States to remain engaged in the South Pacific (but on its own restrictive terms), and the United States, which could see no reason for entering into security agreements in a part of the world that it now regarded as of secondary importance.

Over the next few years American interest in Manus Island waned, and a 1949 basing review placed Australia, New Zealand, and their islands "outside of any important strategic area in any prospective war of the near future."[26] That situation changed a little in the late 1970s, when the U.S. Senate considered Darwin and Cockburn Sound (now HMAS Stirling naval base) as potential alternatives to Subic Bay if the U.S. Navy ever had to leave the Philippines.[27]

Meanwhile, however, the foundation for U.S. basing in Australia during the Cold War had been established with the signing by Britain and the United States on 5 March 1946 of the United Kingdom–United States (UKUSA) Agreement for the sharing of signals intelligence;[28] Canada and Australia became signatories over the following year or so.[29] It is considered to be possibly the most secret agreement ever entered into by the English-speaking world.[30] The UKUSA Agreement enabled a web of American intelligence-gathering and strategic communications facilities to be established in Australia over the following twenty or so years.

The impetus provided by UKUSA was boosted by enactment of the ANZUS Treaty in 1951; American recognition of Australia's concerns over the peace treaty with Japan and its rapid move to support the UN in the Korean War had overcome earlier reluctance to provide a security guarantee.[31] Australia's attraction was also increased by the realization in the early 1960s that the Southern Hemisphere had become a vital location for U.S. facilities associated with strategic reconnaissance programs.[32] The status of the bases (more often called "facilities") and the extent to which Australia had access to them was a source of some controversy for many years. There were two clear categories of facilities: the three major ones at North West Cape, Pine Gap, and Nurrungar, and a set of generally much smaller and less strategically important ones spread throughout the country.

The Major Facilities

Exmouth Gulf, on the northwest coast of Western Australia and, as noted, a Second World War site of U.S. and Australian communications stations, became the site of the first of the major U.S. defense facilities in Australia during the Cold War. Agreement to host the naval communications station was announced by Prime Minister Robert Menzies in May 1962. Menzies denied that the station would play any part in communicating with U.S. ballistic-missile submarines.[33] But the North West Cape communications station, as the new facility was known, was in fact the largest of three such very-low-frequency (VLF) stations around the world designed to provide global communications coverage for U.S. Navy fleet ballistic-missile submarines.[34] North West Cape is also likely to have had a signals intelligence function.[35] Initially North West Cape was simply an American facility, but in January 1974 it became a "joint" facility with the establishment of a separate RAN communications station and the appointment of a RAN officer as deputy commander.[36] North West Cape continues to function but is now fully manned by civilian contract staff.

The other two major U.S. facilities in Australia—Pine Gap, near Alice Springs, and Nurrungar, near Woomera (closed in October 1999)—both functioned as defense satellite ground stations. They acted as part of the Defense Support Program (DSP), a satellite-based ballistic-missile-attack early-warning system.[37] Nurrungar is said to have been a principal link between DSP East and what is now known as the North American Aerospace Defense Command.[38] Both facilities are also believed to have been involved in communications interception. Pine Gap was established as a U.S. Department of Defense program but has apparently been a Central Intelligence Agency (CIA) activity from the beginning.[39] There is also believed to have been CIA involvement in Nurrungar.

Pine Gap became operational in 1970, and Nurrungar is reported to have controlled its first satellite in May 1971.[40] Both facilities employed substantial numbers of people; in 1978, for example, there were 454 at Pine Gap and 396 at Nurrungar. They employed Australian nationals but very few in technical positions.[41]

The Lesser Facilities

Most political and public attention in Australia has focused on the three main U.S. facilities. Several others have operated from time to time, and at least some of these remain in use today. The exact number of U.S. facilities operational during the Cold War is not known, because of the secrecy with which both the American and Australian governments shrouded them. What we do know is that the first of the Cold War U.S. facilities in Australia was the Project Oak Tree seismic station, operated by the U.S. Air Force in Alice Springs from 1955. While its real purpose was to monitor nuclear tests, for many years Australians understood it to be a weather station.[42] Several other similar seismic stations were established around Australia in 1976.

Of the lesser facilities, the Omega navigation station on the south coast of Victoria is probably best known because of the protest activity associated with it.[43] This facility was operational from 1982 to 2008.[44] As part of a global VLF system, it provided navigation information to U.S. aircraft, ships, and submarines. American authorities denied that it provided a service for fleet ballistic-missile submarines, but the fact that its signals could be read underwater perhaps suggests otherwise.

The U.S. Navy Doppler Tracking System (TRANET) receiving station, located at Smithfield, in South Australia, was much more clearly associated with the fleet ballistic-missile submarines. This small station, operated solely by Australian personnel, was part of the global transit-navigation satellite program. It provided all-weather global navigation, especially for fleet ballistic-missile submarines.[45]

Other lesser facilities of note included the Project HIBAL (high-altitude balloon) launching facility at Mildura, in Victoria. Established in 1960 by the U.S. Atomic Energy Agency, the facility measured high-altitude radiation associated with nuclear explosions.[46] Full operational responsibility for the station was assumed by Australia in 1975.[47] In a similar vein, the U.S. Air Force had a solar observatory at Learmonth, near North West Cape. This jointly manned facility, which opened in 1978, examined solar activity for its impact on communications, including on the interception of Soviet communications.[48]

Finally, one of the least-known facilities was Project Flowerless, thought to be an underwater passive sonar array located off Christmas Island in the Indian Ocean. While this facility has never been formally acknowledged, it may well have been part of the U.S. Navy's Sound Surveillance System for submarine detection.[49]

Secrecy and the U.S. Bases in Australia

The issue that characterized American basing in Australia during the Cold War was the lack of information from the U.S. government, especially in respect of the base functions, combined with the almost obsessive secrecy and evasion practiced by the Australian government over the matter.[50] For the most part, American authorities appeared to pass as little information as possible relating to the purposes of the various facilities.[51] For example, as late as December 1978, John Gorton, who was prime minister from 1968 to 1971, noted that he still did not know what Pine Gap's function was, and he had never felt the need to ask when in office.[52] In May 1977 former prime ministers William McMahon and Gough Whitlam also indicated that they were not sure that they had complete knowledge as to the functions of U.S. facilities in the country.[53] Furthermore, there were occasions when U.S. activities at the facilities were conducted without Australian knowledge. One instance was the use of the North West Cape communications station to issue a general nuclear alert in October 1973. Another related to subsequent modifications made to North West Cape without reference to the Australian government.[54]

At least some blame for the way in which this matter was handled belongs with the Australian government. Information about the matter appeared in the Australian media before any proposal had been put to Australia, but while Australian politicians may not have been aware of the plans at that time, Australian officials were.[55] Fault also lies with Australia in other respects. Even the limited information passed to the Australian government was often considered too sensitive to be passed on to the general public. Liberal Party (coalition government) politician Don Chipp said publicly in 1969 that "the government does not deem it wise or necessary to tell the public what is going on at Pine Gap."[56] The same politician castigated the Labor opposition for wanting joint control of North West Cape.[57] Incredibly, the Australian Department of Defence in 1973 refused offers of additional information from its U.S. counterpart.[58] Labor, when in power in the early 1970s, was no less evasive, using the need for secrecy to prevent the left wing of the party from politicizing the issue. Ironically, however, public opinion surveys conducted at the time showed general acceptance of the facilities.

Opposition to the Bases

One explanation for the reluctance of Australian officials to inform the public of the nature and roles of the U.S. facilities was the sense that discussion would encourage debate and that debate would be fueled by misinformation and could lead to opposition to the bases.[59] Inevitably, however, debate and opposition did occur, not least over the potential for the bases to be targets in a nuclear war. Of course, the secrecy itself encouraged speculation.[60] American officials were relatively open in asserting that the facilities in Australia (the three major ones anyway) were likely to be targets, and then-classified Australian strategic assessments admitted as much.[61]

Opposition to the bases was sporadic and limited mainly to left-wing political activists. That said, it has been long lasting, beginning against Pine Gap even as the facility was being built and continuing into the present decade.[62] However, there was little publicly expressed opposition to North West Cape before the Whitlam Labor government came to power at the end of 1972.[63] All of the major facilities were subjected to protests by the same groups at various times during the Cold War and since. Those protesting against Nurrungar made it clear that they opposed the foreign-owned bases themselves and the secrecy associated with them.[64] A more open and honest approach on the part of the Australian government—from the beginning of the establishment of the Cold War facilities—would most likely have rendered these protests even less effective than they have proved to be. This is especially so given that the facilities were very useful, if not central, to maintaining détente with the Soviet Union.[65]

The Facilities and Australian Sovereignty

No aspect of the U.S. facilities in Australia was more contentious than their impact on Australian sovereignty. The Australian government of the day made a conscious decision to host the facilities, motivated no doubt by a desire to see the United States committed to its security in some way.[66] Yet by not insisting on knowing substantially more about the roles of the facilities than the United States appeared willing to share, the Australian government put itself in a most invidious position.[67] It became party to activities of which it had no knowledge and over which it had no control. Furthermore, for years it was less than truthful as to those roles and activities with the Australian people.[68] The Labor opposition claimed that Australia had in fact abrogated its sovereignty.[69]

During its own time in government from late 1972 to late 1975, Labor, especially its left wing, doubted the benefits of the bases;[70] however, it failed to convince the U.S. government to allow Australia a greater say in the operation of the major facilities.[71] American authorities could not have been reassured by Prime Minister Whitlam's statement in Parliament during April 1974 to the effect that his government did not favor extending the agreements covering the U.S. facilities then located in Australia. He made the statement during a debate on a Soviet request (ultimately rejected) to establish a joint space research station in Australia.[72]

Beyond that, elements of the security relationship between Australia and the United States developed without government oversight. There are suggestions, for example, that the relationship between the U.S. National Security Agency (NSA) and Australia's Defence Signals Directorate was unknown to Australian government ministers until the late 1970s.[73] Reports that the NSA, through its presence at Pine Gap, monitored internal Australian communications simply added fuel to an already healthy fire.[74]

A former head of Australia's Department of Foreign Affairs, Alan Renouf, has made scathing comments about the country's foreign-policy making during his years of service, noting "the reluctance by most Australian governments to formulate and execute a foreign policy designed to promote a distinctive Australian interest."[75] He went on to claim that policy making had involved little more than determining what first Britain, and later the United States, thought and then falling in line.

Implications for Australian Domestic and Foreign Policy

Australia enjoys a long-standing and close security relationship with the United States, formalized by the 1951 ANZUS Treaty. The closeness of the relationship is illustrated by frequent high-level political and diplomatic contacts and military ties that see Australian and U.S. forces frequently operating together. Despite this, the presence of the U.S. facilities has complicated Australia's political landscape from time to time.

No matter how close the relationship between the two countries, their national interests have not always been the same. Consequently, at times the United States has used the facilities for purposes to which Australia was not necessarily committed and without informing Australian authorities that it was doing so.[76] Furthermore, the U.S. government took advantage of a politically conservative coalition government that served in Australia throughout the period in which the American facilities were established.[77] The Labor government that came to power in December 1972 was distrusted by Washington, which had already, in 1969, prepared to remove sensitive facilities from Australia in the event of a Labor victory in that year's election. While Labor was in power from 1972 to 1975, the United States threatened three times to cut off intelligence flows to Australia.[78] This suggests that despite being the host of U.S. facilities, Australia had little control over them. It also suggests that Washington had little confidence in the Labor government.[79]

Furthermore, the presence of the facilities also complicated Australia's foreign-policy making. It meant that other countries assessed Australia as being very much "hand in glove" with the United States on a range of security issues. This in effect reduced Australia's credibility on occasions when it took independent initiatives in its region. An example was the 1973 Labor government proposal for a zone of peace in the Indian Ocean. Indian prime minister Indira Gandhi referred specifically to the U.S. facilities in rebuffing Australia's proposal.[80]

U.S. Military Activities: Places Not Bases

Although very few U.S. military units or formations were based in Australia during the Cold War, there was certainly an American military presence through frequent visits by ships and aircraft of the U.S. Navy, Marine Corps ground forces, and Air Force aircraft. Ship visits were mostly for participation in combined exercises with Australian forces or for crew rest during deployments.[81] Air Force U-2 and RB-57 aircraft were based at some southern Royal Australian Air Force (RAAF) bases in the early and mid-1960s as part of the High Altitude Sampling Program.[82] Subsequent U.S. Air Force visits, mainly to Darwin, related to deployments to and from Diego Garcia in the Indian Ocean and to training opportunities in northern Australia for bomber aircraft. The Air Force training flights began in May 1981, with the arrival of the first B-52s, marked by a demonstration involving some 250 people.[83]

During the 1980s significant protest activity was aimed at U.S. Navy ship visits, with the focus primarily on the potential for the ships to be armed with nuclear weapons as well as nuclear powered.[84] With seventy-three ship visits in 1981, there was considerable scope for protest activity, and some (Labor) state governments expressed opposition to the visits. Federally, Labor—again in opposition—had difficulty expressing a clear policy on the visits. The position was simplified when the 1982 ANZUS Council communiqué announced that without U.S. Navy ship visits to Australia, there would be no ANZUS Treaty.[85] Ship visits have continued to this day, and American ships and submarines visiting HMAS Stirling in Western Australia and other ports around the country are now a common and welcome sight.

U.S. Basing in Australia after the Cold War

The closing of the Cold War chapter in world history did not signal any diminution of the ANZUS Treaty relationship between Canberra and Washington. Indeed, shared values and broadly shared strategic interests in regional and international stability at a time of uncertainty have ensured the alliance's current and likely future sustainability. The events of 11 September 2001, ongoing mutual engagement with Middle Eastern turmoil, and the challenges posed by rising Asian powers have only increased the salience of the relationship. In the context of Australian domestic politics, it has become almost an article of faith that any prospective government must first assure the electorate of its national security credentials, including a strong commitment to the alliance.

There is a strong bipartisan political consensus that a nonnegotiable aspect of Australian foreign and defense policies is to ensure that the United States remains heavily and strategically engaged in the Asia-Pacific region. As Australia's 2009 Defence White Paper asserts, "The Government's judgment is that strategic stability in the region is best underpinned by the continued presence of the United States through its network of alliances and security partnerships."[86] The Australian joint facilities play an important role in supporting those policies: "The contributions of these facilities to global U.S. capabilities both strengthen the alliance and greatly enhance our own capabilities."[87]

Australia has, as least in theory, become a rather more "equal" partner in terms of the shared defense facilities on its territory over the past two decades than it had been previously. The notion of independent U.S. bases on Australian soil has long since been replaced by a stronger assertion of Australian sovereignty by which all such bases are viewed as joint facilities or Australian facilities to which the United States has access. In this context the Australian government follows a policy of "full knowledge and concurrence," which it claims to be "the key underlying principle for all joint Australia-U.S. facilities." This principle is described as the Australian government's

> fundamental right to know what activities foreign governments conduct in, through or from Australian territory or national assets. "Full knowledge" equates to Australia having a "full and detailed understanding" of any capability or activity with a presence on Australian territory or making use of Australian assets. "Concurrence" does not mean Australia approves every activity or tasking; rather, we approve the presence of a capability or

function in Australia in support of its mutually agreed goals, based on our full and detailed understanding of that capability and the uses to which it can be put.[88]

Opposition to the facilities, mainly by an umbrella group called the Australian Anti-Bases Campaign Coalition, is only occasionally vocal or visible, peopled by the generally marginalized political radicals of what remains of the "peace" movement.[89] The group lacks obvious support in mainstream Australian politics, although the minor Greens Party is somewhat sympathetic to its ideals. In government, both main political parties in turn have expressed at least rhetorical support in recent years for the prospect of an expanded American strategic presence in Australia, should such a request be received from Washington.[90]

Despite that fact, sensitivities about a permanent U.S. military presence remain, and it is commonplace for public communications by the Australian government regarding joint facilities and U.S. training activities to include assurances that the activities in question do not equate to U.S. military bases on Australian soil. For its part, the United States recognizes these prevailing conditions and has consistently stated that formal basing in Australia is not planned.[91] Nevertheless, Robert Gates, then secretary of defense, noted at a joint press conference following the November 2010 Australia–United States Ministerial Consultations (AUSMIN) that "efforts to enhance our presence and posture in the Pacific" had been discussed at the talks in the context of the ongoing Global Posture Review and that the two allies had agreed "to create a bilateral force posture working group to begin developing options for enhanced joint defense cooperation on Australian soil."[92] At the 2011 Shangri-La Dialogue, Gates further noted that the working group was considering options that would contribute to the objectives for U.S. force-posture development in the Asia-Pacific region, which include "enhancing our presence in Southeast Asia and into the Indian Ocean."[93]

Options were set out in the AUSMIN 2011 joint communiqué as increased American access to training facilities, prepositioning of American equipment in Australia, increased use of Australian ports and facilities by U.S. forces, and "joint and combined activities in the region."[94] An initial announcement on an enhanced U.S. force posture in Australia involving both training and greater access to existing Australian Defence Force facilities was made during President Barack Obama's visit to Australia in November 2011.[95] Although the initiatives are evolutionary in nature, Australia's defense minister has nonetheless described them as "the single most important development in the operational arrangements under the alliance since the striking of the joint facilities in the 1980s."[96]

The importance of the joint facilities for communications, early warning, surveillance, and intelligence gathering meant that their continued operation after the Cold War was never in doubt. American use of Australian territory over the past twenty years has been built on three elements: the ongoing salience of the joint facilities, expanded training and combined exercising, and access to Australian bases and facilities as points for transit, logistic support, and repair for U.S. ships or aircraft. Using the terminology employed by a 2004 report to Congress on U.S. global defense posture, a 2005 presidential commission categorized the American military presence in Australia in the third rank of facilities, that of a "cooperative security location" (CSL).[97] A CSL is defined as possessing "little or no permanent U.S. presence . . . [and] will be maintained with periodic service, contractor, or host-nation support. CSLs will provide contingency access and be a focal point."[98] However, the options outlined in the 2011 AUSMIN joint communiqué and the subsequent force-posture initiatives of November 2011 suggest that Australia may soon be better described as a "forward operating site," the second category of facilities, involving rotational deployments of U.S. forces, a training focus, and a possibility of hosting prepositioned equipment.[99]

The Major Joint Facilities, 1990–2011
With the status of Naval Communications Station Harold E. Holt having been changed to that of a joint facility in 1974, its command was transferred from the United States to Australia in 1992.[100] Its status changed again in May 1999, when it became an Australian facility "to which the U.S. has full access."[101] In July 2008 a new agreement, the Harold E. Holt Treaty, was signed to extend joint use of the facility for a further twenty-five years.[102] An exchange of letters was made at AUSMIN 2010 regarding the full knowledge and concurrence arrangements for the agreement.[103]

As noted earlier, the Nurrungar ballistic-missile early-warning facility at Woomera, South Australia, closed in 1999. It was replaced by a new relay ground station (RGS) at Pine Gap. Compared to Nurrungar, which had supported around four hundred staff, the new facility is designed to accommodate only fifteen to twenty people.[104] The RGS supports U.S. satellites used to detect ballistic-missile launches and then transmits launch information to the United States. For example, the system was involved with the detection of Iraq's Scud missile launches against Israel during Operation Desert Storm.[105] The data are important for any ballistic-missile-defense system. Joint Defence Facility Pine Gap itself continues to be the largest and most important of the joint facilities in Australia. The treaty governing Pine Gap was extended for another decade in 1998;[106] the existing arrangements remain in place even without formal extension of the agreement beyond 2008. Detailed public information on the facility is by its very nature limited. However, in 2002 there were 448 Australian and 428 American citizens working there, including personnel from "all arms of the Australian Defence Force and U.S. Armed Services." At that time there were twenty-six satellite antennas located at Pine Gap, four of which are associated with the (U.S.) Defense Support Program RGS.[107]

The Joint Geological and Geophysical Research Station is jointly operated by Geoscience Australia and the U.S. Air Force. As part of the International Monitoring System of the Comprehensive Test Ban Treaty, it continues to monitor any nuclear explosions that may occur as well as monitoring earthquakes.[108]

A new Australia-U.S. Joint Communications Facility was announced in early 2007, to be hosted at the Australian Defence Satellite Communications Station at Geraldton, Western Australia. The unmanned ground station will support American and Australian users of a satellite-based communications network known as the Mobile User Objective System.[109]

Further joint facilities are also being considered. At AUSMIN 2010 a "Joint Statement on Space Security" was issued and a "Space Situational Awareness Partnership Statement of Principles" signed.[110] Space situational awareness (SSA) refers to the monitoring and tracking of orbiting objects in space, including satellites and accumulated debris, which can endanger satellites and manned space missions alike. As dependence on space grows, and with threats to space security also on the rise from accidents, collisions with debris, and dedicated antisatellite weaponry, SSA has become essential. However, an SSA partnership document argues that global SSA is constrained by limited surveillance coverage of space in the Southern Hemisphere.[111] Therefore, one element of the partnership is the consideration given to the establishment of ground-based SSA radars in Australia as joint facilities, which could improve the overall coverage of the U.S. Space Surveillance Network. Australia has expressed a preference that any future sensors established for this purpose be colocated with Naval Communications Station Harold E. Holt.[112]

Training and Exercising, 1990–2011

Australia has consistently offered the United States enhanced access to its training and exercise facilities since the end of the Cold War as part of Canberra's policy to enmesh the American regional strategic presence. For example, as early as 1992 Australia invited U.S. forces to make use of its Delamere Air Weapons Range in the Northern Territory and the underwater tracking range off the Western Australian coast.[113] It was subsequently announced, at the 1996 AUSMIN talks, that U.S. forces, particularly the Marine Corps, would increase both the number and scale of exercises conducted in northern Australia. By 2007 the number of exercises was to increase from four to seven, each involving up to 2,500 American personnel, whereas previous exercises had been limited to company size (150 personnel). A small permanent Marine Corps cell was established in Australia to assist with coordination. In addition, the largest Australia-U.S. combined exercise held since perhaps the end of the Second World War, Tandem Thrust 1997, was announced, involving around 17,000 American and 5,000 Australian personnel in joint and combined exercises during March 1997 in Queensland.[114]

The AUSMIN 2005 talks noted the agreement of a memorandum of understanding on the Joint Combined Training Centre (JCTC), which had been initiated at the previous year's discussions. This included an Australian agreement to develop the Shoalwater Bay Training Area in central Queensland in preparation for Talisman Sabre 2007, the latest iteration of the large combined exercises in Queensland that had begun with the Kangaroo series and then Tandem Thrust. At the talks, Australia also agreed to host training visits of B-52, B-1, and B-2 long-range bombers at the Delamere Air Weapons Range and RAAF Base Darwin.[115]

Later renamed the "Joint Combined Training Capability," the new combined training system is described as an "initiative designed to enhance high-end bilateral training, increase and measure operational capability, improve interoperability, and facilitate capability development." JCTC links headquarters facilities of the two partners with various force units, training areas and systems, and "constructive simulations and virtual simulators" to create a single, integrated system for sophisticated combined training.[116] Live training action in geographically disaggregated training ranges can thus be linked, even at sea, in the United States, or at U.S. facilities elsewhere. Simulators can also be used to add virtual capabilities that are not physically available or appropriate for a particular exercise.

The JCTC established the Australian Defence Training and Experimentation Network, which is in turn connected to the U.S. Joint Training and Experimentation Network. Employing network-centric concepts, the system collects data from the distributed training systems and exchanges them among those systems.[117] As part of the JCTC, the Shoalwater Bay Training Area and the Delamere Air Weapons Range and Bradshaw Field Training Area in the Northern Territory have received enhancements enabling them to be linked with U.S. facilities. At Shoalwater Bay, an Exercise Control Facility and an Urban Operations Training Facility have been constructed. Management of the JCTC involves the posting of a small number of American personnel to Australia; it is possible that U.S. military equipment may be prepositioned for future exercises.[118]

The JCTC has been explicitly linked not only to Australia's alliance interests but also to the U.S. Global Posture Review: "The collaborative development of a JCTC in Australia is an example of how high-technology initiatives are being employed to support the development of a more agile force and how Australia is able to assist the U.S. in the achievement of the review objectives."[119] The United States budgeted $10 million in FY 2009 toward JCTC development, including money for studies to develop instrumentation for the Shoalwater Bay Training Area, the Bradshaw Field Training Area, and the Cultana Training Area in South Australia.[120]

The biennial Talisman Sabre exercise series continues to grow in size and complexity. In 2011 it involved approximately 15,000 American and 12,000 Australian personnel distributed throughout training areas on land, at sea, and in the air, in and around Australia and (by networked connection) in the

United States. The exercise will involve three key sites: the East Australian Range Complex, including the Shoalwater Bay Training Area and the Townsville Field Training Area; the North Australian Range Complex, including the Delamere Range Facility, the Bradshaw Field Training Area, and Mount Bundy Training Area; and designated parts of the Coral, Timor, and Arafura seas. A number of ports, civilian airports, RAAF bases, and other Department of Defence sites function as lesser, supporting sites for the exercise.[121] Talisman Sabre 2011 was a vast undertaking, employing the JCTC and involving both simulated command-post and field-training exercises, many of which involve live firing of weapons. The range of live field-training exercises includes amphibious landings, naval gun and missile firings, mine countermeasures, and antisubmarine, antiair, and antisurface naval warfare; Special Forces training, land force maneuver, parachuting, and urban and air operations by land forces; and aerial combat and intercept training, low-flying maneuvers by both fixed-wing aircraft and rotorcraft, unmanned aerial vehicles operation, and air-to-air refueling.[122]

The November 2011 initiatives announced by President Obama and Prime Minister Julia Gillard involve six-month rotational deployments of U.S. Marines to Darwin and northern Australia for training and exercises. The first deployment under the arrangement began in April 2012 and consisted of a company of 250 Marines plus a liaison group.[123] The rotations are expected to grow to an entire 2,500-strong Marine air-ground task force (MAGTF) by 2016–17, and negotiations are continuing on the specific attribution of costs, with those associated with deployment to Australia to be borne by the United States and combined exercise costs shared, "consistent with existing practice."[124] Training and exercises are to take place at Bradshaw and Mount Bundy; increased rotations of U.S. Air Force aircraft and personnel will also occur, particularly through RAAF Base Tindal, and will include greater use of the Delamere Air Weapons Range.[125] It has been reported that this enhanced U.S. presence will occur under the existing 1963 status of forces agreement, and that American forces will be able to conduct unilateral as well as combined training with the Australian Defence Force. The MAGTF deployments are likely to include U.S. Navy amphibious ships and their embarked fixed-wing combat aircraft and rotorcraft.[126]

Logistics and Maintenance Support

An Australian Department of Defence submission to a parliamentary inquiry noted that Australia had expended "considerable effort" to become a location offering "strategic support" to the U.S. military, especially with respect to maintenance and logistic support for U.S. ships and aircraft, communications, and training. The submission noted in particular an arrangement between industry in Western Australia and the U.S. Navy regarding maintenance and repair services for Military Sealift Command ships.[127] Ship repairs undertaken in Australia are coordinated by Commander, Logistics Group Western Pacific, based in Singapore.[128]

Australian industry and governments perceive considerable commercial opportunity in offering support services for U.S. forces. For example, the South Australian state government has advertised its new Techport facility in Port Adelaide to the U.S. Navy as a repair-base alternative to those in Japan and Singapore, potentially closer to theaters of operations, especially for Indian Ocean missions. The facility was developed to build Australia's new Aegis-equipped air warfare destroyers and the next generation of RAN submarines, and it can handle ships of almost any dimension other than full-size U.S. Navy aircraft carriers. Techport has the added benefit to the U.S. Navy that all the major American naval systems defense contractors already operate from the facility.[129]

U.S. Navy port visits to Australia are frequent, especially to the RAN's Fleet Base West, HMAS Stirling, near Fremantle. This was also the location for the U.S. Navy's two "Sea Swap" multicrewing experiments in 2003, wherein the destroyer USS *Fletcher* exchanged crews to extend its deployment without needing to return to home port.[130] The Navy Criminal Investigative Service maintains offices in both Sydney and Perth, subordinate to the Singapore Field Office.[131] American military aircraft also visit Australia regularly.

Future Developments

Although increased naval deployments to HMAS Stirling were not included in the November 2011 force-posture initiatives, Australia's defense minister has indicated that greater access for both U.S. surface ships and submarines is a possible future development.[132] Indeed, the 2012 *Australian Defence Force Posture Review* describes the possibility as a "third priority" after the Marine Corps and U.S. Air Force deployments.[133] Among the review's recommendations are the development of HMAS Stirling to include improved support facilities and expanded wharf capacity sufficient to enable greater use of the base by U.S. Navy assets, including aircraft carriers and submarines.[134] It also envisions the establishment of a second submarine base on the east coast, with a preference for Brisbane as a port approved for use by nuclear-powered vessels, in order to "optimise interoperability" with U.S. submarines.[135] Perhaps the greatest benefit to the U.S. Navy of improved access to HMAS Stirling is its easy access to the West Australian Exercise Area and Underwater Tracking Range off the Western Australian coast, as well as to such maintenance and support facilities as a heavyweight torpedo maintenance center.[136] However, as is the case with the 2009 Defence White Paper's proposed Australian Defence Force structure, there is no strong Australian government commitment to fund the review's recommendations in the context of ongoing fiscal constraints.

The possibility of actually forward basing a carrier strike group at HMAS Stirling is one of the options for a potential future enhanced U.S. force posture canvassed in the June 2012 Center for Strategic and International Studies report: *U.S. Force Posture Strategy in the Asia Pacific Region.*[137] The study pointed out, though, that HMAS Stirling is not necessarily ideally located for carrier strike group operations. Situated in the southern part of Western Australia, it is a great distance from possible areas of operation such as the Persian Gulf and the South China Sea and would require significant and costly infrastructure development.[138] In this sense, expansion of the existing helicopter support facility to take fixed-wing aircraft is probably not feasible, for space and environmental reasons, but RAAF Base Pearce is just forty miles to the north. The approach to HMAS Stirling, through a single lengthy channel, is another issue that could demand attention in any further consideration of carrier basing.

Australia's defense minister, Stephen Smith, subsequently reaffirmed that there would be no U.S. bases in Australia, but noted once again that more visits by U.S. Navy warships to HMAS Stirling were possible in the future.[139] Smith also emphasized that greater U.S. access to RAAF bases in the north is currently a higher priority.[140]

Australia's own *Australian Defence Force Posture Review*, driven by Canberra's concerns with strategic developments in the western Pacific and Indian Ocean, the protection of the northern maritime border, and the security of infrastructure related to Australia's resources boom, including vast gas deposits off the coasts of northern and northwestern Australia, was also developed in the context of its alliance relationship with the United States, the November 2011 announcements of increased U.S. military presence in the country, and the ongoing U.S. Global Posture Review. The independent review recommends a substantial expansion of Australian basing and support infrastructure across northern and northwestern Australia. If fully implemented, such improvements would have positive implications for both announced and possible future U.S. force-posture arrangements in Australia. The Australian government has stated explicitly that the review will "complement" the efforts already being made by the bilateral force-posture working group.[141]

In addition to the review's recommendations already mentioned, one further possibility has salience for U.S. forces: an upgrade of the airfield on the Cocos (Keeling) Islands—located in the Indian Ocean some 2,750 km northwest of Perth—to allow operations by Australia's intended P-8A Poseidon maritime patrol aircraft and long-range, high-endurance, maritime surveillance unmanned aerial vehicle (UAV) capability.[142] The U.S. Air Force has at times made use of this facility, which currently needs significant maintenance work, and in theory the Cocos facility could host Global Hawk surveillance UAVs and other aircraft. However, the Australian government seems to have ruled out significant investment on the runway and associated facilities at this time.[143]

Strategic Context

Australia remains one of the closest allies of the United States. In recent years alliance ties have grown even closer as a consequence of shared combat experiences in Iraq and Afghanistan as well as a multitude of other noncombat operations across a spectrum of contingencies. The two states cooperate closely in intelligence sharing, in responding to the radical extremist militant Islamist threat, in countering the proliferation of weapons of mass destruction (and their associated materials and delivery vehicles), and in dealing with rising regional powers. China's military modernization and growing influence, in particular, have become a shared strategic concern. This issue has resulted in a significant public attitudinal shift by Australian governments, whose earlier more sanguine views have now been largely replaced by expressions of mistrust and concern, as reflected in the 2009 Defence White Paper.[144]

The evolving strategic situation in Asia has elevated the geostrategic importance of Australia, with its extensive coasts on both the Pacific and Indian oceans. In the words of Australia's ambassador to the United States and former defense minister Kim Beazley, the changed international circumstances mean that the situation today is unlike during the Cold War, when "Australia was in a strategic backwater and owed its influence to its hosting of the joint intelligence and communications facilities. . . . Now things are different. . . . We are the southern tier of the focal point of the global political system"—that is, the Indo-Pacific region.[145] Australia's position will allow an enhanced U.S. force posture in the north of Australia (especially the future MAGTF deployments), much faster access to crises in Southeast Asia and the Indian Ocean, and easier access to regular bilateral exercise programs undertaken by U.S. forces in those regions.

The 2009 Defence White Paper outlined a significant medium-term expansion of Australian maritime capabilities. However, it is also worth noting that considerable concern remains in Australia over the long-term fiscal viability of the United States and its ability to maintain its regional strategic presence at current levels. The possibility that the United States may falter financially raises the possibility that Australia may over time need to boost yet further its own contributions to national defense, to its alliance commitments, and to regional stability. It suggests also the possibility of offering additional access to Australian facilities to U.S. forces to mitigate the costs borne by Washington as part of the burden sharing required to keep the United States fully engaged in the region over the long term. However, concern over the United States' fiscal prospects increasingly coincide with Canberra's own budgetary pressures and changing domestic priorities, thereby creating uncertainty over its longer-term defense spending commitments and delivery of Defence White Paper and recommended posture review programs.

This chapter has demonstrated how American strategic engagement with Australia continues to grow both in extent and intensity. In part, this reflects the fact that Canberra is undoubtedly one of Washington's closest alliance partners, with recent and ongoing shared combat experiences. It also reflects a maturing of Australia's foreign-policy making, even though the apparently permanent need for a major security ally remains evident. From an American perspective, some of the joint facilities in Australia remain vital to U.S. nuclear forces. Perhaps more salient for the future, though, are shared concerns over the particular character of geopolitical dynamics in the Asia-Pacific region.

Australian encouragement of an expanded American presence is driven by the need for strategic reassurance, especially given the challenges posed by a rising and more assertive China. Other attractions for Canberra include improved access to American defense technology, enhancements to Australian Defence Force capabilities, better interoperability with its primary ally, and even commercial opportunities in the defense, support, and maintenance sectors. For its part, the United States can use the agreeably vast expanse of the Australian continent and surrounding waters to maintain its vital communications and intelligence-gathering infrastructure, enhance its regional presence with improved flexibility for force deployments, enhance its own capabilities through better training and exercising facilities, and improve the strategic effectiveness of its alliances by deepening its engagement with the Australian Defence Force.

The evolution of U.S. regional force-posture arrangements reflects in part a political and financial need to encourage its strategic partners to shoulder greater shares of the burden for regional and world order. Australia may have no choice but to eventually increase its share of the common defense, whether by increasing its own defense outlays directly, facilitating the regional U.S. force posture, or, most likely, a combination of both. All of the factors discussed here point to a dynamic future for the American force posture in Australia. The deepening relationship does not mean, however, that Australian acquiescence to the use of facilities and assets on, or to operations from, Australian territory in any given future conflict can be assumed by Washington. The precise circumstances will matter. But Canberra is, under most scenarios, likely to be a pliable and valuable ally.

Notes

1. David J. Berteau, Michael J. Green, Gregory Kiley, and Nicholas Szechenyi, *U.S. Force Posture Strategy in the Asia Pacific Region: An Independent Assessment* (Washington, D.C.: Center for Strategic and International Studies, 15 August 2012), 92–94, http://csis.org/publication/pacom-force-posture-review.
2. Graham Freudenberg, *Churchill and Australia* (Sydney: Macmillan, 2008), 370–71.
3. Ibid., 393.
4. Ibid., 395.

5. Michael McKernan, *All In! Australia during the Second World War* (Melbourne: Nelson, 1983), 187.
6. Ibid., 191.
7. Ibid., 204.
8. Ibid.
9. T. B. Millar, *Australia in Peace and War* (Canberra: Australian National University Press, 1978), 150–51.
10. Ross Gillett, *Warships of Australia* (Adelaide: Rigby, 1977), 67.
11. James Goldrick, "World War II: The War against Japan," in *The Australian Centenary History of Defence*, vol. 3, *The Royal Australian Navy*, ed. David Stevens (South Melbourne: Oxford University Press, 2001), 133–34.
12. Ibid., 134.
13. Tom Frame, *Pacific Partners: A History of Australian-American Naval Relations* (Sydney: Hodder and Stoughton, 1992), 72.
14. Ibid. Harkavy also makes the point that Australia objected to a permanent U.S. postwar presence in its territories. Robert E. Harkavy, *Great Power Competition for Overseas Bases: The Geopolitics of Access Diplomacy* (New York: Pergamon, 1982), 113.
15. Coral Bell points out that Evatt had personal ambitions that perhaps influenced his professional outlook. Coral Bell, *Dependent Ally: A Study in Australian Foreign Policy* (Melbourne: Oxford University Press, 1988), 34.
16. Ibid.
17. Ibid., 36.
18. Ibid., 35.
19. Frame, *Pacific Partners*, 74–75.
20. Exmouth became the site for the North West Cape U.S. Navy and, ultimately, joint U.S. and Royal Australian Navy communications station.
21. Frame, *Pacific Partners*, 73.
22. W. David McIntyre, *Background to the ANZUS Pact: Policy-Making, Strategy and Diplomacy 1945–1955* (Basingstoke: Macmillan, 1995), 71.
23. Frame, *Pacific Partners*, 79.
24. McIntyre, *Background to the ANZUS Pact*, 72.
25. Ibid., 73–78.
26. Ibid., 82.
27. U.S. Senate, *U.S. Foreign Policy Objectives and Overseas Military Installations* (Washington, D.C.: Congressional Research Service for Committee on Foreign Relations, 1979), 160.
28. HW80/4, *British-US Communication Intelligence Agreement*, 1946, p. 10, National Archives, Kew, United Kingdom, available at www.nationalarchives.gov.uk.
29. David Horner, *Defence Supremo: Sir Frederick Shedden and the Making of Australian Defence Policy* (St. Leonards, NSW: Allen and Unwin, 2000), 249.
30. Ibid.
31. Thomas B. Millar, "Australia and the American Alliance," *Pacific Affairs* 37, no. 2 (Summer 1964): 149.

32. Bell, *Dependent Ally*, 54.
33. Desmond Ball, *A Suitable Piece of Real Estate: American Installations in Australia* (Sydney: Hale and Iremonger, 1980), 19.
34. Ibid., 15. See also Robert E. Harkavy, *Strategic Basing and the Great Powers, 1200–2000* (Abingdon, U.K.: Routledge, 2007), 162.
35. Robert E. Harkavy, *Bases Abroad: The Global Military Foreign Presence* (New York: Oxford University Press for the Stockholm International Peace Research Institute, 1989), 181.
36. Ball, *Suitable Piece of Real Estate*, 56.
37. Ibid., 58.
38. Harkavy, *Bases Abroad*, 190.
39. Ball, *Suitable Piece of Real Estate*, 63.
40. Ibid., 65.
41. Ibid., 64.
42. Ibid., 83.
43. The Australian Anti-Bases Campaign Coalition Web site is found at www .anti-bases.org.
44. Jessica Bennett, "Omega Tower Shuts Down," *Gippsland Times and Maffra Spectator*, 30 December 2008, available at http://www.gippslandtimes.com.au/.
45. Ball, *Suitable Piece of Real Estate*, 99.
46. Harkavy, *Bases Abroad*, 199.
47. Ball, *Suitable Piece of Real Estate*, 116.
48. Ibid., 120.
49. Ibid., 111–12.
50. Ibid., 19.
51. One Australian defense official was noted as saying during the negotiations that "they [the Americans] are trying to treat us like Thais"! Bell, *Dependent Ally*, 65–66.
52. Ball, *Suitable Piece of Real Estate*, 22.
53. Ibid., 154.
54. Ibid., 52.
55. Alan Renouf, *The Frightened Country* (South Melbourne: Macmillan, 1979), 487.
56. Ibid., 24.
57. Australia, House of Representatives, *Commonwealth Parliamentary Debates*, vol. 63, 22 May 1969, 2179.
58. Ball, *Suitable Piece of Real Estate*, 23.
59. Joseph A. Camilleri, *ANZUS: Australia's Predicament in the Nuclear Age* (South Melbourne: Macmillan, 1987), 95.
60. Australia, House of Representatives, *Commonwealth Parliamentary Debates*, vol. 63, 29 April 1969, 1420.
61. Stephan Frühling, ed., *A History of Australian Strategic Policy since 1945* (Canberra: Department of Defence, 2009), 370.
62. For further details, see "Pine Gap Protests: Historical," *Nautilus Institute*, http://nautilus.org/publications/books/australian-forces-abroad/defence-facilities/pine-gap/pine-gap-protests/protests-hist/#axzz2etU4fYwo.

63. Bell, *Dependent Ally*, 66.
64. Melanie Sjoberg, "Nurrungar '93: Close the Bases!" *Green Left*, 7 April 1993, http://www.greenleft.org.au/node/4290.
65. Coral Bell, "The Changing Central Balance and Australian Policy," in *Agenda for the Nineties: Australian Choices in Foreign and Defence Policy* (Melbourne: Longman Cheshire, 1991), 20.
66. Camilleri, *ANZUS*, 24.
67. Ball, *Suitable Piece of Real Estate*, 153.
68. Ibid., 20.
69. Australia, House of Representatives, *Commonwealth Parliamentary Debates*, vol. 63, 22 May 1969, 2179.
70. Harkavy, *Great Power Competition*, 210.
71. Camilleri, *ANZUS*, 42.
72. Peter King, "Whither Whitlam?" *International Journal* 29, no. 3 (Summer 1974): 426.
73. Ball, *Suitable Piece of Real Estate*, 153.
74. Ibid., 48.
75. Renouf, *Frightened Country*, 14.
76. Ball, *Suitable Piece of Real Estate*, 144.
77. The Liberal–Country Party Coalition government served from 1949 to 1972.
78. Bell, *Dependent Ally*, 131.
79. As Coral Bell suggests, there was little or no reason for the United States to fear the Labor government of that time. Ibid., 127.
80. Gary Brown, "The ANZUS Alliance: The Case Against," in *Security and Defence: Pacific and Global Perspectives*, ed. Desmond Ball and Cathy Downes (North Sydney: George Allen and Unwin, 1990), 244.
81. Exercise Kangaroo One in 1974 was one such combined exercise; it involved U.S. Navy ships and aircraft and amphibious operations by the U.S. Marine Corps in Shoalwater Bay, Queensland. See "HMAS Melbourne (II)," *Royal Australian Navy*, http://www.navy.gov.au/hmas-melbourne-ii.
82. See "U-2 and SR-71 Units, Bases and Detachments," *Art and Aerospace Page of Kathryn and Andreas Gehrs-Pahl*, http://www.ais.org/~schnars/aero/ol-det.htm.
83. Camilleri, *ANZUS*, 106.
84. Ibid.
85. Ibid., 86.
86. Commonwealth of Australia, *Defending Australia in the Asia-Pacific Century: Force 2030* (Canberra: Department of Defence, 2009), 43.
87. Ibid., 94.
88. Australia–United States Ministerial Consultations [hereafter AUSMIN] 2010, "Australia–United States Exchange of Letters Relating to Harold E. Holt Naval Communications Station," fact sheet, www.dfat.gov.au/geo/us/ausmin/Exchange-of-Letters-Relating-to-Harold-E.pdf.

89. For an example of the highly ideological, pathologically anti-American arguments of antibases campaigners, see Hannah Middleton, "U.S. Bases in Australia," *Peace Review: A Journal of Social Justice* 22, no. 2 (2010), 144–49.

90. See Nick Butterly, "PM Welcomes U.S. Bases," *Advertiser* (Adelaide), 20 June 2006; and Matthew Franklin, "No More Bases but Gillard Sees Closer Military Ties with U.S.," *Australian,* 8 March 2011.

91. See, for example, *Report to the President and the U.S. Congress* (Arlington, Va.: Commission on Review of Overseas Military Facility Structure of the United States, May 2005), http://www.fas.org/irp/agency/dod/obc.pdf [hereafter, Military Facility Structure Report], H4.

92. Quoted in Hillary Rodham Clinton, "Remarks at the Australia–United States Ministerial," Melbourne, 8 November 2010, http://www.state.gov/secretary/rm/2010/11/150663.htm. The AUSMIN bilateral talks replaced the annual ANZUS Council meetings in 1985, beginning with the suspension of U.S. treaty obligations to New Zealand.

93. Secretary of Defense Robert Gates, speech delivered to the Shangri-La Dialogue, Singapore, 4 June 2011, *Department of Defense*, http://www.defense.gov/speeches/speech.aspx?speechid=1578.

94. AUSMIN, "Australia–United States Ministerial Consultations Joint Communiqué," San Francisco, 15 September 2011, *Hon. Kevin Rudd MP*, http://foreignminister.gov.au/releases/2011/kr_mr_110916b.html.

95. "U.S.-Australia Relations: Remarks by President Obama and Prime Minister Gillard of Australia in Joint Press Conference," *Embassy of the United States (Australia)*, 16 November 2011, http://usrsaustralia.state.gov/us-oz/2011/11/16/wh1.html.

96. Stephen Smith MP, "Minister for Defence: Response to Question without Notice in the House of Representatives," House of Representatives, *Commonwealth Parliamentary Debates*, 21 November 2011, p. 12942, http://parlinfo.aph.gov.au/parlinfo/search/display.

97. Military Facility Structure Report, H11. The first and second categories are, respectively, the main operating base and forward operating site. The commission also lists the prepositioning site and sea basing as fourth and fifth categories (ibid., GL01–GL02). For the 2004 report to Congress, see Douglas J. Feith, Under Secretary of Defense for Policy, *Strengthening U.S. Global Defense Posture*, Report to Congress (Washington, D.C.: Office of the Under Secretary of Defense for Policy, September 2004).

98. Feith, *Strengthening U.S. Global Defense Posture*, 10.

99. Ibid.

100. AUSMIN, "Australia–United States Ministerial Consultations Joint Communiqué," Washington, D.C., 1 October 1992, http://usrsaustralia.state.gov/us-oz/1992/10/01/communique.html.

101. Hon. Dr. Brendan Nelson, Minister for Defence, "Australia–U.S. Joint Communications Facility to Be Hosted at Geraldton," media release 007/2007, 15 February 2007, http://www.defence.gov.au/minister/49tpl.cfm?CurrentId=6375.

102. In full, the "Agreement between the Government of Australia and the Government of the United States of America Relating to the Operation of and

Access to an Australian Naval Communications Station at North West Cape in Western Australia."

103. AUSMIN, "Australia–United States Exchange of Letters," fact sheet.

104. AUSMIN, "Transcript: SecDef Perry and MinDef McLachlan On-the-Record Press Conference at Hotel Intercontinental, Sydney," Sydney, 26 June 1996, http://usrsaustralia.state.gov/us-oz/1996/07/26/dod1.html.

105. Department of Defence submission to the Joint Standing Committee on Foreign Affairs, *Defence and Trade Defence Sub-Committee Inquiry into Australia's Defence Relations with the United States*, submission no. 6, February 2004, 12, http://www.aphref.aph.gov.au_house_committee_jfadt_usrelations_subs_sub6.pdf.

106. In full, the "Agreement between the Government of Australia and the Government of the United States of America relating to the Establishment of a Joint Defence Facility at Pine Gap, done at Canberra on 9 December 1966," as amended and extended.

107. Australia, House of Representatives, *Commonwealth Parliamentary Debates*, Questions on Notice, "Defence: Pine Gap," question 286, 28 May 2002.

108. Nelson, "Australia–U.S. Joint Communications Facility to Be Hosted at Geraldton."

109. Ibid.

110. AUSMIN 2010, "Joint Statement on Space Security," 8 November 2010, http://www.dfat.gov.au/geo/us/ausmin/Australia-United-States-Joint-Partnership-on-Space-Security.pdf.

111. AUSMIN 2010, "Australia–United States Space Situational Awareness Partnership," fact sheet, http://www.dfat.gov.au/geo/us/ausmin/Space-Situational-Awareness-Partnership-fact-sheet.pdf.

112. Ibid.

113. AUSMIN, "Australia–United States Ministerial Consultations Joint Communiqué," Washington, D.C., 1 October 1992, http://canberra.usembassy.gov/irc/us-oz/1992/10/01/communique.html.

114. AUSMIN, "Transcript: SecDef Perry and MinDef McLachlan," 26 June 1996.

115. AUSMIN, "Australia–United States Ministerial Consultations Joint Communiqué," Adelaide, 18 November 2005, http://usrsaustralia.state.gov/us-oz/2005/11/18/wf1.html.

116. "Joint Combined Training Capability," *Department of Defence*, www.defence.gov.au/. For discussion on the use of the JCTC during Talisman Sabre 2007, see Wing Cdr. Thomas Wickham and Darren McFarlane, "The Australian Joint Combined Training Capability: Reality or Fiction," in *Improving M&S Interoperability, Reuse and Efficiency in Support of Current and Future Forces*, Meeting Proceedings RTO-MP-MSG-056, Paper 2 (Neuilly-sur-Seine, France: RTO, NATO, 2007), 2.1–2.12.

117. Lt. Gen. David Hurley, Vice Chief of the Defence Force, keynote address presented to SimTecT 2009, Adelaide, 16 June 2009.

118. "Joint Combined Training Capability."

119. Ibid.

120. Office of the Secretary of Defense, *RDT&E Project Justification, Project 760 Joint Combined Training Centre (JCTC)* (Washington, D.C.: February 2010), 20.

121. Australia, Department of Defence, draft *Talisman Sabre 2011 Public Environment Report* (Canberra: 2010), 3.

122. Ibid., 5–7.

123. Meagan Dillon, "Who Foots Bill for Marines?," *Northern Territory News*, 3 August 2012, 6.

124. Allan Hawke and Ric Smith, *Australian Defence Force Posture Review*, for the Australian Government, 30 March 2012, 53, http://www.defence.gov.au/oscdf/adf-posture-review/docs/final/Report.pdf.

125. Australian Government, Department of Prime Minister and Cabinet, Prime Minister Julia Gillard Media Release, "Australia–U.S. Force Posture Initiatives," 16 November 2011, http://pmtranscripts.dpmc.gov.au/browse.php?did=18272.

126. Brendan Nicholson, "Elite Northern Unit Gives U.S. Access in a Crisis," *Australian*, 17 November 2011.

127. Department of Defence submission to the *Defence and Trade Defence Sub-Committee Inquiry into Australia's Defence Relations with the United States*, 14, http://www.aphref.aph.gov.au_house_committee_jfadt_usrelations_subs_sub6.pdf.

128. See Commander, Navy Installations Command, "NRCS: Tenant Command—COMLOG WESTPAC/CTF 73," http://www.cnic.navy.mil/regions/sac/about/tenant_commands/commander_logistics_group_western_pacific_task_force_73.html.

129. Greg Kelton, "Ship Shape: U.S. Navy Considers Adelaide Maintenance Base," *Advertiser* [Adelaide], 22 August 2009.

130. Department of Defence submission to the *Defence and Trade Defence Sub-Committee Inquiry into Australia's Defence Relations with the United States*, 19.

131. NCIS: Naval Criminal Investigative Service, Singapore Field Office, Republic of Singapore, http://www.cnic.navy.mil/regions/sac/about/tenant_commands/navy_criminal_investigation_service_ncis.html; http://www.ncis.navy.mil/About NCIS/Locations/Singapore/Pages/default.aspx.

132. "Minister for Defence: Response to Question without Notice in the House of Representatives," 21 November 2011.

133. Hawke and Smith, *Australian Defence Force Posture Review*, 53.

134. Ibid., 33, 35.

135. Ibid., 29–31.

136. Berteau et al., *U.S. Force Posture Strategy*, 32–33.

137. Ibid., 74.

138. Ibid., 33, 74–75. For example, Stirling is about 2,800 nautical miles from Diego Garcia and 2,100 from Singapore.

139. Brendan Nicholson, "No US Bases Here, Says Smith, but Washington Confirms Plan as Part of Asia-Pacific Pivot," *Australian*, 3 August 2012, 2.

140. "Minister for Defence: Interview with Paul Murray, 6PR—Perth," 2 August 2012, *Australian Government: Department of Defence*, http://www.minister .defence.gov.au/2012/08/02/minister-for-defence-interview-with-paul-murray-6pr-perth.

141. "Minister for Defence: Australian Defence Force Posture Review," Department of Defence press release, 22 June 2011, http://www.minister.defence.gov .au/2011/06/22/minister-for-defence-australian-defence-force-posture-review/.

142. Hawke and Smith, *Australian Defence Force Posture Review*, 26.

143. Stephen Smith MP, Minister for Defence, "Interview with Ashleigh Gillon, SKY PM Agenda," transcript, 2 August 2012, http://www.minister.defence.gov .au/2012/08/02/8079/.

144. See Commonwealth of Australia, *Defending Australia in the Asia-Pacific Century*; and, for analysis, Jack McCaffrie and Chris Rahman, "Australia's 2009 Defense White Paper: A Maritime Focus for Uncertain Times," *Naval War College Review* 63, no. 1 (Winter 2010): 64–67.

145. Quoted in Brendan Nicholson and James Massola, "Global Position Puts Us on the Map, Says Kim Beazley," *Australian*, 16 November 2011. On this point see also Iskander Rehman, "From Down Under to Top Center: Australia, the United States, and This Century's Special Relationship," *Transatlantic Academy Paper Series* (Washington, D.C.: Transatlantic Academy, May 2011).

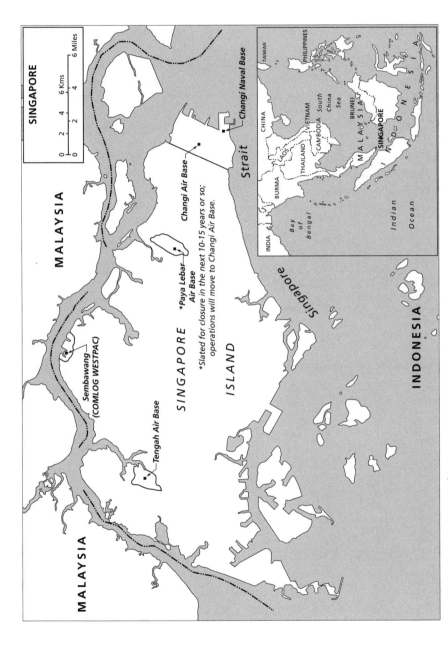

Map 5. Military Facilities in Singapore

5

Singapore: Forward Operating Site

Chris Rahman

Historically, Singapore functioned as a major naval hub supporting the British Empire's position in the Far East. The island was viewed by Admiral Sir John "Jackie" Fisher as one of the world's five key locations enabling Britain's global naval superiority.[1] The fortification of the British strategic position on Singapore reached both its zenith and its nadir with the development in the interwar years of the "Singapore Strategy," which was designed to buttress the empire's Far Eastern defenses against possible Japanese aggression. That controversial plan failed miserably in the breach.[2] However, the island continued to host a significant British military presence after the Second World War, including its use by British Commonwealth forces to counter the communist insurgency in preindependence Malaya and to protect Malaysia during Indonesia's 1963–66 Confrontation (*konfrontasi*). Map 5 depicts Singapore's present military facilities.

Singapore as a Regional Strategic Hub

Britain's presence was reduced post-Confrontation due to its declining economy and a consequent decision to wind down its military posture East of Suez. The existing Anglo-Malaysian Defence Agreement was replaced by the consultative Five Power Defence Arrangements (FPDA) involving British, Australian, and New Zealand assistance to help Singapore and Malaysia provide for their own external defense;[3] the FPDA involved the stationing of components of an Australia–New Zealand–United Kingdom (ANZUK) Force in Singapore and Malaysia. The Australian and British elements of the ANZUK Force were withdrawn from

Singapore by the mid-1970s. That withdrawal spurred the establishment of New Zealand Force South East Asia in Singapore in January 1974, involving the 1st Battalion Royal New Zealand Infantry Regiment, No. 41 Squadron Royal New Zealand Air Force, and an "assigned" Royal New Zealand Navy frigate as well as support elements variously based at Dieppe Barracks, Kangaw Barracks, and the former Royal Navy base at Sembawang. Among other things, New Zealand Force South East Asia provided port clearances for visiting British and American warships using Stores Basin Sembawang.[4]

The small New Zealand military presence remained until 1989, but it was not until the final decade of the twentieth century that the island again took on a role as a regional strategic hub with a constant and significant foreign military presence.

The United States and the Singapore Hub

The United States does not operate its own military bases in Singapore. Nevertheless, the island city-state has become increasingly important to U.S. Pacific Command, particularly the U.S. Navy, since the end of the Cold War as the foremost Southeast Asian location for in-region support facilities. Initially, though, during the city-state's independence period, Singapore's prime minister, Lee Kuan Yew, adopted an anti-American foreign policy, publicly stating in 1965 his opposition to American use of Singapore's bases. This position was designed both to win diplomatic recognition for the newly independent state from the nonaligned states of the Third World and to manipulate international acceptance of a politically tenuous balance between nonalignment and the continued British military presence deemed essential for Singapore's security, even its survival.[5]

Despite the difficult start to the Singapore-U.S. relationship, even prior to the early 1990s the U.S. Navy maintained a minor presence on the island, with Navy Regional Contracting Center (NRCC) Singapore acting as the coordinator of ship maintenance within Southeast Asia from 1968.[6] Also, despite its initial public rhetoric, Singapore at that time was highly supportive of the American strategic role in Southeast Asia, including in the Vietnam War, which served to insulate Singapore and other states in the region from the expanding communist menace. As Lee Kuan Yew explained in 1970, "What America has done and is doing by helping the Republic of Vietnam survive the Communist attack is buying time for other Southeast Asian people to consolidate their independence as legitimate sovereign states. If the U.S. were not fighting in Vietnam, Singapore would be gone by now!"[7]

Close economic ties between Singapore and the United States developed in the late 1960s, whereby Singapore in effect coupled its economy to the American production system, assembling and exporting manufactured goods for the U.S. market, enabled by the development of the Port of Singapore and containerization.[8] Those links were supplemented strategically with a military relationship that grew steadily during the 1970s. In terms of the American military presence on the island, from at least early 1978 U.S. Navy aircraft conducted long-range Indian Ocean patrols from Tengah Air Base, while the U.S. Air Force supported transiting transport flights from Paya Lebar Air Base in the 1980s.[9]

The regional strategic changes following the global geopolitical discontinuity of 1989–91 included not only the collapse of Soviet/Russian power and a drawdown of U.S. forces but also the prospect that the United States would lose access to major Philippine basing facilities. The possibility of being denied access to the Subic Naval Base, Naval Air Station Cubi Point, and Clark Air Base led to the signing in 1990 of a "Memorandum of Understanding [MoU] Regarding United States Use of Facilities in Singapore." The MoU provided for expanded American access to the Singaporean facilities of Sembawang wharves and Paya Lebar Air Base. The agreement resulted in increased use of Singaporean facilities by U.S. air and naval forces, with the 497th Tactical Fighter Training Squadron established at Paya Lebar to support U.S. Air Force detachments. The value of these facilities for transiting ships and aircraft was soon demonstrated during operations Desert Shield and Desert Storm. The regional contracting center was expanded during this period, and the number of American military support personnel based in Singapore grew from twenty to ninety-five.[10]

The MoU with Singapore became the most formal of the arrangements negotiated with a number of Southeast Asian states as the U.S. Department of Defense shifted its "post-Philippines" focus from permanent bases to access agreements (often referred to as "places, not bases"), with the express intent of maintaining the ability of U.S. forces "to deploy quickly to any location within the region and to sustain that deployment as long as necessary."[11] The timing of the long-term lease arrangement with Singapore may have been somewhat fortuitous in maintaining the U.S. military presence in Southeast Asia, yet it was no accident. The proactive role of Singapore and its intent to ensure that the United States remained strategically engaged in Southeast Asia should be stressed; Prime Minister Lee Kuan Yew took the initiative in 1989 to invite U.S. forces publicly to use Singaporean facilities.[12]

The final rejection in 1991 by Manila of a new treaty to allow continued American use of Philippine bases resulted in an agreement with Singapore in January 1992, under the existing MoU, to move the Commander, Logistics Group Western Pacific (COMLOG WESTPAC) from Subic Bay to Singapore in July of that year.[13] The proactive Singaporean stance was reiterated in early 1998 with the announcement that it was constructing a new $60 million naval base at Changi, with the express purpose of accommodating American warships, including aircraft carriers and submarines. Singapore's attitude was encapsulated by the deputy prime minister and defense minister of the time, Tony Tan, who stated that "the presence of U.S. forces is a positive influence for regional peace and stability, and the access that the U.S. has to facilities in Singapore is important in facilitating that presence."[14] The Singaporean attitude was demonstrated even more clearly by trade and industry minister George Yeo after the opening of the Changi facility in 2001 and the berthing of the aircraft carrier USS *Kitty Hawk* in March of that year: "We built [the Changi Naval Base] at our own expense to facilitate the deployment of the U.S. 7th Fleet in Southeast Asian waters. . . . At a time when the region is going through dramatic political change, the presence of these ships has a stabilizing effect."[15]

An addendum to the MoU in 1998 allowed U.S. Navy vessels access to the Changi base. During the 1990s U.S. Navy service and civilian personnel in Singapore numbered around 150, with a small number of Air Force personnel.[16] By the end of that decade U.S. Navy ship visits to the island state numbered more than a hundred annually, while the Air Force on average deployed 6 one-month fighter aircraft detachments per year. In addition, reciprocal logistics support between American and Singaporean forces was enabled by a March 2000 Acquisition and Cross-Servicing Agreement.[17]

The relationship was further strengthened by the signing of a Strategic Framework Agreement in July 2005. Recognizing both Singapore's status as a "major security cooperation partner" and Singapore's and Washington's common interests in maintaining regional stability and combating global terrorism, they agreed, inter alia, to "increased defense cooperation through the provision of facilities in Singapore for United States military vessels, aircraft, personnel, equipment and materiel; supporting deployments of the Parties' respective forces; conducting bilateral and multilateral exercises in the region and in the United States and exchanging military training."[18]

In June 2011 Robert Gates, then the U.S. defense secretary, outlined in Singapore the ways in which the two partners were enhancing their defense ties and operational engagement under the Strategic Framework Agreement. These included prepositioning supplies in Singapore, particularly for use in disaster-response missions; enhancing command and control capabilities; and increasing training cooperation. He also noted in the context of operational engagement that the U.S. Navy would deploy its new small warship class of littoral combat ships (LCS) to Singapore.[19] President Obama later implicitly linked future LCS deployments to "America's enhanced presence across Southeast Asia."[20] The chief of naval operations, Adm. Jonathan Greenert, has further explained that "forward stationing" of LCSs in Singapore is one of a number of "initiatives to establish [the U.S. Navy's] forward posture."[21]

Singapore and the United States jointly acknowledged in April 2012 the proposed forward deployment of "up to four" LCSs to Singapore. In a reflection of the political sensitivities involved, the joint statement notes that the ships "will be deployed on a rotational basis and will not be based in Singapore."[22] A second joint statement in June announced Singapore's "in-principle agreement" to the proposal and expanded upon the arrangement: "The LCS will not be based or homeported in Singapore, and the LCS crew will live on board the LCS for the duration of their deployment."[23] Despite this public sensitivity, the lead company of one of the two LCS industry design teams, Lockheed Martin, claims that "Singapore officials specifically asked the Navy to deploy the LCS there."[24] The first littoral combat ship, USS *Freedom*, began an initial ten-month "demonstration deployment" to Singapore in March 2013, with the second ship of the Lockheed Martin-built LCS class, *Fort Worth*, scheduled to be the first to deploy there on a regular basis, possibly beginning in late 2014.[25]

Although Singapore lacks the status of a formal U.S. ally, the extent of the relationship in practical terms can now be viewed as being considerably greater than that which exists between the United States and its lesser regional alliance partners the Philippines and Thailand. In some respects, it could be argued that Singapore has become the most important partner in the U.S. Pacific Command security network after the three main formal allies—Japan, South Korea, and Australia. In terms of American foreign basing infrastructure in the East Asian region, the importance of Singapore is secondary only to that of Japan and South Korea, with their main operating bases. Indeed, in the terminology of the September 2004 Department of Defense report to Congress on U.S. global force posture, Singapore hosts the only "forward operating site" (FOS) in the PACOM region.[26] The report describes a FOS as "an expandable . . . [facility] maintained with a limited U.S. military support presence and possibly prepositioned equipment. FOSs will support rotational rather than permanently stationed forces and be a focus for bilateral and regional training."[27]

With respect to bilateral training and exercises, the June 2012 Singapore–United States joint statement also emphasized an intent to deepen and expand the bilateral exercise program, and to increase U.S. use of Singaporean facilities for combined training. Specific proposals include incorporating naval participation into the existing bilateral air force exercise, Commando Sling, and instituting regularized training between U.S. Marines and the Singapore Armed Forces at Singapore's Murai Urban Training Facility from 2013.[28]

Facilities and Commands

The American military presence in Singapore, located primarily in the former British facilities at Sembawang, involves 15 commands numbering over 800 military and civilian personnel and their family members.[29] The Defense Department's *Base Structure Report* placed the Singapore Area Coordinator numbers as of 30 September 2009 at 128 military, 28 civilian, and 19 "other" personnel.[30] The Navy Region Center Singapore (NRCS), established in 2007, now manages all shore support services for the U.S. military in Singapore in its capacity as the Singapore Area Coordinator.[31] The NRCS replaced the NRCC, delegating the latter's supply and contracting functions to other commands;[32] it is staffed by 4 American naval personnel and around 75 American civil service and Singaporean employees.[33]

Commander, Logistics Group, Western Pacific (COMLOG WESTPAC; also Commander, Task Force 73) is the largest of the fifteen commands, comprising around ninety military and civilian personnel. It coordinates logistics for the Seventh Fleet across the vast area of Indian and Pacific oceans. Located within the Maritime Port Authority of Singapore's Sembawang Terminal, it also coordinates voyage repairs to U.S. Navy vessels in Southeast Asia and maintains responsibility for diving, towing, and salvage needs for the Seventh Fleet. To enable its primary logistics role, COMLOG WESTPAC at any one time has "operational oversight" of more than forty ships of U.S. Military Sealift Command.[34]

Military Sealift Command Far East (MSCFE) operates on average forty-eight vessels providing sealift, fleet support, and other support functions for PACOM. Its fleet-support function provides essential underway replenishment of fuel and other supplies to naval forces deployed in or transiting through the PACOM area of responsibility.[35] MSCFE relocated to Singapore from Japan in July 2006 so as to be situated close to COMLOG WESTPAC.[36] It has provided important logistics support for both military and humanitarian assistance/disaster relief missions, including operations Desert Storm and Iraqi Freedom, Operation Unified Assistance (the 2004 Indian Ocean tsunami response), and the hospital ship USNS *Mercy*'s humanitarian and civic-assistance mission to parts of Southeast Asia during Pacific Partnership 2010.[37] Military Sealift Fleet Support Command Ship Support Unit Singapore (MSFSC SSU) provides a range of engineering and logistics support throughout Southeast Asia, including contracting regional shipyards to carry out repairs to ships owned and operated by the U.S. government; it employs a staff of seventeen.[38] A Naval Criminal Investigative Services (NCIS) field office manages other regional NCIS offices; and a Fleet Industrial Support Center (FISC) Detachment Singapore manages supply, warehousing, and transportation in support of U.S. facilities.[39] FISC Detachment Singapore also provides logistics support, including fuel and provisions, for U.S. warships at ports stretching from India to the Philippines and from Hong Kong to Australia.[40]

The U.S. Air Force maintains facilities at the Republic of Singapore Air Force's Paya Lebar base. The 515th Air Mobility Group, Detachment 2, coordinates the movement of both personnel and cargo to and from Singapore and other locations within the region. The 497th Combat Training Squadron (CTS)—a detachment of the 36th Wing, Andersen Air Force Base, Guam—coordinates air-to-air combat exercises between units of six U.S. Air Force F-15s, F-16s, or U.S. Navy or Marine Corps F/A-18s and the Republic of Singapore Air Force. These exercises now take place approximately three to four times per year. During such deployments the squadron expands to involve approximately 80 to 120 personnel and becomes the 497th Air Expeditionary Group under the 13th Air Expeditionary

Task Force. The squadron also carries out other functions, including participation in and support of regional exercises.[41] In March 2012 the 13th and 14th Fighter Squadron and 35th Maintenance Group from Misawa Air Base, Japan, deployed to Singapore to support the three-week Exercise *Commando Sling* 12-2, which involved different aspects of air combat training.[42]

Other commands include a small-boat-team unit, the Special Operations Command Pacific Logistics Support Facility, and the Army Veterinary Services and Defence Contract Management Agency.[43] In addition, the U.S. Coast Guard Marine Inspection Detachment (MIDET) Singapore comprises seven Coast Guard officers who inspect U.S.-flagged ships operating in and repaired in Asia, inspect foreign-flagged ships that trade with the United States, and investigate maritime casualties involving U.S. vessels. MIDET Singapore also implements the International Port Security Program in Asia, congressionally mandated Coast Guard inspections of foreign ports to assess their compliance with the provisions of the International Maritime Organization's International Ship and Port Facility Security Code.[44]

The Singapore Hub in Strategic Context

The primary function of American facilities in Singapore is to act collectively as a logistics support center and support transiting U.S. forces. These have in recent years become particularly important roles, given the high tempo of operations in Iraq (until recently), Afghanistan, the Persian Gulf, the Arabian Sea, the Gulf of Aden, and the western Indian Ocean. In this context, the NRCS coordinates support to more than 150 visiting ships and 400 aircraft each year; and 30,000 service personnel transit through Singapore annually.[45] The ship-visit total includes around 10 calls by nuclear-powered attack submarines.[46]

The second major function is the coordination of bilateral and multilateral exercises for Southeast Asia. For example, the Operations, Plans and Policy Directorate of COMLOG WESTPAC coordinates and supports the annual Cooperation Afloat Readiness and Training (CARAT) series initiated in 1995 of bilateral maritime exercises with Brunei, Indonesia, Malaysia, the Philippines, Singapore, and Thailand.[47] Cambodia became the seventh participant in 2010. Bangladesh too has joined, as the first South Asian participant, and a separate regular program has been initiated with Vietnam.[48] Such exercise programs are leading elements of American regional engagement and theater security cooperation strategies, which have been expanded significantly since the terrorist attacks of September 11 and in Bali (2002, 2005), with Southeast Asia becoming an important secondary front in the fight against radical extremist Islamist terrorism.

The use of Singaporean facilities, however, has created a potential vulnerability for U.S. forces, given the island state's geopolitical location in the midst of the Muslim Malay core of maritime Southeast Asia. Indeed, attacks against a U.S. Navy ship at the Changi Naval Base and at a bar popular with American service personnel as well as against other non-American targets were planned in late 2001. Twenty-one suspects were arrested by Singaporean authorities, nineteen of whom were believed to be members of the regional terrorist group Jemaah Islamiah, acting on the orders of the leading Jemaah Islamiah operative, Hambali.[49] The plan to target a U.S. warship most likely was inspired by the successful October 2000 al-Qaeda terrorist attack against USS *Cole* in Aden. Nevertheless, and despite the inherent difficulties of protecting extremely busy maritime thoroughfares and working harbors, Singapore's security apparatus and protective measures are impressive and thus far have proved successful. Its programs include the enforcement of a number of restricted areas and maritime security measures far beyond those required by international regulations; an example is the harbor craft transponder system, mandated for tracking the some 2,800 small vessels licensed by the Maritime Port Authority of Singapore.[50]

Further maritime security support is provided by the Command and Control Centre, established by Singapore at the Changi Naval Base, which monitors shipping in the Malacca and Singapore straits and shares the data with partners such as the U.S. Navy. The United States is one of ten states that have thus far posted an international liaison officer to the center's Information Fusion Centre.[51] Singapore, in fact, is a leading U.S. partner in promoting naval cooperation and sharing maritime security information, which is consistent with the concepts of improving maritime domain awareness and enhancing response capabilities as developed by the U.S. Navy's Global Maritime Partnership initiative.[52]

Force-protection and counterterrorism measures at the Sembawang facility are complicated by its location on the Singapore side of the Johor Straits opposite the Malaysian coast. Physical security there is provided by Singapore Armed Forces personnel while Singapore police officers of the Installation Auxiliary Police Forces, administered by the New Zealand Defence Support Unit, provide law enforcement. This situation obtains largely due to the shared nature of the Sembawang facilities, whereby U.S. facilities are colocated with those of Singapore, Australia, New Zealand, and the United Kingdom. The NRCS coordinates "overarching anti-terrorism services" for American units at Changi Naval Base and Paya Lebar Air Base.[53]

Potential sensitivities among Singapore's neighbors regarding the U.S. military's presence and constant use of the island seem not to be a significant factor. This may be in part because American use of Singapore has built up slowly over two decades and remains relatively low-key. Also, all parties have a common interest in combating regional and international terrorist threats, and the U.S. contribution to regional stability is widely acknowledged, if not always publicly. Further, Washington maintains less-formal access arrangements with Malaysia, making it difficult for that country to object to Singapore's. However, the suggestion of Adm. Thomas Fargo, then commander, U.S. Pacific Command, in

March 2004 in connection with the proposed Regional Maritime Security Initiative, that U.S. forces undertake patrols to protect the Malacca Strait was enthusiastically received by Singapore but shrilly rejected by both Indonesia and Malaysia.[54] The incident is a reminder that Singapore constantly must conduct its regional relations carefully, including those involving its strategic relationship with the United States.

Potentially more problematic for Singapore is the possibility of conflict between mainland China and Taiwan, most likely also involving the United States. With its Cold War anticommunist foreign policy now consigned to the distant past, Singapore's economic and political relationship with China has both normalized and grown substantially. Social links have grown, with Singapore—of which a majority of the population is ethnically Chinese—increasingly embracing its cultural links to China and importing mainland Chinese immigrants, whether as guest workers or permanent residents. Complicating matters further, Singapore also has long-standing defense cooperation links with Taiwan and, in particular, the Republic of China Navy.[55] These factors, as well as the close economic relationship with China, would place Singapore in an unenviable position were conflict to occur. Although Singapore is most unlikely to become directly involved in such a conflict, it would be unable to avoid a high degree of political discomfort and potentially long-term strategic consequences. For, unlike most of its neighbors, Singapore would be forced to decide whether to allow U.S. forces to use its facilities in support of actions against China. The issue was recognized by the 2005 Overseas Basing Commission, which stated, "Freedom of operations for unilateral actions [by U.S. forces using Singapore] is not guaranteed and Singapore could fall out with the United States should a China-Taiwan conflict erupt."[56] Indeed, the same problem could pertain in the event of other potential conflicts involving China and the United States, possibly regarding, for example, American alliance obligations to Japan, crises on the Korean Peninsula, disputes in the South China Sea, or freedom of navigation.

Singapore's continued strategic significance derives from its physical location—guarding, as it does, the eastern entry (or exit) point of one of the most vital choke points for global trade as well as transit routes for major navies, the straits of Malacca and Singapore, which link the Indian Ocean to the South China Sea. Consequently, Singapore will remain a magnet for maritime forces intent on ensuring the security of seaborne trade. Singapore emerged at the outset of the post–Cold War period in Asia as an important host for U.S. naval and air support forces. As a consequence of the loss of its bases in the Philippines, the United States has had to rely upon access arrangements with Singapore to support both its regional presence in Southeast Asia and its forces transiting to and from the Persian Gulf and the western Indian Ocean region.

As has been documented throughout this chapter, Singapore represents the prime example of the transformation of U.S. force posture in Southeast Asia demanded by the political circumstances of the post–Cold War world, from the era of permanent bases to flexible arrangements enabling constant forward presence and enhanced security cooperation. U.S. arrangements with Singapore remain limited in their scope, albeit relatively stable; they are likely to persist without significant change unless a major strategic discontinuity occurs. A shared concern with "regional stability" after the Cold War and a commonly perceived threat from radical extremist Islamist militancy post–September 11 have ensured a high level of mutual dependence. In this relationship Singapore provides access to its facilities while the United States provides the regional strategic reassurance the city-state desires.

But the problem of China looms as the potential limiting factor in the U.S.-Singapore relationship. Singapore may be comfortable with a posture aimed at maintaining regional "stability," a term that perhaps functions primarily as a euphemism for deterrence of adventurism by China or other dissatisfied states. Yet the access arrangements may be severely tested should deterrence fail and consequent military action by U.S. forces be required. Perhaps the need to avoid such a dilemma can explain why Singapore so strongly supports the stabilizing American role in Asia in the first place. Although there may be a degree of circularity in the logic, it also reflects the limited choices Singapore and other smaller regional states have to contribute substantively to peace among the major powers of the Asia-Pacific region. That is, by providing U.S. forces access to Singaporean facilities and thus enabling America's regional force posture, Singapore is contributing indirectly to the U.S. deterrent effect that seeks to prevent the outbreak of future conflict.

Notes

1. Paul Kennedy, *The Rise and Fall of British Naval Mastery* (London: Penguin, 1976), 205–6.
2. See, for example, James Neidpath, *The Singapore Naval Base and the Defence of Britain's Eastern Empire, 1919–1941* (Oxford: Clarendon, 1981); and Ian Hamill, *The Strategic Illusion: The Singapore Strategy and the Defence of Australia and New Zealand, 1919–1942* (Singapore: Singapore University Press, 1981).
3. Michael Leifer, *Singapore's Foreign Policy: Coping with Vulnerability* (London: Routledge, 2000), 63.
4. Christopher Pugsley, *From Emergency to Confrontation: The New Zealand Armed Forces in Malaya and Borneo 1949–1966* (South Melbourne, Victoria: Oxford University Press, 2003), 340.
5. Leifer, *Singapore's Foreign Policy*, 62, 101–2.

6. COMLOG WESTPAC Singapore Area Coordinator, "Welcome to Singapore" guide, 5, http://www.cnic.navy.mil/regions/sac.html.

7. Quoted in Charles Hill, *Grand Strategies: Literature, Statecraft, and World Order* (New Haven, Conn.: Yale University Press, 2010), 248.

8. Jeffrey D. Sachs, "The Geography of Economic Development," *Naval War College Review* 53, no. 4 (Autumn 2000): 100–101.

9. U.S. Defense Department, "A Strategic Framework for the Asian Pacific Rim: Report to Congress," 27 July 1992, reproduced in *Asia-Pacific Defense Forum* (Winter 1992–93): 21–22; and Tim Huxley, *Defending the Lion City: The Armed Forces of Singapore* (St. Leonards, NSW: George Allen and Unwin, 2000), 209.

10. Huxley, *Defending the Lion City*, 209.

11. U.S. Defense Department, *Annual Report to the President and the Congress* (Washington, D.C.: DoD, January 1994), 21.

12. Patrick E. Tyler, "U.S. near Agreement to Base Aircraft, Ships in Singapore," *Washington Post*, 6 July 1990, A26.

13. Singapore Area Coordinator, "Welcome to Singapore," 5.

14. Quoted in Bill Gertz, "Singapore Prepares for U.S. Warships," *Washington Times*, 16 January 1998, A10.

15. Quoted in Trish Saywell, "'Places Not Bases' Puts Singapore on the Line," *Far Eastern Economic Review*, 17 May 2001, 21.

16. Singapore Area Coordinator, "Welcome to Singapore," 5.

17. Huxley, *Defending the Lion City*, 209–10.

18. Strategic Framework Agreement between the United States of America and the Republic of Singapore for a Closer Cooperation Partnership in Defense and Security, Washington, D.C., 12 July 2005, article 2.2a.

19. Robert M. Gates, speech delivered to the Shangri-La Dialogue, Singapore, 4 June 2011, http://www.defense.gov/speeches/speech.aspx?speechid=1578.

20. Barack Obama, "Remarks by President Obama to the Australian Parliament," Parliament House, Canberra, 17 November 2011, *White House*, http://www.whitehouse.gov/the-press-office/2011/11/17/remarks-president-obama-australian-parliament.

21. Jonathan Greenert, "Statement of Admiral Jonathan Greenert, Chief of Naval Operations, before the Congress on FY 2013 Department of Navy Posture," March 2012, http://www.navy.mil/cno/120316_PS.pdf, 7.

22. "Joint Statement from Secretary Panetta and Singapore Minister for Defence Ng," 4 April 2012, http://www.defense.gov/releases/release.aspx?releaseid=15160.

23. "Joint Statement of U.S.-Singapore Meeting at Shangri-La," 2 June 2012, http://www.defense.gov/releases/release.aspx?releaseid=15337.

24. "LCS Headed for Singapore: Will Play Key Role in New U.S. Defense Strategy," *Lockheed Martin*, http://www.lockheedmartin.com/us/news/trade-shows/farnborough/stories-from-the-show/lcs-singapore.html.

25. Christopher P. Cavas, "U.S. Navy Creates LCS 'Council' to Guide Development," *Defense News*, 22 August 2012, http://www.defensenews.com/article/20120822/DEFREG02/308220009/U-S-Navy-Creates-LCS-8216-Council-8217-Guide-Development.

26. *Report to the President and the U.S. Congress* (Arlington, Va.: Commission on Review of Overseas Military Facility Structure of the United States, May 2005), http://www.fas.org/irp/agency/dod/obc.pdf [hereafter Military Facility Structure Report], H11.

27. Douglas J. Feith, Under Secretary of Defense for Policy, *Strengthening U.S. Global Defense Posture*, Report to Congress (Washington, D.C.: Office of the Under Secretary of Defense for Policy, September 2004), 10.

28. "Joint Statement of U.S.-Singapore Meeting at Shangri-La."

29. Singapore Area Coordinator, "Welcome to Singapore," 5.

30. U.S. Defense Department, *Base Structure Report Fiscal Year 2010 Baseline (A Summary of DoD's Real Property Inventory)* (Washington, D.C.: Office of the Deputy Under Secretary of Defense [Installations & Environment]), DOD-91.

31. Singapore Area Coordinator, "Welcome to Singapore," 6.

32. CNIC [Commander, Navy Installations Command]: Singapore Area Coordinator, "History," http://www.cnic.navy.mil/regions/sac/about/history.html.

33. CNIC: Singapore Area Coordinator, "Command," www.cnic.navy.mil/.

34. Singapore Area Coordinator, "Welcome to Singapore," 6.

35. Ibid.

36. CNIC: Singapore Area Coordinator, "MSC Sea Logistics Group Far East," http://www.cnic.navy.mil/regions/sac/about/tenant_commands/msc_sea_logistics_group_far_east.html.

37. Military Sealift Command, "Sealift Logistics Command Far East," http://www.cnic.navy.mil/regions/sac/about/tenant_commands/msc_sea_logistics_group_far_east.html.

38. Singapore Area Coordinator, "Welcome to Singapore," 6–7; and Military Sealift Command, "Ship Support Unit Singapore," http://www.cnic.navy.mil/regions/sac/about/tenant_commands/ship_support_unit_singapore_ssu.html. The Singapore MSFSC SSU is one of six worldwide; the others are located in Bahrain, Guam, Italy, Japan, and San Diego.

39. Singapore Area Coordinator, "Welcome to Singapore," 7.

40. CNIC: Singapore Area Coordinator, "Fleet Industrial Support Center (FISC), Detachment Singapore," http://www.cnic.navy.mil/regions/sac/about/tenant_commands/fleet_industrial_support_center_flsc_det_singapore.html.

41. Singapore Area Coordinator, "Welcome to Singapore," 7; CNIC: Singapore Area Coordinator, "497th Combat Training Squadron," http://www.cnic.navy.mil/regions/sac/about/tenant_commands/497th_combat_training_squadron.html; and Embassy of the United States Singapore, "497th Combat Training Squadron (497th CTS)," http://singapore.usembassy.gov/497cts.html.

42. Kaleb Snay, "Airmen Deploy for Commando Sling," 26 March 2012, http://www.misawa.af.mil/news/story_print.asp?id=123295255.

43. Singapore Area Coordinator, "Welcome to Singapore," 7.

44. Ibid.; and Embassy of the United States Singapore, "U.S. Coast Guard Marine Inspection Detachment Singapore," http://singapore.usembassy.gov/coast.guard.html.

45. CNIC: Singapore Area Coordinator, "Operations and Management," www.cnic .navy.mil/; and Timothy J. Keating, "Statement of Admiral Timothy J. Keating, U.S. Navy, Commander U.S. Pacific Command, before the Senate Armed Services Committee, on U.S. Pacific Command Posture," 19 March 2009, 17, http://www.almc.army.mil/ALU_INTERNAT/CountryNotes/PACOM/2.PA COM%20Posture%20Statement.pdf.

46. Jermyn Chow, "New U.S. Nuclear Sub Makes Port Call," *Straits Times*, 19 January 2011.

47. COMLOG WESTPAC, "N3: Operations, Plans and Policy," www.clwp.navy.mil /ops.htm.

48. COMLOG WESTPAC, "CARAT," https://www.facebook.com/Exercise.CARAT.

49. Alexa Olesen, "Singapore Says 21 Men Planned to Attack a U.S. Ship," *San Diego Union-Tribune,* 20 September 2002, A18.

50. See Joshua Ho, "Managing Port and Ship Security in Singapore," in *Lloyd's MIU Handbook of Maritime Security*, ed. Rupert Herbert-Burns, Sam Bateman, and Peter Lehr (Boca Raton, Fla.: CRC, 2009), 307–14.

51. Lt. Col. Nicholas Lim, "The Information Fusion Centre (IFC): A Case for Information Sharing to Enforce Security in the Maritime Domain," *Pointer: Journal of the Singapore Armed Forces*, "The Information Fusion Centre: Challenges and Perspectives" supplement (April 2011), 7. Colonel Lim is head of the Information Fusion Centre.

52. See Chris Rahman, *The Global Maritime Partnership Initiative: Implications for the Royal Australian Navy*, Papers in Australian Maritime Affairs 24 (Canberra: Sea Power Centre–Australia, 2008), 11, 44–45.

53. CNIC: Singapore Area Coordinator, "Force Protection," http://www.cnic.navy .mil/regions/sac/om/force_protection.html.

54. See Chris Rahman, "The International Politics of Combating Piracy in Southeast Asia," in *Violence at Sea: Piracy in the Age of Global Terrorism*, ed. Peter Lehr (New York: Routledge, 2007), 193–94.

55. Huxley, *Defending the Lion City*, 198–200.

56. Military Facility Structure Report, H6.

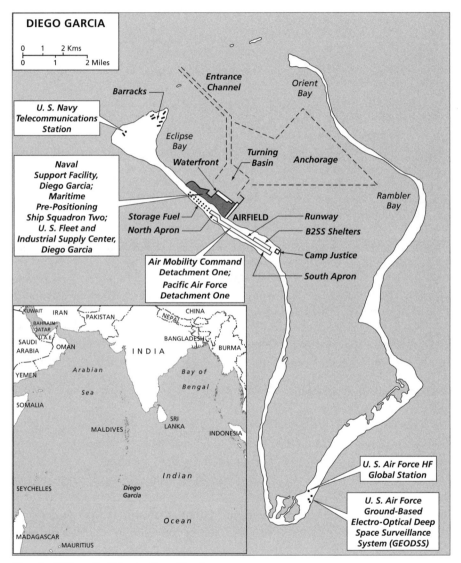

DIEGO GARCIA

0   1   2 Kms
0   1   2 Miles

Entrance Channel

Orient Bay

Barracks

U. S. Navy Telecommunications Station

Eclipse Bay

Turning Basin

Anchorage

Waterfront

Naval Support Facility, Diego Garcia; Maritime Pre-Positioning Ship Squadron Two; U. S. Fleet and Industrial Supply Center, Diego Garcia

Rambler Bay

Storage Fuel

AIRFIELD

Runway

North Apron

B2SS Shelters

Air Mobility Command Detachment One; Pacific Air Force Detachment One

Camp Justice

South Apron

KUWAIT   IRAN   PAKISTAN   CHINA
BAHRAIN   NEPAL
QATAR   BANGLADESH
SAUDI   U.A.E.
ARABIA   OMAN   I N D I A   BURMA
YEMEN   Arabian   Bay of
Sea   Bengal
SOMALIA
SRI LANKA
MALDIVES   INDONESIA
Indian
SEYCHELLES   Diego Garcia
Ocean
MADAGASCAR
MAURITIUS

U. S. Air Force HF Global Station

U. S. Air Force Ground-Based Electro-Optical Deep Space Surveillance System (GEODSS)

Map 6. Military Facilities in Diego Garcia

6

Diego Garcia and American Security in the Indian Ocean

Walter C. Ladwig III, Andrew S. Erickson, and Justin D. Mikolay

After more than a decade of war, the U.S. military is returning to an expeditionary force posture across the Middle East and South Asia.[1] To project power, deter adversaries, and maintain a credible contingency response capability, the United States must sustain a robust, continuous, and enduring maritime presence throughout the region. For decades the American base on the British island of Diego Garcia has played an important role in helping the United States sustain a forward presence in the region. Yet questions remain about the military importance of Diego Garcia and how the island might be used by the American military in the future.

U.S. forces operate from a network of bases and military facilities across the Indian Ocean littoral, stretching from Northeast Africa to the Middle East, the Arabian Peninsula and the Gulf, and South Asia. The United States maintains strong military-to-military relationships with several Gulf states, and these states host tens of thousands of U.S. troops at a number of land-based facilities. Such facilities do not come cheap or without liabilities, from host nation demands to popular opposition to the close proximity of Iranian missiles. Map 6 depicts Diego Garcia's location and current facilities.

Diego Garcia helps facilitate regional military operations because of its central geographic location in the Indian Ocean littoral. The U.S. military uses Diego Garcia for long-range bomber operations, special forces staging, the replenishment of naval surface combatants and guided-missile nuclear-powered submarines (SSGNs) capable of carrying out strike and special operations, and the prepositioning of Army and Marine Corps brigade sets.

Diego Garcia is the sovereign territory of a close ally and does not present the uncertainty that periodically plagues other overseas bases. Elsewhere, host nations may question long-term American commitments or demand "tacit or private goods, which risks future criticism and contractual renegotiation in the event of regime change."[2] Meanwhile, from a military standpoint, Diego Garcia's isolated location introduces operational challenges but also mitigates vulnerability to terrorist or state-based attacks.

Potential conflict involving Iran drives a significant portion of future U.S. force posture planning in the region. Such a contingency requires maritime assets continuously on station in the Gulf and the northern Indian Ocean as well as the use of land-based platforms operating from Gulf states. Specific components of U.S. military planning for possible Iran scenarios are classified, but the Iranian threat dictates a mix of maritime and land-based response options far closer to the point of action than Diego Garcia.

Our analysis proceeds in four sections. The first section examines the emerging strategic importance of the Indian Ocean littoral. The second, and most extensive, section concentrates on American interests in the Indian Ocean and surveys the history and development of the American presence on Diego Garcia as part of an expeditionary, networked basing strategy in the region. A third section examines India's and China's interests and activities in the region. The final section assesses the likelihood of great-power cooperation in the region, suggests how the United States might best develop and maintain basing and access there, and underscores the need for the further development of a U.S. regional strategy.

Geographical Pivot of the Twenty-First Century

Stretching from the Persian Gulf and the coast of East Africa on one side to the Malay Archipelago and the shores of Australia on the other, the Indian Ocean comprises an area of over 28 million square miles. The thirty nations that constitute the ocean's littoral region contain one-third of the world's population. Rich in natural resources, this geographical space contains 62 percent of the world's proven oil reserves, 35 percent of its gas, 40 percent of its gold, 60 percent of its uranium, and 80 percent of its diamonds.[3] In addition, a host of important minerals such as iron, titanium, chromate, and manganese as well as raw materials like rubber and tin are found in abundance in various parts of the littoral region.[4]

The Indian Ocean is not just a source of raw materials; it is also a vital conduit for bringing those materials to market. Most notably, it is a key transit route for oil making its way from the Persian Gulf to consumers in Europe and Asia: 17 million barrels of oil a day (20 percent of the world's oil supply and 93 percent of oil exported from the Gulf) transit by tanker through the Strait of Hormuz and into the western reaches of the Indian Ocean.[5] While large amounts of oil make their way to Europe and the Americas via the Suez Canal and the

Cape of Good Hope, the more important route is eastward—Gulf oil provides nearly 75 percent of Asia's import needs.[6] Roughly $70 billion worth of oil annually crosses the Indian Ocean from the Strait of Hormuz to the Strait of Malacca, bound for markets in Japan, China, and Korea, while another $16 billion worth flows to India.[7] Such is the importance of this route that some commentators have termed it the "new Silk Road."[8] Japan's economy is almost totally dependent on Gulf oil, with 89 percent of its imports shipped via the Indian Ocean, while Asia's two rising powers, China and India, are increasingly reliant on oil transiting the region. At present, more than 89 percent of China's hydrocarbon imports come via the Indian Ocean, and Gulf oil will soon account for 90 percent of India's imports.[9]

In terms of global trade, the Indian Ocean is a major conduit linking manufacturers in East Asia with markets in Europe, Africa, and the Persian Gulf. In addition to more than two-thirds of the world's oil shipments, half of the world's containerized cargo and one-third of its bulk cargo travels the Indian Ocean's busy sea-lanes annually.[10] The Asia–Europe shipping route via the Indian Ocean has recently displaced the transpacific route as the world's largest containerized trading lane.[11]

In 1904 British geographer Halford Mackinder described the Eastern Europe/Central Asia region as the "geographical pivot" on which the control of the Eurasian landmass, and potentially global hegemony, turned.[12] While this formulation accurately reflected the patterns of geopolitical conflict during the twentieth century, it is not an exaggeration to suggest that the Indian Ocean littoral could be the twenty-first century's pivot, with the potential to influence the global balance of power.[13] Indeed, Robert Kaplan argues that the Indian Ocean is a key geographic space that melds energy, commerce, and security.[14]

Continued economic growth in both the developed and developing worlds depends in part on uninterrupted access to the Indian Ocean littoral's oil and mineral resources and the goods that transit it—particularly because 80 percent of the trade conducted across the Indian Ocean is extraregional.[15] This causes the region and its sea-lanes to assume a strategic significance for many nations because political and military developments that adversely affect the flow of oil, raw materials, or trade goods could impact global economies.

The Indian Ocean littoral spans a great proportion of what Thomas Barnett has termed "the Non-Integrating Gap."[16] This region has a high potential for producing dysfunctional polities—*Foreign Policy* magazine's 2010 index of failed states included nine littoral states in its top twenty-five.[17] Moreover, the potential for interstate conflict remains high as many states have unresolved maritime or territorial disputes in a region that lacks substantial collective security arrangements.

The particular geography of the ocean itself, which is bounded on almost all sides by choke points—the Strait of Malacca to the east and the Suez Canal,

Cape of Good Hope, and Strait of Hormuz to the west—imposes challenges to maritime security. As two maritime analysts have noted, "If there was ever a case to be made for the relevance of strategic choke points, it is here, at the aquatic juncture between the world's largest sources of petroleum and the world's most import- and export-dependent economies."[18] Not only are ships in these narrow sea-lanes vulnerable to attack by terrorists or capture by pirates, but control of these bottlenecks has been the key to dominating this ocean since the Portuguese first arrived in the fifteenth century.

In addition to conventional security challenges, the littoral is plagued by a host of irregular security threats. A syndicate of violent extremist networks, including al-Qaeda and associated movements, operates from poorly governed spaces. While maritime trade routes are at risk from piracy on the high seas, the very same waterways that transport goods are also used for human smuggling, drug trafficking, and gunrunning as well as proliferation of munitions among insurgent groups. Several other challenges exacerbate existing ethnic, tribal, and religious tensions, including a large youth population, a growing surplus of males, and competition for increasingly scarce natural resources (fresh water is particularly limited).

Finally, the region also has the potential to be the scene of great-power conflict. In the context of the simultaneous rises of both India and China, Kaplan argues that "the Indian Ocean is where global struggles will play out in the 21st century."[19] It is not an exaggeration to suggest that the Indian Ocean littoral could be pivotal geopolitically. Any country that exercised a dominant role in the northern Indian Ocean would have the ability to affect the oil and trade routes from the Middle East to Europe and Asia—and thereby exercise negative influence over the industrialized world. As the world's strategic center of gravity shifts from the Euro-Atlantic region to the Asia-Pacific, therefore, the Indian Ocean is increasingly seen as "the ocean of destiny in the 21st century."[20]

The United States and the Indian Ocean

As outlined by Christopher Layne, U.S. strategic priorities since the end of the Second World War have been preventing the emergence of a rival hegemon in Europe or Asia while guaranteeing order in key areas of the periphery—most notably the Persian Gulf.[21] In this light, developments in the Indian Ocean are important to the United States because they affect the achievement of these broader goals. Among Washington's most significant interests are securing the sea lines of communication (SLOCs) that pass through the region, preventing hostile powers from dominating the littoral, and disrupting the operations of al-Qaeda–affiliated groups.

Indeed, the Indian Ocean region links the land and maritime theaters that most concern American strategic thinkers. The U.S. National Security Strategy identifies two land theaters of vital interest: Iraq and the greater Middle East, and Afghanistan/Pakistan.[22] Similarly, the nation's maritime strategy identifies the western portion of the Indian Ocean, which includes the piracy-plagued Horn of Africa, and the western Pacific as theaters of vital interest.[23]

The United States has an interest in preventing the emergence of a hostile regional power that could threaten the flow of commodities in the region.[24] To the West, Iran could threaten to shut the Strait of Hormuz, the world's most important maritime choke point. Iran's ability to employ attack submarines, sea mines, antiship cruise missiles, and perhaps even an antiship ballistic missile (*Khalij Fars*) will make it difficult to prevent Iran from shutting the Strait, although senior U.S. officials have declared that the United States can and will prevent Iran from doing so, if necessary.[25] Moreover, in the context of the ongoing dispute over Iran's nuclear program, Tehran conducted a series of naval maneuvers in 2006 that appeared to be intended to signal its ability to block the Strait of Hormuz in a crisis.[26] Lt. Gen. Ronald Burgess, director of the Defense Intelligence Agency, has testified that "if attacked, or if sanctions on its oil exports are enacted, Iran has threatened to control traffic in or temporarily close the Strait of Hormuz with its naval forces, a capability that it likely has."[27]

At the same time, from Southeast Asia to the coast of East Africa, China has increased its extraregional presence and political influence in its quest for energy. There is widespread speculation that Beijing is cultivating an informal set of access rights to local ports that could increase the Chinese navy's ability to project power into the littoral.[28] Although Chinese expeditionary naval capability remains limited, the mismatch between expressed concerns over the security of energy flows through regional choke points and China's actual behavior to date bears monitoring. Should one or both of these nations, Iran or China, achieve a more influential role in the littoral, it could have significant implications for American strategic interests.

Finally, U.S. interests in the region are also conditioned by the fact that the littoral has been ground zero for its nearly decade-long struggle against violent extremists. Prior to 11 September 2001, the United States had been the victim of al-Qaeda-backed terrorist attacks in Kenya, Tanzania, and Yemen. Today the United States is conducting a global counterterrorism campaign through a network of special operations forces. Given its location at an intersection of two main reservoirs of Islamic extremism, the Middle East and Southeast Asia, the Indian Ocean is, as one commentator has branded it, a "lake of Jihadi terrorism."[29] Al-Qaeda has repeatedly proclaimed its desire to cripple the West economically by targeting the oil-rich Gulf sheikdoms in the western reaches of the Indian Ocean that are friendly to the United States. In the past decade, agents acting in al-Qaeda's name have targeted American civilian and military entities in Yemen, Jordan, Bahrain, the United Arab Emirates (UAE), the Strait of Hormuz, and the Strait of Malacca.

The globalized nature of financial and commodity markets ensures that major political and economic tremors in the Indian Ocean are soon felt in America. Moreover, as American naval analysts have recently noted, "As the world's greatest trading nation, the U.S. economy . . . would not be so prosperous or dynamic were American or foreign-flagged shipping unable to use the world's oceans at will, free from restriction and interference."[30] In recognition of the importance of this region to American interests, the 2007 U.S. maritime strategy reoriented the two-ocean focus of the Navy and Marine Corps from the traditional Atlantic and the Pacific to the Indian Ocean and the Pacific, thereby declaring the intent to maintain sufficient forces in these latter regions to deter or defeat any hostile power.[31] In 2011 the U.S. Department of Defense released a new defense strategy with a key element of rebalancing the force to emphasize the Asia-Pacific region.

As an extraregional power, the United States can play a key role in managing stability in the region, whether by leading multilateral responses to irregular security threats, such as piracy, or by preventing the escalation of interstate conflict to dangerous levels. To achieve its regional objectives, the United States does not require a major ongoing military commitment to the Indian Ocean; rather, regular military deployments coupled with the ability to surge forces into the area during a crisis would provide the ability to deter most threats to U.S. interests there. These factors combine to make the centrally positioned island of Diego Garcia "one of the most strategic American bases in the world."[32]

The Malta of the Indian Ocean

The Indian Ocean has long been a crucial conduit for transit and commerce in the region. Since 2500 BC, traders and explorers from ancient Egypt, Phoenicia, the Persian Empire, the Indian subcontinent, the Arab states, and even China have all plied its waters in search of gold, incense, spices, and silks.[33] The ocean's role as a strategic base from which naval power could be employed to dominate the littoral regions did not develop until the arrival of the Portuguese in 1497. The rounding of the Cape of Good Hope by Vasco de Gama changed the strategic value of naval power in the Indian Ocean. Previously navies had played only a minor role in a region where land power had been the primary means by which the Persians, Hindus, and Arabs built large empires.[34]

Employing a strategy that would be duplicated by other European powers, the Portuguese sought to cement their position in the littoral region by establishing a series of strongholds, supported by naval power, along the strategic approaches to the Indian Ocean.[35] Control of key choke points such as Socotra, Hormuz, and Malacca secured Portuguese influence over the Indian Ocean. The goal was not territorial conquest per se but rather control of the trade routes that brought spices, raw materials, and goods from Asia to markets in Europe.[36]

The ensuing centuries saw the Dutch, the French, and the British joining the Portuguese in bids for supremacy in the region.

The maritime dominance Britain achieved following the battle of Trafalgar in 1805 was solidified after the defeat of Napoleon in 1815. Unrivaled dominance at sea, together with control of India, Singapore, and the Persian Gulf, allowed the Royal Navy to transform the Indian Ocean into a British lake—a condition that lasted until the end of the Second World War. British influence was felt throughout the littoral region.

Of the various bases available for projecting power into the Indian Ocean region, the Europeans favored island strongholds. These facilities, which could also serve as supply stations, allowed the desired control of trade routes yet did not have large populations to be governed or hinterlands from which rebellions could be launched.

Diego Garcia, named after the Portuguese navigator who discovered it in 1532, is the largest of seven islands that constitute the Chagos Archipelago. Located in the Indian Ocean, Diego Garcia is approximately 1,000 miles south of India, 700 miles southwest of Sri Lanka, and 2,500 miles southeast of the Strait of Hormuz. The island consists of a wishbone-shaped coral atoll, 14 miles long and 4 miles wide, surrounding "one of the finest natural harbors in the world."[37] With a total surface area of 11 square miles, Diego Garcia has an average elevation of 4 feet; the highest point on the island reaches 22 feet above sea level. Regarding climate change and rising sea levels, Secretary of the Navy Ray Mabus stated in a 2013 interview, "You won't begin to see impacts until the middle of this century, and major impacts until well into the next century. So, it will remain crucial for us as far out into the future as we are able to see right now."[38]

Diego Garcia was largely ignored for two and a half centuries until the French laid claim to it in 1783.[39] African slaves were introduced onto the originally uninhabited atoll by the French East India Company. Slave labor was used to harvest copra (dried coconut meat) and to produce oil from it. This oil was exported via Mauritius to France, where it was used for illumination and as a fuel for motors.

The board of directors of the British East India Company became increasingly concerned with France's footholds in the Indian Ocean, leading the company to launch in 1786 an expedition to Diego Garcia that succeeded in capturing the island. In the Treaty of Paris that ended the war between Napoleonic France and the Sixth Coalition in 1814, the majority of France's Indian Ocean territories, including Diego Garcia, were formally relinquished to Britain. The British government was largely unconcerned with Diego Garcia, and little changed appreciably following the change of control. A survey conducted at the time of its seizure had indicated that despite the quality of its harbor, the cost of fortifications and a permanent garrison would far outweigh the island's benefits.[40] Under British rule, the islands of the Chagos Archipelago were administered by

Mauritius, 1,500 miles to the southwest, much as they had been by the French. The former slaves, now freed and hired on Diego Garcia's three plantations as contract workers, were supplemented by laborers from Mauritius and the Seychelles, yet copra production remained the island's sole industry.[41] By the mid-1880s there were approximately three hundred contract laborers on Diego Garcia. The island featured a hospital, a church, a jail, and a "police officer, with a proper staff of constables."[42] Diego Garcia's deep harbor made it a useful coaling station for steamships traveling from the Suez Canal to Australia.[43]

During the Second World War, the British government established a small base and communications facility on Diego Garcia. The primary mission of this facility was to reconnoiter for German submarines and naval raiders preying on Allied shipping transiting between India and Australia. Two battalions from the British Indian Army were deployed to the island, as was a contingent of PBY Catalina flying boats. The German submarine threat in the Indian Ocean declined by 1942; the Diego Garcia garrison was withdrawn, and the island resumed its status as a forgotten corner of the British Empire. Matters remained so in the first decades of the Cold War.[44]

Despite being a maritime power with a long seagoing tradition, the United States had not traditionally possessed an integrated strategy for the Indian Ocean littoral. Instead, ad hoc responses to emerging challenges characterized its regional approach. During the first half of the twentieth century, Britain's dominance at sea and its imperial role in South Asia led the United States to regard the Indian Ocean as a British preserve.[45] Reliance on British power to "police" the region extended into the early decades of the Cold War. Until the early 1960s the Indian Ocean remained largely neglected in American strategic planning. American postwar strategy concentrated on the Atlantic, the Pacific Basin, and, to a lesser extent, the Mediterranean as Western Europe and Japan were viewed as essential territories in the struggle against global communism.[46] Involvement in the Indian Ocean littoral consisted primarily of economic and military aid rather than the deployment of military forces. A token U.S. naval presence—three obsolete destroyers of the Middle East Force—was based in Bahrain. American strategic interests in the region were narrowly conceived and focused exclusively on securing access to Gulf oil. Given Britain's naval and political dominance in the region, many American policy makers continued to see the security of the Indian Ocean and adjacent Persian Gulf as Great Britain's responsibility.

Some elements within the U.S. Navy, however, recognized the need to acquire a logistics base in the Indian Ocean that could support local contingency operations. Requirements included a communications station for ships and aircraft in the area, an airfield capable of operating long-range reconnaissance aircraft, and a supply depot that could sustain a U.S. naval presence. Such a facility would have to be strategically located, based on a site that was not heavily populated, and free from political restrictions on its use.[47] (These attributes remain Diego Garcia's key strategic advantages.)

As Third World nationalism swept through the Indian Ocean region in the wake of decolonization, the Navy became increasingly aware of the susceptibility of shore-based facilities to popular opinion in host nations.[48] Lightly populated islands, on the other hand, would presumably be relatively free from coups and political protests, and the presence of foreign bases might be less likely to aggravate local opinion. As part of what became known as the "strategic island concept," therefore, naval planners advocated securing basing rights on strategically located and "sparsely populated islands."[49] Among the most promising "strategic islands" identified by American naval analysts was the British-held territory of Diego Garcia. Adm. John McCain noted, "As Malta is to the Mediterranean, Diego Garcia is to the Indian Ocean—equidistant from all points."[50] Gaining access to Diego Garcia became a top priority for the Navy as the concept for a facility there received high-level support from the chief of naval operations, Adm. Arleigh Burke, and Secretary of the Navy Paul H. Nitze.[51]

Events in the early 1960s appeared to compel a greater U.S. involvement in the Indian Ocean region. In 1961 Britain began to discuss the possibility of withdrawing its forces from "East of Suez."[52] The following year the United States found itself hard-pressed to render emergency assistance to India during its 1962 war with China.[53] Concerns about a power vacuum in the region should the British actually draw down their forces coincided with a recognition that a U.S. military presence was necessary "to lend muscle to American diplomacy in the region."[54]

In 1963 the United States initiated talks with the British government about establishing a shared Anglo-American defense facility on Diego Garcia, which was by then a dependency of the self-governing crown colony of Mauritius.[55] The British welcomed the proposal because an American presence would complement their efforts to deter "communist encroachment in the littoral countries and might assist in dealing rapidly with local disturbances." London also saw Diego Garcia as a potential base for a military presence in the Indian Ocean, should Britain lose access to Aden or Singapore.[56]

As Britain's Indian Ocean colonies moved toward independence, London took action to secure strategic islands for defense purposes. As a condition of independence, the government of Mauritius had been persuaded to surrender its claims to the Chagos Archipelago. This island chain was subsequently combined with three islands that had been detached from the Seychelles to form a new crown colony, the British Indian Ocean Territory (BIOT), which came into being on 8 November 1965. As the colonial secretary told the House of Commons in announcing the formation of the new colony, "The islands will be available for the construction of defense facilities by the British and United

States governments."[57] The government of Mauritius was given $8.4 million in compensation for the loss of its territory.[58]

An exchange of notes between the United States and the United Kingdom in December 1966 made the entire BIOT available "for the defense purposes of both governments as they may arise."[59] Although the agreement made the territories available to the United States "without charge," the United States entered into a confidential agreement to compensate the United Kingdom for half the costs of establishing the colony.[60]

Although ideal in many respects and never self-governing at any time in history, at the time of the creation of the BIOT Diego Garcia had a population of 483 men, women, and children. All but 7 of these were employees (or their dependents) of the copra plantations owned by the Seychelles-based Chagos-Agalega Company.[61] Both the British and American governments believed that establishing defense facilities on the island would require closing the copra plantations and resettling the workers and their families.[62] After the formation of the BIOT, the government of Mauritius informed its nationals working in the Chagos Archipelago that they should seek alternate employment.[63] It was hardly exceptional to close plantations and transfer workers—the copra plantations on three other islands in the Chagos Archipelago had been discontinued during the interwar period and their employees relocated.[64] Between 1965 and 1971, under the direction of the British government, the Chagos-Agalega Company ceased renewing work contracts for existing employees. This natural attrition took its toll; by the time the plantations stopped operating in 1971, only 359 inhabitants remained on the island.[65] In preparation for the start of construction on the joint communications facility, the company evacuated the remaining civilian population by ship to Mauritius.[66] The British government paid the government of Mauritius a total of $8.6 million to cover the costs of resettlement.[67]

Construction commenced on an austere communications facility and an eight-thousand-foot runway in March 1971. This was quickly followed, in October 1972, by a second Anglo-American agreement on Diego Garcia that formally approved the construction plans for the communications facility as well as "an anchorage, airfield, associated logistics support and supply and personnel accommodations."[68] The communications post became operational in early 1973—a dynamic time in the Indian Ocean littoral. In January 1968 the Labor government of Harold Wilson surprised the world by announcing its intention to withdraw all British forces from the Far East and the Persian Gulf by 1971.[69] From a Western perspective, Wilson's decision could not have come at a worse time. The increasingly unpopular war in Vietnam constrained Washington's ability to assume military commitments in other parts of the globe in order to fill the void left by the British, whereas the Soviet Union and China appeared to be expanding their influence around the world.[70] In the wake of the British announcement, the Soviet navy began regular deployments to the Indian Ocean.[71]

In response, the United States undertook a "major shift" in its regional strategy, one that saw a significant increase in the frequency of naval patrols in the Indian Ocean.[72] The logistical difficulties of supporting these increased deployments, combined with a noticeable growth in the Soviet naval presence, led the Navy to the conclusion that Diego Garcia had to be expanded.[73] In February 1976 a third British-American agreement approved an upgrade from a "limited communications facility" to a "support facility of the U.S. Navy," which one scholar calls "a diplomatic euphemism for a full-scale American naval/air base."[74]

The need for such a facility in the region was made clear in 1979, when revolution swept through Iran and the Soviet Union invaded Afghanistan. Under the Nixon Doctrine, the shah's Iran had been America's self-professed policeman in the Persian Gulf—defending the West's economic, political, and strategic interests. With the shah's overthrow, the United States lost a security buffer between the Soviet Union and the Gulf, and lost access to the strategically located Iranian ports of Bandar Abbas and Chah Bahar. Washington feared that radical extremist Islamist militancy could undermine the pro-Western states of the region and provide an avenue for Soviet intrusion, which had been on display in the Middle East and the Horn of Africa even before Soviet combat troops entered Afghanistan in December 1979. The 1973–74 oil embargo had alerted Western leaders to their vulnerability to an oil-supply disruption. With up to 80 percent of the strategic minerals consumed by Japan, Europe, and the United States transiting the Indian Ocean, Washington believed that a base was needed to maintain resource supplies and deter threats to disrupt them.[75]

In the early 1980s Diego Garcia saw a host of construction projects as the facility was turned into a logistical hub for naval forces in the Indian Ocean. This upgrade involved deepening the lagoon so that it could berth a dozen ships, establishing a fuel storage depot that could supply a carrier battle group for a month, and extending the runway to 12,000 feet to accommodate America's largest tanker and cargo aircraft as well as SR-71 reconnaissance aircraft.[76] Such a facility would provide the United States a secure naval base in the Indian Ocean, a hub to project power into the region, under the control of America's closest ally. While not ideal in every respect, it would add a significant component to the U.S. force structure. In this way concerns that the United States would be denied access to local bases in a regional crisis, as they had been in the 1973 Yom Kippur War, were allayed.

The extension of the island's airfield and upgrade of its communications suite allowed the temporary basing of long-range bombers, such as the B-52. Diego Garcia also became the home of a fleet of seventeen maritime prepositioning ships that carried enough equipment, ammunition, and fuel to outfit a mechanized Marine amphibious brigade.[77] The improvement of Diego Garcia's facilities and the prepositioning of military equipment significantly enhanced the

United States' capability to project power into the Indian Ocean littoral and created the potential to take a more active role in the region's affairs.

Defense Planners and the Footprint of Freedom

From these beginnings, America's use of Diego Garcia as a forward operating base has grown over time. Diego Garcia's status as a modern base materialized gradually over the last thirty years, growing out of its value as an in-transit supply and repair station and its dependability. These traits make the island useful for both routine operations and crisis response. The island also serves as a prepositioning point for a collection of ships in the island's harbor that carry logistical equipment for contingency operations.

Even for assets that possess extended endurance, Diego Garcia remains a natural service stop when entering and exiting the Indian Ocean. The island routinely receives long-range bombers, fast-attack submarines, and medium-sized surface ships between missions as part of Central Command task forces. In its current state, then, Diego Garcia fulfills an important regional support role for logistics and operations. Planned construction presages a much-expanded role for the island as a primary maintenance and upkeep facility for naval assets.

The island suffers from a number of challenges similar to other forward-support locations.[78] First, the "tyranny of distance" both adds and detracts value from the island. Diego Garcia, while centrally placed, is too far—seven degrees south of the equator—from the locations of likely regional threats for immediate response. With flexibility and speed as their priorities, planners prefer bases closer to anticipated points of action—a forward posture that calls for more bases in more places.

Diego Garcia contains only one runway and one quay wall (to which ships can moor), and that small footprint is far less than required for a buildup of material to support a major military engagement. Nonetheless, should the need arise to surge units and equipment to the area, planners could expect to use Diego Garcia without delay.

Planners understandably place a high priority on assured access to regional bases. If the atoll is thousands of miles from any given area of interest, it is central to many others. Absent advance notice of the next hot spot, it is sensible to concentrate on the center of the overall operating area. Accordingly, quasi-sovereign access to the island remains critical to continued operations in the theater.

The new U.S. defense strategy calls for the future force to remain agile and flexible in order to respond to regional threats and defeat any adversary, anytime. Diego Garcia helps to provide such flexibility, but it is relatively far removed from likely contingency locations in the northern Indian Ocean. A submarine takes five days to transit from the island through the Strait of Hormuz into the Persian Gulf and even longer to travel through the Bab al Mandeb into the Red Sea. Critically, though, planners much prefer the guarantee that Diego Garcia represents. The U.S.-British military agreement in the BIOT is expansive, long-term, and steadfast. The unified maritime strategy explicitly reinforces the importance of that agreement: "Credible combat power will be continuously postured in the Western Pacific, the Gulf, and the Indian Ocean to protect America's vital interests, assure our friends and allies of the continuing commitment of the U.S. to regional security, and deter and dissuade potential adversaries and peer competitors. This combat power can be selectively and rapidly repositioned to meet contingencies that may arise elsewhere."[79]

Beyond the military agreement, American and British officials meet annually for a two-day political-military dialogue to examine treaty arrangements and procedures for the U.S. use of British territories (not only Diego Garcia but Ascension Island as well, among others). In recent years, the discussions on Diego Garcia have focused on advance notification of British travelers to the island, U.S. munitions storage, the Chagos population, taxation of international communications, and environmental issues. The lease between the United States and the United Kingdom will be up for renewal in 2014; though no major disagreements are expected, discussions involving renewal will offer an opportunity for both parties to press for concessions on payment and infrastructure development plans.[80] Like its Pacific counterpart, Guam, Diego Garcia is a preferred launching point for prepositioned stock and munitions to surrounding hot spots. Unlike with Guam, however, defense planners long hesitated to modernize the island's aging infrastructure. This is no longer the case. After a ten-year hiatus in structural improvements to the pier, a refit and facilities upgrade have returned to the budget priority list. This is no coincidence. The U.S. military will continue to confront violent extremism, Iran's nuclear ambitions and destabilizing actions, and other regional threats over the long term. In this context, Diego Garcia offers a stable platform from which to protect the promise and opportunity of the Indian Ocean. Absent interference from rogue elements, the ocean links the Middle East and Africa to the trade routes of the western Pacific. The island links—and helps to coordinate the efforts of—three nearby combatant commands, each of which endeavors to remove these elements of interference.

The island sits a few hundred miles southeast of the vertical seam of the Central and Pacific Commands (CENTCOM and PACOM). That seam divides the Indian Ocean and then cuts due west along the equator toward Kenya and Africa Command (AFRICOM). CENTCOM retains the upper-left quadrant of the Indian Ocean. The corner of this area of responsibility (AOR) juts to within a day's transit of Diego Garcia. As a result, many units changing operational command between PACOM and CENTCOM naturally employ facilities on Diego Garcia to receive deliveries and for crew rest. This is especially important for B-1 and B-2 pilots on missions (often longer than forty hours) that originate from theaters other than CENTCOM. After these fatigued bomber crews complete their missions and withdraw from harm's way, they need a safe haven in which to fuel, rest, and prepare to return home.

Other practical reasons validate frequent stops at the island. In particular, units—particularly ships—in transition between commands must adjust to different operational rules, communications circuits, and command relationships. Diego Garcia acts as a gateway for ships en route from one AOR to another to pause, fix equipment, train, and demonstrate material readiness and crew proficiency for certification to higher-level commanders. The president and the secretary of defense authorize platforms to execute sensitive national-security tasking in-theater. No other base affords similar flexibility on the rim of the Indian Ocean in such a key mission area as the Horn of Arica.

As operational tempo increases throughout the region, the need to improve basic services on the island has grown. The military practicality of the island, then, justifies further American investment to this narrow strip of land to meet combatant commander requirements. These requirements include increased payloads for vertical strike (often quantified in terms of the number of serviceable Tomahawk missiles in-theater at a given time), increased surveillance capabilities, and increased operational flexibility for short- and long-range aircraft.

But although planners agree on the general utility of Diego Garcia, they find it difficult to reach consensus on how best to capitalize on the island's central placement. The parochial interests of three nearby combatant commanders confuse the setting of regional priorities that would contribute to a coherent, long-term construction plan for the island. The U.S. Unified Command Plan, as noted, splits the Indian Ocean in two along the line that separates the AORs of CENTCOM and PACOM. This axis, at 68 degrees east longitude, divides "ownership" of the region and thereby promotes indifference to the unique aspects of Indian Ocean security as a whole.[81] In particular, the United States too often overlooks the concerns of Indian leaders about U.S. military development on Diego Garcia (discussed later). Consequently, Diego Garcia's role within the region remains unclear, and construction plans for the island are often delayed or derailed by the lack of a comprehensive regional strategy for the Indian Ocean.

Diego Garcia at Present

Diego Garcia acts as a fixed warehouse from which the U.S. Navy and Air Force support operational units throughout the region with fuel, food, routine supplies, spare parts, munitions, aircraft shelters, maintenance services, and communications. The Navy is impacted minimally by the island's remoteness (with the important exception of potential escalation involving Iran, which could happen faster than ships could respond from Diego Garcia). However, the island cannot accommodate large Navy platforms at its small pier. Conversely, Air Force fighters cannot traverse the Indian Ocean to Diego Garcia without help from tankers, an operationally burdensome reality, but the long runway on the island accommodates any aircraft in the inventory.

The atoll serves four primary functions for American commanders: a full one-third of the entire U.S. Afloat Prepositioning Force occupies the lagoon; fast-attack submarines and surface ships use the deep-draft wharf; an Air Expeditionary Wing supports tactical and long-range aircraft; and a telecommunications station tracks satellites and relays fleet broadcasts to units in the area. We will treat each function in separate sections and then consider the current status of island utilities in support of the overall effort.[82]

The Afloat Prepositioning Force

The U.S. military prepositions stock at three primary locations: in the Mediterranean, on Diego Garcia, and on Guam. Combatant commanders would enjoy tremendous flexibility should it become necessary to call upon these nearby assets. The design basis for prepositioned stock enables an Army and Marine Corps brigade to mobilize within twenty-four hours anywhere within the region without additional support for up to thirty days.[83]

Several layers of command oversee these stocks. The Afloat Prepositioning Force, including strategic sealift forces commonly referred to as "prepositioning ships," falls under the authority of the Military Sealift Command (MSC), itself a component of U.S. Transportation Command. Diego Garcia hosts Maritime Prepositioning Squadron 2 (MPSRON 2), one of three squadrons under MSC authority operated by professional civilian mariners.[84] MPSRON 2 maintains between ten to fifteen forward-deployed prepositioning ships within Diego Garcia's dredged lagoon, which ranges from sixty to a hundred feet deep.

Three primary clients demand MSC support: the Army, the Marine Corps, and a joint-service group. The Army loads its forward equipment on Afloat Prepositioned Stocks 3 (APS-3) ships. Diego Garcia's eight APS-3 ships provide Army commanders a thirty-day buffer during which replacement equipment for an advance brigade can be sent from within the region. These ships, designated T-AKRs, carry combat-support and combat-service-support elements. As hostilities escalate, APS-3 ships can position heavy armor, land-based reconnaissance equipment, artillery, and combined-arms battalions in-theater from Diego Garcia within a week.

The Marine Corps benefits from similar readiness in the Indian Ocean should commanders exercise the dedicated MSC Maritime Prepositioning Force. Five of these ships in Diego Garcia, designated T-AK, enable the decisive speed of a Marine expeditionary brigade. Together the ships can equip 15,000 Marines already on the beach and conduct simultaneous helicopter operations. The concepts of operations of the Marine Corps Maritime Prepositioning ships and Army APS-3 ships are matched in terms of self-sufficiency and roll-on/roll-off capability.

A group comprising a mix of other customers makes up the third major client of the Afloat Prepositioning Force: the Navy, Defense Logistics Agency, and Air Force ships (known collectively as the Prepositioning NDAF) transport Navy and Air Force munitions and ordnance for transfer to smaller carriers on land or via at-sea replenishment. The Prepositioning NDAF includes separate petroleum-delivery ships, high-speed vessels, and aviation-logistics support ships, all of which can be vectored to Diego Garcia for urgent availability.

With sustained speeds in excess of thirty knots, sealift ships are considered the fastest cargo ships in the world. As a result, CENTCOM can dispatch these prepositioned assets to a regional crises; in the Indian Ocean region especially, this has meant humanitarian as well as combat missions.[85] Of note, however, a typhoon approaching Diego Garcia would force the local operational commander, a Navy captain, to send the squadron out to sea, as the low-lying island affords little protection from the wind.

Naval Forces Support

A general-purpose, deep-draft wharf or quay wall 2,000 feet long and 150 feet wide serves the island. The wall sits within the island's interior lagoon to the northwest and contains two main berths (Berth A, or "Alpha Wharf," to the north, and Berth B, or "Bravo Wharf," on the south). Typically the pier receives a T-AKR for a week each month at Alpha Wharf; in the current configuration, the supply ship moors starboard side to. The pier can accommodate a fast-attack submarine (SSN) at Bravo Wharf. In rare circumstances, the pier accepts up to two nested SSNs (one alongside the pier, the other outboard).

Naval Support Facility Diego Garcia consolidates the services available to personnel on the island. Shore support facilities include buildings for spare equipment, housing for electrical power cables and associated distribution breakers, pier space for service craft, and bachelor quarters for residents and flyaway maintenance teams. Recreation options, however, remain limited for shipboard personnel visiting the island.[86] By comparison with other overseas U.S. military installations, Diego Garcia has only modest amenities and little room for expansion.

Air Force

Various U.S. Air Force planes land on Diego Garcia's generous runway, and an Air Expeditionary Wing occupies its airfield. Detachments of Pacific Air Forces operate and maintain aircraft temporarily posted on the island. On a continual basis, shore support elements service about ten long-range bombers with munitions, fuel, and supplies. B-1 and B-52 bombers line the landing field, while visiting B-2s use four special hangars designed to protect the planes' sensitive skins. The hangars, constructed in 2003, represent the latest significant upgrade to Diego Garcia's structural facilities. The Air Force has established Diego Garcia as an en-route base for the Air Mobility Command.[87]

Long-range bombers based at Diego Garcia have been—with the possible exception of unmanned intelligence surveillance aircraft—the Air Force's most important asset in Operation Enduring Freedom.[88] Throughout the initial air campaign, gunships and fighters based in Turkey and elsewhere encountered logistical difficulties and soon ceded their strike taskings to the bomber fleet based on Diego Garcia. Bombers were able to operate in Afghanistan with relative impunity after the first few days of strikes due to the limited antiaircraft capabilities of the Taliban. Unimpeded bomber operations from Diego Garcia could be expected only in future conflicts against similarly disorganized and poorly armed terrorist groups—not against a modern military force such as Iran's.[89]

For tactical air operations, Diego Garcia's distance from other land introduces far greater levels of complexity and demands multiplatform coordination. Practical endurance limitations of modern-day fighter aircraft limit their tactical radii (the maximum distances from which aircraft can return unrefueled) to less than five hundred miles. Fighters that take off from Diego Garcia require in-flight refueling from escort tankers on their way to CENTCOM missions.[90] Fighter squadrons therefore take up permanent stations in bases closer to the areas of operations.[91]

Long-range bombers on missions originating from the island do not require such support. The Air Expeditionary Wing's B-52s can reach CENTCOM targets and return without refueling. Bombers based on the island took advantage of their forward location to prosecute targets in Afghanistan after 11 September 2001.[92]

The Telecommunications Facility

The U.S. Naval Computer and Telecommunications Station (NCTAMS) Far East Detachment oversees a small communications suite on Diego Garcia (NCTAMS DET DG). The station broadcasts and relays operational information to units in the region, tracks satellites, and operates shore information-technology services on the island. Shore relay stations still serve a critical function in the U.S. military's worldwide communications. Submarines in the Indian Ocean, for example, establish satellite links while under way and must report and receive real-time intelligence data to accomplish their missions. Satellite dishes on Diego Garcia transmit data to satellites over the Indian Ocean to provide deployed commanders (and those on shore) with the current status and locations of U.S. and enemy forces. Joint operations in the Indian Ocean rely upon secure tactical circuits maintained by NCTAMS DET DG. Its operators perform critical functions for units in the area: they assist in troubleshooting satellite connectivity issues (through geolocation, remote technical advice, and verification of circuit operability), and they enforce strict rules that govern the sharing of scarce satellite bandwidth.

Utilities

Electrical capacity, sewage treatment capacity, and water supply limit the number of assets that can call on Diego Garcia simultaneously. To a lesser extent, units also require compressed air, nitrogen, amine to scrub CO_2 from the air in submarines, and "controlled pure water" for various shipboard uses.[93] Finally, tended ships and submarines must off-load oily waste generated from lubricating oil leak-off and other sources. (Nuclear-powered ships on deployment normally transport radiological waste on board for transfer to facilities only upon return to home port; thus, facilities for its stowage and disposal are not required at remote locations such as Diego Garcia.) The pier facilities must have hoses and cables, with their fittings and connections, that match American standards. Incompatibility issues sometimes occur at foreign ports, strengthening the appeal to some commanders of the dependable services at a U.S.-operated pier like Diego Garcia. The U.S. military has proven adept at overcoming a variety of tactical challenges of this sort, but the availability of standardized U.S. equipment only reinforces the value of long-term access to Diego Garcia for routine missions.

The waterfront electrical complex draws from the island grid, requiring Air Force, Navy, and Army facilities to share amperage.[94] Should pier configuration change to receive additional units alongside, total electrical capacity will be insufficient to meet demand.[95] This will require surface ships to continue steaming to provide their own electrical power and SSNs to keep their reactors critical, with the electric plant in self-sustaining operation.[96]

Sewage from land facilities and shipboard sanitary tanks either drains or is pumped to a single-pool waste-retreatment facility on the island. The resident population is expected to remain constant, but additional naval functions will raise waste treatment facility usage. An upgrade is overdue: a report for FY 2010 military construction Project 182 finds "the sewage lagoon that services the island is [only] marginally treating the sewage" under current loads.

Water treatment also remains problematic. Potable water contains unacceptable levels of trihalomethanes, a contaminant not readily removed by existing facilities.[97] Improved filtration systems are needed to raise water quality for use throughout the island and, perhaps more important, service submarines, which observe strict potable-water standards.

Looking Ahead

The coming years will bring additional construction to Diego Garcia, substantively upgrading the existing forward operating naval base. The significant U.S. construction planned for the island—four phased projects totaling around $200 million—will be the second such effort in the island's history. The first effort, completed in 1986, established the berthing facilities currently in use and transformed the island from a simple communications facility to its present role as an important support facility in the India Ocean.

The construction program is an outgrowth of two additional requirements laid on the island:

- To support a nuclear-powered guided-missile submarine (SSGN) with limited repairs, which began in 2011.
- To act as the forward operating base for the submarine tender *Emory S. Land*, transferred from La Maddalena, Italy, to Diego Garcia in 2010.[98]

The SSGN

SSGNs conduct multimonth special operations missions, calling at Guam for brief refit periods and planned crew swaps. This concept of operations is similar to the type from which the current SSGNs were converted, the Trident ballistic-missile nuclear-powered submarine (SSBN).[99] After refit and crew swap, the SSGN conducts additional missions before returning to home port for a longer refit period. This deployment cycle maximizes time at sea, achieving a deployment rate over 70 percent.[100] With parallel deployment schedules, USS *Michigan* (SSGN 727) and USS *Ohio* (SSGN 726) will provide constant presence in the Pacific. In the same way, rotation of USS *Florida* (SSGN 728) and USS *Georgia* (SSSGN 729) from the Atlantic Fleet will establish coverage in the Indian Ocean.[101]

Diego Garcia is the natural choice to host a guided-missile submarine in the Indian Ocean for reasons of security and stability. In terms of security, the SSGN would not need to transit a dangerous choke point to arrive at the island. Basing at Bahrain and Dubai, for example, would require a tricky transit through the busy and shallow Strait of Hormuz. In addition, a fully loaded SSGN makes an attractive and conspicuous target for terrorists. The platform could also face potential harassment by a regional aggressor, such as Iran. The isolated pier at Diego Garcia, therefore, represents a safer alternative to many options closer to likely objectives. The island also provides stability. SSGNs require unique—and therefore expensive—support facilities to load and maintain their vertical-launch systems and special operations forces modules and associated equipment. A flexible and short-term basing structure (facilities at multiple locations throughout the theater) would not afford suitable support for the complex platform. Finally, Diego Garcia contains adequate housing and shore facilities to conduct an in-theater crew swap while the submarine undergoes a three-week refit.

The reasons for bringing SSGNs into the theater itself are even more compelling. The platform exploits an enormous "dwell time" on station and provides two unique capabilities in addition to covert intelligence collection. First, with a full "maximum strike" complement of 154 Tomahawk land-attack missiles (TLAM), the SSGN offers enormous vertical-strike power, twelve times that of an improved *Los Angeles*–class SSN. The overwhelming cruise-missile support represented by the SSGN is a joint enabler for other forces. On its own, one SSGN satisfies the vast majority of the theater-level TLAM requirements of combatant commanders, which frees up TLAM-equipped SSNs and surface ships for other tasks, such as surveillance and interdiction. Commanders are therefore understandably eager to acquire the operational flexibility generated by constant SSGN presence in the region.

Second, the SSGN can be configured for simultaneous strike and special operations forces (SOF) missions. Strike canisters can be converted to accommodate over 60 SOF personnel and their equipment. Advanced SEAL delivery vehicles or dry dock shelters can attach to and detach from missile canisters from which the weapons have been removed. As a result, the submarine can covertly insert a SOF mission close to land and then stand by for strike tasking with the remaining 140 operational TLAMs. In the future the SSGNs may also employ unmanned underwater vehicles for special operations.

Several upgrades were required to permit Diego Garcia to accommodate the SSGN, including installing a pneumatic fender system, dredging Bravo Wharf to accommodate the boat's forty-foot keel depth, and improving waterfront electrical capabilities.[102]

USS *Emory S. Land*

Local political pressure forced the closure of *Emory S. Land*'s previous home port on the Italian island of Sardinia. The compulsory base closure at La Maddalena reinforces concern that "guaranteed access" is a chimera—even on the territory of otherwise reliable NATO allies. The circumstances surrounding *Emory S. Land*'s relocation tell a cautionary tale: local concerns often balloon into unfavorable domestic political conditions that can unhinge even strong basing agreements.[103] The choice of Diego Garcia over other potential homeports demonstrates an appreciation of the island's strategic location. Planners considered a number of options but settled on Diego Garcia even though it was more costly and involved a number of housing upgrades and pier improvements.

A significant number of submarine missions take place east of the Suez Canal. Typically Atlantic submarines coordinate with Combined Task Force 69 in the European Command (EUCOM) and moor alongside a tender in the Mediterranean during the first few weeks of six-month deployments. Thereafter, if critical equipment fails beyond the capability of the ship's force to repair during a CENTCOM mission, either the item must remain out of commission until the boat returns through the canal and visits the tender or a flyaway team must attempt to restore or replace the casualty in Bahrain or Diego Garcia. Neither repair scenario is ideal: one requires a lengthy and expensive transit that could preclude follow-on tasking in CENTCOM, and the other limits the repair team's immediately available resources.[104] Similarly, if a TLAM-capable unit launches a full salvo, reload is available only at the tender, after a northbound Suez transit.

As EUCOM missions dwindled, accordingly, the argument to base *Emory S. Land* at Diego Garcia gained force.

CENTCOM and PACOM will benefit from the enormous capabilities of the tender. Submarine tenders serve as floating shipyards to repair and supply submarines and surface combatants. Specialized personnel—berthed on board the auxiliary ship itself or temporarily assigned in flyaway teams from the United States—can provide virtually any service the tended ship requests, from repair of a small valve to complete replacement of steam piping, electrical cables, pumps, ventilation fans, or components of weapons systems. The tender can also accept transfer of radioactive and hazardous materials that build up on nuclear-powered boats during long at-sea periods. Aside from mechanical and structural repair and maintenance, the tender offers full legal, dental, medical, and assorted other services for shipboard personnel. The tender houses fifty shops that can make and install spares for electronic, metal, or wooden components. Multiple ships can be served, moored along both sides of the tender (if anchored) simultaneously.

Only two submarine tenders exist in the U.S. fleet. USS *Frank Cable* (AS 40), redeployed to Guam since 1997, serves as the model that *Emory S. Land* will emulate. After completing a refit overhaul in Bremerton, Washington, that started in February 2008, *Emory S. Land* arrived at its new Indian Ocean home port in August 2010.

A Contested Space

The United States is not operating alone in the Indian Ocean. America increasingly encounters Indian and Chinese military influence, making it unlikely that it can achieve military predominance in the Indian Ocean theater. The next two sections address, respectively, Indian and Chinese efforts to establish influence in the region.

India and the Indian Ocean

India's strategic orientation toward the Indian Ocean has increased markedly in the past decade. In the time of the Raj, British India managed the empire "from the Swahili coasts to the Persian Gulf and eastward to the Straits of Malacca."[105] When India achieved independence in the wake of the Second World War, senior British officials assumed that the Raj's dominance in the region would pass to the Republic of India.[106] Early Indian strategic thinkers argued, accordingly, that India required a navy that could pick up where the Royal Navy had left off. Keshav Vaidya argued that "the Indian ocean must become an Indian Lake. That is to say India must become the supreme and undisputed power over the waters of the Indian Ocean . . . controlling the waves of that vast mass of water making the Indian Ocean, and its two main offshoots, the Arabian Sea and the Bay of Bengal."[107] Historian Kavalam Panikkar echoed the view that India should be the dominant power in the Indian Ocean, predicting that "the future of India will undoubtedly be decided on the sea."[108] As a result, it was necessary that India exercise control over the Indian Ocean: "While to other countries, the Indian Ocean is only one of the important oceanic areas, to India it is a vital sea. . . . The Indian Ocean must therefore remain truly Indian."[109]

Despite these expectations and entreaties, the country took a different route following independence. India's political leaders turned their strategic attention northward to the threats posed to India's territory by Pakistan and China. In an environment where a focus on economic growth constrained the size of the defense budget, the Indian army and air force received shares of military expenditures double that of the navy. Instead of blue-water operations as envisioned by Vaidya and Panikkar, the navy's role in India's defense plans was to support army operations on land against Pakistan. The idea of controlling, let alone dominating, the Indian Ocean was ignored for decades.

Neglect of the Indian Ocean came to an end in the late 1990s, when the right-of-center Bharatiya Janata Party government launched an ambitious program of naval acquisition paired with a "forward-leaning" foreign policy that sought to cement India's access and political leverage across the littoral region from East Africa to the Asia-Pacific.[110] These political and economic developments were tied to a renewed appreciation of the value of maritime power to an emerging power. India's 1998 *Strategic Defense Review* argued that "the Navy must have sufficient maritime power not only to be able to defend and further India's maritime interests, but also to deter a military maritime challenge posed by any littoral nation, or combination of littoral nations of the Indian Ocean Region, and also be able to significantly raise the threshold of intervention or coercion by extra-regional powers."[111]

In April 2004 the Indian navy released its first doctrinal publication, *India's Maritime Doctrine*. According to this document, "for the first quarter of the 21st century [India] must look at the arc from the Persian Gulf to the Straits of Malacca as a legitimate area of interest."[112] Indian naval strategists are staking an explicit claim to the legacy of the British Empire as identifying the natural boundaries of India's influence. The 2004 doctrinal document notes explicitly the link between maritime power and the protection of economic interests. In terms of concrete tasks, protecting India's maritime economic interests requires that the navy be able to carry out sea-denial missions throughout the country's expansive exclusive economic zone (EEZ). To protect the valuable SLOCs that carry India's trade and energy resources, the navy requires the capability to exercise sea control out to the perimeter of the Indian Ocean littoral. The doctrine describes explicitly the means by which India can control these SLOC-based trade routes. It emphasizes in particular the importance of dominating important islands and maritime choke points. Such actions are not merely defensive measure. Their coercive value is explicitly noted: "Control of these choke points could be a useful bargaining chip in the international power game."[113] India's growing maritime capabilities and expanding strategic vision suggest a desire to be the dominant naval power in, if not the regional hegemon of, the entire Indian Ocean littoral.[114]

India's focus on the Indian Ocean is driven by three interrelated factors: geography, economics, and concern about extraregional actors. India's landmass protrudes into the ocean at its midpoint. This places India adjacent to the primary maritime trade routes that link the Strait of Hormuz, the Arabian Sea, and the Horn of Africa, on one hand, with the Bay of Bengal and the Strait of Malacca, on the other. A substantial portion of the country—nearly 3,500 miles of coastline—physically touches the Indian Ocean. To this must be added a host of island chains and atolls in both the Arabian Sea and Bay of Bengal that add an additional 1,300 miles of coastline.[115] Altogether this provides India with a massive EEZ of 2.54 million square miles—nearly 10 percent of the Indian Ocean's total area.[116]

The sustained economic growth that India has experienced over the past fifteen years has given it sufficient wealth and power to start considering its security interests beyond South Asia.[117] At the same time, economic growth and the need to sustain it require that India focus increasingly on the Indian Ocean littoral, on which India's continued economic growth will depend heavily. In recent years, official statements have underscored increasingly the importance India attaches to energy security, which "is vital for an assured high rate of [economic] growth."[118] India's oil consumption is expected to double by 2025, which would make it the world's third-largest energy consumer, after the United States and China.[119] Roughly 30 percent of India's oil and gas comes from offshore fields in the Bombay High and Krishna-Godavari Basins.[120] However, India imports more than half of its natural gas and 70 percent of its oil, the supermajority of which comes from the Persian Gulf. With roughly 90 percent of its external trade by volume and 77 percent by value traveling by sea, it is not surprising that the security of shipping lanes in the Indian Ocean is a major concern for India. Indeed, a host of observers have argued that India's economy is "at the mercy of the power which controls the sea."[121]

India's extended neighborhood offers significant opportunities for beneficial economic engagement. India considers the Persian Gulf region to be not only a source of energy but, in the words of Prime Minister Manmohan Singh, "part of our natural economic hinterland."[122] The importance of the Persian Gulf / North Africa to India's economy generally can be seen in the fact that the UAE is India's third-largest trading partner while the combined region as a whole accounts for more than 20 percent of India's exports and nearly 30 percent of its imports.[123] At the opposite end of its extended neighborhood, India's focus is driven by economic engagement with Southeast Asia. During 2007–8 Indian trade with the Association of Southeast Asian Nations (ASEAN) reached $40 billion.[124] As of early 2009, the ASEAN countries as a whole accounted for 11 percent of India's exports and 9 percent of its imports.[125]

The need for India to secure its own interests in the Indian Ocean littoral points to the third and final factor driving India's attention to the region—concern about extraregional actors. While some Western scholars have argued that New Delhi desires primacy or hegemony in the Indian Ocean, Indian analysts suggest that it instead seeks, more modestly, to develop the capability to "balance the influence of other powers and prevent them from undercutting" India's interests in this zone.[126] The latter goal is significantly more achievable in the near term because while India's navy ranks as the world's fifth largest, it is currently contracting as obsolete ships leave service faster than they are being replaced, albeit by more capable modern platforms. The present fleet is built around the aging aircraft carrier INS *Viraat*, which is supplemented by fewer than 60 surface combatants—many of them at the end of their service lives—and more than a dozen diesel-electric submarines. The navy's ambitious goal is to have a "160-plus ship navy, including three aircraft carriers, 60 major combatants, including submarines, and close to 400 aircraft of different types" by 2022.[127] However, even this fleet would possess only a modest ability to project Indian power to the farthest reaches of the Indian Ocean or to influence military operations on land. At present, India's naval capabilities allow it to defend its territorial waters and police the sea-lanes of the northern Indian Ocean; they would need to be significantly greater to achieve primacy in the littoral region or to deter the unwanted interventions of extraregional actors.

The issue of extraregional actors in the Indian Ocean is particularly acute for New Delhi because, as the 2004 Indian maritime doctrine predicts, all "major powers of this century will seek a toehold in the [Indian Ocean region]."[128] India has long sought to preclude other powers from gaining a lasting presence in the Indian Ocean, a goal that assumes added force in light of the popular belief that India lost its independence when it lost control of the Indian Ocean in the sixteenth century.[129] Since the end of the Cold War, China has replaced the United States as the extraregional actor of primary concern. There is long-standing friction in the relationship between New Delhi and Beijing. The 1962 war between the two countries inflicted a humiliating defeat on India and created a yet-unresolved border dispute; furthermore, China has been a principal supplier of weapons technology, both conventional and nuclear, to Pakistan, India's South Asian bête noire. Moreover, China's perceived efforts to establish a network of ports and partnerships with countries in the littoral region—including in several nations that have traditionally been hostile to India—are viewed by some as part of a coherent strategy to encircle India and confine its influence to South Asia.[130]

The goal of this strategy would be to maximize access to resource inputs and economic growth in peacetime while making it politically difficult for hostile naval powers to sever seaborne energy supplies in times of crisis. To the west, China is financing and building a major deepwater port complex for Pakistan at Gwadar.[131] Some Indian media sources claim that the People's Liberation Army

Navy (PLAN) will have access to this facility, which will give it a strategic position in the Arabian Sea, close to the mouth of the Persian Gulf. A Singaporean journalist speculates that Gwadar will help China "to monitor American military movements from Diego Garcia."[132] To the east, Indian sources allege, the Chinese military has assisted Burma with the construction of several naval facilities on the Bay of Bengal—particularly at Kyaukpyu and Hainggyi Island.[133] As with Gwadar, it is presumed in the Indian press that these facilities are being upgraded to serve China's needs in a future military contingency. However uninformed by existing facts on the ground, such concerns reflect apprehension over the PLAN's ongoing expansion, which is viewed as a possible threat to India's strategic interests in the region.[134]

India's attitude toward the U.S. presence in the Indian Ocean in general, and the base at Diego Garcia in particular, has evolved significantly since the end of the Cold War. In the wake of the British withdrawal from "East of Suez" in 1968, India sought to make the Indian Ocean "a zone of peace from which great power rivalries and competition, as well as bases concerned in the context of such rivalries and competition either army, navy, or air force, are excluded."[135] Prime Minister Indira Gandhi made it clear that India was "opposed to the establishment of foreign military bases, and believed that the Indian Ocean should be an area of peace, free from any kind of military base."[136] In keeping with the pro-Soviet orientation of the "nonalignment" policy pursued by the Gandhi government, the joint British-U.S. facility at Diego Garcia was a particular target of left-leaning politicians from the Congress Party while similar Soviet facilities at Berbera in Somalia were largely ignored.[137] In the words of one Indian foreign minister, Diego Garcia "epitomized U.S. imperialistic tendencies and neo-colonial policies."[138]

Indian hostility to Diego Garcia stemmed in part from the assumption that the establishment of a U.S. naval facility indicated that American naval power would be a permanent fixture of the region. Again, successive Congress governments, which dominated Indian politics throughout the Cold War period, characterized American naval power as a significant threat to regional peace while largely ignoring the Soviet navy's deployment to the region.[139]

The collapse of the Soviet Union in 1991 and the subsequent reorientation of India's economic and foreign policies created the opportunity for significant improvements in Indo-American relations. A recognition of common interests and concerns in areas ranging from securing the free flow of commerce to halting the spread of radical Islam have led to enhanced economic and security ties between the two nations. This improved relationship culminated in the George W. Bush administration's declared policy to "help India become a major world power in the 21st century."[140]

Indian attitudes toward American naval power in the Indian Ocean have adjusted accordingly. Indian strategists recognize that the United States will remain the world's preeminent economic and military power for at least the next several decades. As such, American power will likely be committed to defending the status quo in the international system—thereby also defending the stability India requires to sustain its own economic development. In the context of the Indian Ocean, U.S. military presence is now seen as a stabilizing factor in an otherwise fragile region.

In addition, there appears to be a recognition and acceptance by the Indian government that Diego Garcia is an important and permanent hub for U.S. power projection in the Indian Ocean littoral. As evidence that India has lost its aversion to the "neocolonial" Anglo-American facility, in 2001 and again in 2004 the Indian navy participated in combined exercises with the United States at Diego Garcia. Furthermore, there have been suggestions that the Indian government has encouraged Mauritius to reach a final settlement on the sovereignty of the Chagos Archipelago that would allow for the continued presence of the British/American facility at Diego Garcia.[141]

The absence of criticism of Diego Garcia and U.S. military presence in the region has been notable at a time when military operations against violent extremism have brought a significant increase in U.S. forces in Central Asia and the Horn of Africa region as well as a significant use of the air and naval facilities at Diego Garcia. For example, in June 2007 the nuclear-powered aircraft carrier USS *Nimitz* (CVN 68) made a port call at Chennai. In accordance with American policy, *Nimitz* refused to confirm or deny that it carried nuclear weapons. While the transit of nuclear weapons through the Indian Ocean by external powers had been a major issue for New Delhi in the past, the *Nimitz* visit was notable for the lack of objection by the left-leaning government, by this time the Congress Party–led United Progressive Alliance coalition. When a small group of Indian intellectuals released a letter decrying the "reversal of past policy opposing the transit of nuclear weapons in its neighbourhood and the U.S. base at Diego Garcia, and its demands for a 'zone of peace' in the Indian Ocean," they were dismissed by the *Times of India* as "purveyors of selective indignation" who were motivated by pious anti-Americanism rather than logic.[142] This is a marked change from the Indian rhetoric of the 1960s, 1970s, and 1980s.

Although India ultimately seeks strategic autonomy in its foreign affairs, New Delhi has looked favorably, in light of these latter developments, on its strategic ties with Washington as a means to reinforce its position in the Indian Ocean. Given the U.S. ability to base substantial air assets at Diego Garcia and to deploy naval forces from the Gulf and the Pacific to the Indian Ocean, there is recognition that American presence in the littoral can complement India's quest for a peaceful and stable regional order.

Diego Garcia and Chinese Interests in the Indian Ocean

Where Indian observers increasingly see a Chinese "string of pearls" encircling India, Chinese observers see a rapidly developing Indian navy gradually complementing the overwhelming U.S. naval power in the Indian Ocean to challenge the security of China's seaborne trade there. Since the Cold War's end, U.S. forces in Diego Garcia have been seen by Chinese analysts as part of a larger strategy of maintaining American control of East Asia at China's expense.[143] An article in *PLA Daily*, the newspaper of the General Political Department of the People's Liberation Army, states that Diego Garcia is viewed as anchoring an inner network of bases, or "First Island Chain," that constrains Chinese military power projection:

> The Asia-Pacific region has always been one of the focal points of U.S. contention for world hegemony. For the purpose of structuring a strategic "containment" posture vis-à-vis the Asia-Pacific countries, the U.S. military has from beginning to end built a three-layer chain of bases west from Japan, South Korea and Southeast Asian countries and east to the western coast of the continental United States. The first layer of chains consists of bases extending from Japan and South Korea all the way to the Indian Ocean island of Diego Garcia. They are an "island chain" type of "forward bases" that control very important navigation channels, straits and sea areas. The second stretch consists of various islands with the island of Guam as the center plus the bases in Australia and New Zealand. They serve as the backing for the first stretch as well as major intermediary bases for sea and air transportation. The third stretch is composed of bases on the archipelagoes around Hawaii and on the Midway Island, Alaska and the Aleutian Islands. These bases are the main command center of the Pacific theater and serve as relay stations for the support coming from the western coast of the continental United States for the forward bases.[144]

Nearly identical wording is used by several other sources.[145] These include Academy of Military Sciences research fellow Wang Weixing, in an interview with a reporter from the Chinese Communist Party's (CCP) primary daily newspaper for intellectuals and professionals, who adds that "since World War II, [Washington] has gradually built up a system of global military bases, backed up by the bases on the American mainland, in order to pursue its global strategy."[146] Chinese analysts thus view the "island chains" alternatively as benchmarks of progress in maritime force projection and as fortified barriers that China must continue to penetrate to achieve freedom of maneuver in the maritime realm.[147] As PLAN senior captain Xu Qi emphasizes, China's "passage in and out of the [open] ocean is obstructed by two island chains. [China's] maritime geostrategic posture is [thus] in a semi-enclosed condition."[148] The authors of the PLA's first

English-language volume on strategy likewise believe that "despite its 18,000 kilometer coastline, China is currently constrained by the world's longest island chain, centering on the strategically-, politically-, and economically-vital territory of Taiwan."[149] However, because neither the PLAN nor any other organization of the People's Republic of China government has publicly made the island chains integral parts of official policy or defined their precise scope, references to them must be interpreted with caution.

A 2006 article in the official PLAN journal *People's Navy* credited Diego Garcia with the following capabilities:

> Diego Garcia Naval Base . . . has a usable area of 44 square kilometers, and a runway over 3,600 meters long that can accommodate heavy long-range bombers such as the B-52, B-1, and B-2. The 370,000 square meter aircraft parking area can hold over 100 military aircraft. The base's harbor has a wharf and two deep water channels. It can berth large aircraft carrier(s), nuclear submarines, and a fleet with prepositioned goods and materials. This base's combined installations are perfect, its strategic position is important. It has already become America's most important sea and air operations and logistics supply base in the Pacific region. It is called "the unsinkable aircraft carrier in the Indian Ocean."[150]

A *Liberation Army Daily* article lists Diego Garcia as "[one of, with Japan and South Korea] the U.S. military's frontline bases in the Asia Pacific region," one that controls "major sea and air navigation channels in the middle of the Indian Ocean."[151] The U.S. Air Force's plan to construct "four overseas relay stations for U.S. strategic bombers" (战略轰炸机的海外继中站) on Guam and Diego Garcia was formally announced on 27 November 2001;[152] it is viewed as part of a larger plan of "quietly stepping up its deployment of modern weapons in forward positions in the Asia-Pacific region."[153] A U.S. Air Force major general is quoted as saying that "[Guam's] Andersen [Air Force Base] is one of the two such important bases built by the United States in the Asia-Pacific region. The other important base is at Diego Garcia in the Indian Ocean."[154] Another *Liberation Army Daily* article concludes that "Diego Garcia not only controls the sea routes, straits, and sea areas in the western Pacific but can also launch attacks both to east and west in support of U.S. combat operations in the Asia-Pacific and Middle East regions. U.S. impatience to build up forward long-range bomber bases at [Diego Garcia and Guam] is bound to bring a real threat to peace and security in the Asian region, and cannot but arouse a high degree of vigilance in the countries concerned."[155] A subsequent Xinhua News Agency article reports that forward bomber basing gives the U.S. Air Force "a capability of striking anywhere in the region within 12 hours."[156] A group of Taiwanese scholars assess that improved access to naval facilities in Singapore will enhance the value of Diego Garcia as a key anchor of America's naval presence in the India Ocean.[157]

Diego Garcia's long-term use as a satellite tracking station is emphasized by Chinese analysts. One lengthy official news analysis notes Diego Garcia's role as one of five "photoelectric observation stations" that support the U.S. Air Force Air Surveillance and Tracking System/Ground-Based Electro-Optical Deep Space Surveillance (GEODSS) to "[monitor] high-orbit satellites." GEODSS, in turn, is part of a "strategic early warning system" to help make the United States "the sole space-dominating power."[158] Chinese news reports have credited Diego Garcia with a role in monitoring Chinese military and civilian space activities.[159] According to a daily paper sponsored by the CCP Central Committee's China Youth League, "U.S. radar tracking and control stations and electronic listening posts will collect all electromagnetic or communication signals related to the launch of *Shenzhou VI* and other Chinese space vehicles.[160]

Chinese Analysis of Diego Garcia's Operational Uses

Chinese articles have repeatedly reported on the use of Diego Garcia to support the Clinton administration's pressure and air strikes on Iraq in December 1998. The official Xinhua News Agency, *People's Daily* (the daily newspaper of the CCP Central Committee), and Central People's Radio Network, for instance, have all noted that, following its expansion, Diego Garcia is capable of accepting long-range bombers, such as B-52s, from Barksdale Air Force Base, Louisiana, as well as B-2s.[161] As one article noted, "The island is within striking range of Iraq, but beyond the reach of Iraqi missiles including Soviet-made Scuds."[162]

Chinese sources likewise observed Diego Garcia's role as a bomber base in Operation Enduring Freedom in Afghanistan (fall 2001).[163] *Naval and Merchant Ships*, a journal of the Chinese Society of Naval Architecture and Marine Engineering, has published a detailed analysis stating that shipping "air-launched precision-guided weapons" such as "cruise missiles and laser-guided bombs" to such "front line" bases as Diego Garcia was a cost-effective strategy for the U.S. military.[164]

Diego Garcia has also attracted significant Chinese attention as a support base for Iraqi Freedom. As early as 2002 a *PLA Daily* reporter anticipated that B-52 and B-1 bombers might be moved from the island to the Middle East, possibly al-Udeid Air Base in Qatar, to support an invasion of Iraq.[165] A *People's Daily* article later that year quoted an Associated Press reporter who anticipated that tanks and other equipment would be transported covertly by ship for Diego Garcia for that purpose.[166] As they had done before previous wars in Iraq and Afghanistan, Chinese observers noted a buildup of military aircraft on Diego Garcia, such as B-2 and B-52 bombers capable of dropping "satellite and laser guided 'smart' bombs."[167] China's official English-language daily asserted that this process began "in October 2002, one month earlier when the Security Council endorsed the Resolution 1441 on disarmament in Iraq."[168] An Army brigade's equipment had been airlifted from Diego Garcia to the Gulf, Academy of Military Sciences researchers documented, while a Marine brigade's prepositioned equipment awaited transport.[169] Similarly, it is speculated that Diego Garcia could support a future U.S. attack on Iran.[170]

In keeping with general Chinese fears of "strategic encirclement" by U.S. force deployments as part of the "Long War" against global terror, there is concern, according to a graduate student at China's National Defense University, that improvements in American-Indian relations offer "conveniences for the U.S.'s military presence in South Asia and the Indian Ocean. Additionally, the U.S. Army further plans to shift a portion of the pre-positioned equipment deployed in Europe to the Diego Garcia base in the Indian Ocean."[171] This is part of a larger assessment, expressed in a magazine published by Xinhua, that "the military bases in Guam can interact with the Diego Garcia Base in the Indian Ocean to make reactions against Central Asia, the Middle East, and Africa."[172] The island has also been called a "northward strategic attack line."[173] A party-sponsored newspaper raised the related concern that a North Korean vessel, *Sosan*, was escorted toward Diego Garcia in December 2002 until the White House determined that there was no legal method of preventing the missiles it was carrying from continuing to Yemen.[174] However, a report in a Hong Kong journal said to have PLA connections, noting points of friction and unmet expectations in U.S.-Indian relations, goes so far as to suggest that strategic considerations impel India not only to assert increasing influence over the Indian Ocean but also to develop capabilities to counter U.S. forces at Diego Garcia as part of a strategic rivalry:

> Dominating the Strait of Malacca is the key part of India's maritime strategy. . . . India set up a base in Blair Port, the Andaman Islands, in 1967 and the Andaman Fortress Headquarters in 1984. In 2001, the Indian Ministry of National Defense expanded this headquarters to the strategic defense headquarters. Once a war breaks out in the future, India will be able to deploy its naval troops in the eastern and western parts of the mainland to echo with the army in the metropolitan territories and to gain the assistance of the air force. In this way, India will be able to form an overall powerful army–navy–air force defense force and to launch corner offenses against the U.S. Diego Garcia Base in the Indian Ocean. . . . After the September 11 Incident, India established a strategic defense headquarters in the Andaman Islands. This headquarters may echo with the other two large naval forces garrisoned in the western coastal areas and rely on the mainland's nuclear attack capabilities to launch corner offenses against the U.S. Diego Garcia base in the south. The U.S. military will surely be worried about this.[175]

More recently there has been substantial concern that Diego Garcia can help Japan to project maritime power and influence, through its alliance with the United States. A Hong Kong newspaper thought to have PLA connections notes that on 21 September 2001 "an Aegis destroyer and a supply ship under Japan's Defense Agency, accompanied by USS *Kitty Hawk,* departed Yokosuka, Japan for the Indian Ocean. The [Self-Defense Force] vessels will ply between Japan and the American base in Diego Garcia in the Indian Ocean to provide supplies to U.S. armed forces and undertake the mission of escorting U.S. aircraft carriers. This was the first time that Japan sent its escort vessels overseas under the pretext of gathering information."[176] China's military press claims that Japan Maritime Self-Defense Force general staff headquarters officers pointed out in a 10 April 2002 meeting with, and subsequent letter to, Robert C. Chaplin, commander, U.S. Forces Japan, that "the Japanese P-3C warning plane has a rather high capability for search and rescue and conducting maritime monitoring. It is hoped that Japan can send this aircraft to increase its support, and the U.S. military would speak highly of the aircraft if the aircraft were to conduct activities in the vicinity of the Diego Garcia Island."[177] (The Chinese claim was dismissed by General Nakatani, director general of the Japan Defense Agency, on 7 May.[178]) Whatever the validity of these claims, Japanese scholars too recognize Diego Garcia's strategic significance. An Osaka University professor writes in a journal on Chinese and East Asian affairs published by the Kazankai Foundation, Japan's oldest organization of China watchers, that the island is "one of [the] strategic deployment positions supporting the U.S. forces' worldwide crisis response capability."[179]

Finally, it must be emphasized that despite an almost visceral distaste for elements of America's global military posture in general, current Chinese analyses of Diego Garcia's significance for Beijing's interests are not nearly as alarmist as those concerning American bases in Guam, Japan, or even South Korea, which are perceived as more directly related (or at least applicable) to military scenarios directed against China and its territorial and maritime claims. This disparity probably stems in part from a present lack of Chinese capability to project power into the Indian Ocean but also from a belief that any U.S. overextension in the "Long War" against global terror would likely be beneficial to China's security. As one Xinhua report concludes,

> Regarding the strategic readjustment of U.S. forces abroad, some U.S. military experts believe it is necessary to readjust military deployments around the globe and cover the globe with rapid-response units to launch a "preemptive first strike" against terrorist organizations that are difficult to track and whose members are scattered as well as those countries the United States believes will pose a potential threat in the future. But there are also some military personnel and defense experts who believe such readjustment carries a certain degree of strategic risk; it spreads out the U.S. forces in various parts of the world and is not favorable for fighting a large scale war against a major power.[180]

China and the Indian Ocean

China's current naval platforms and weaponry still suggest an "access denial" strategy focused on deterring Taiwan from declaring independence and on consolidating its other contested island and maritime claims in the three "near seas" (Yellow, East China, and South China). Beyond these areas and their immediate approaches, the PLAN may not seek to project naval influence substantially into the western Pacific; it may instead look south and west along the strategic sea-lanes through Southeast Asia and past the subcontinent. Persistent fears of oil-supply interdiction together with China's growing interests in maritime resources and commerce may gradually drive more long-ranging naval development.

Already, low-intensity operations driven by overseas commercial and human-security interests are giving China a modest presence in the Indian Ocean. These include the deployment of a frigate and military transport aircraft to safeguard the evacuation of Chinese citizens from Libya in February 2011; sixteen (and counting) anti-piracy task forces to deter pirates in the Gulf of Aden since December 2008; and the dispatch of a hospital ship to treat over 15,500 in Indian Ocean and African nations in the summer of 2010, individuals in the Caribbean in autumn 2011, patients in seven Indian Ocean region countries and on Chinese and foreign naval vessels conducting anti-piracy operations in the Gulf of Aden in summer 2013, and Typhoon Haiyan victims in Tacloban, Philippines in November 2013. However, it should be noted that capabilities will not match Chinese intentions any time soon; Chinese naval ambitions in the Indian Ocean region will run afoul of those of India, another rising great power operating far closer to home; and whatever its leanings in the abstract, Beijing must tend to matters in East Asia before it can apply its energies to building up naval forces able to vie for supremacy in the Indian Ocean region.[181]

Diego Garcia and American Interests in the Indian Ocean

American interests in the Indian Ocean littoral are driven by a mixture of economics and security. Among the most significant concerns are the need to secure SLOCs, the desire to prevent a hostile power from dominating the littoral, and the challenge to existing governments in the region posed by the spread of radical extremist militant Islamist groups. Underpinning all of this is recognition that the Indian Ocean littoral is a fragile part of the world, characterized by Barnett's "Non-Integrating Gap."[182] The potential for interstate conflict remains high as many states in the area have unresolved maritime or territorial disputes. In addition to conventional security challenges, the littoral region is plagued by a host of irregular security threats, such as terrorism, insurgency, and trafficking in arms and drugs.

As the world's largest economy, the United States has a strong interest in the security of the ships that transit the Indian Ocean to bring goods and energy to market. The energy resources of the Persian Gulf are accessible only via the

Indian Ocean's SLOCs. Not only does 22 percent of America's imported oil reach the market in this way, but more than fifty strategic minerals come from or transit through the littoral region. Because the market for hydrocarbons is global, a supply disruption affects world prices for oil and gas. The requirements of trade and energy make the continued free passage of shipping through the Indian Ocean SLOCs of supreme importance for the United States.

Deriving from protection of the freedom of navigation in the Indian Ocean is America's second major interest in the region—preventing the littoral from being dominated by a power hostile to the United States. China has been quite active in securing energy supplies and increasing its strategic political influence across the region from Southeast Asia to the coast of East Africa. As discussed previously, there is even speculation that some informal set of access rights may ultimately increase the PLAN's ability to project power into the littoral while economic ties provide influence over local governments. In the western portion of the region, as explained earlier, Iran has achieved the ability to threaten navigation through the Strait of Hormuz, the world's most important choke point. Should either or both of these nations achieve a dominant role in the littoral, there is a strong potential that American interests would be harmed.

Finally, American interests in the region are driven by the fact that the Indian Ocean littoral encompasses a large portion of the "arc of instability" that stretches from Southeast Asia through Central Asia to the Middle East and East Africa. This zone not only has a high potential for producing failed states but is also home to much of the world's Muslim population. The Indian Ocean is located at an intersection of two main reservoirs of Islamic extremism. Prior to 11 September 2001, the United States was the victim of al-Qaeda–backed terrorist attacks in Kenya, Tanzania, and Yemen. Today, the United States and its allies are conducing military operations against Muslim extremists in the East African, Central Asian, and Southeast Asian subregions that abut the Indian Ocean.

Diego Garcia's Strategic Future

The security situation in the Indian Ocean region, long characterized by uncertain relations between its major power brokers, is prone to strategic miscalculation. More than ever before, the interests of the United States, India, and China coincide and collide in the Indian Ocean littoral. These key states, one predominant and the others ascendant, may find themselves at odds as they protect national interests in a region with great potential and numerous challenges, including:

- Volatile and fragile states, which are often beset by, and sometimes facilitate, irregular threats, irredentist powers, sectarian divides, and religious tensions
- A rich flow of resources through constrained and vulnerable shipping lanes

- Often skittish host nations
- Restive and newly hopeful populations seeking more responsive governance as well as improved economic and social conditions
- Newly capable actors possibly seeking to undermine others' influence by sustained projection of power

It has been widely argued that the world is undergoing a significant geopolitical realignment, and that the global "center of gravity" is shifting from the Euro-Atlantic to the greater Asia-Pacific region.[183] The National Intelligence Council envisions "fast developing powers, notably India and China," joining the United States "atop a multipolar international system."[184] As India and China continue to accrete military might, they pull the center of gravity toward the Indian Ocean. To maintain its preponderant position in so dynamic an international environment, the United States will have to shift its geostrategic focus from the Euro-Atlantic (which, after decades of American attention, is prosperous, secure, and self-sustaining) to regions of the world that were once dismissed as peripheral to American interests. One such area is the Indian Ocean, the littoral of which is emerging as a key strategic region in the "Asia-Pacific Century." All this particularly affects the maritime dimension, where the U.S. Navy guarantees the free flow of goods at sea worldwide.

Sustained American preeminence in the greater Indian Ocean region will be increasingly difficult to realize without an appreciation for the need to invest in a versatile and enduring basing structure. With a flexible constellation of bases and other facilities in place, American strategists must shield these bases and the larger region from any interference, whether physical or political, by state and substate actors. In doing so, the United States must avoid an insular approach, instead crafting a coherent Indian Ocean policy that accounts for the reactions of India and China as well as the interests of its regional partners. Such an approach will strengthen U.S. command of the commons in partnership with India and may open ways to engage with China in the Indian Ocean. The Department of Defense would do well to reprise the approach taken in the late 1990s by its Office of International Security Affairs, which issued a series of unclassified regional policy documents.[185] A direct evaluation of Indian Ocean policy, which could assist in forming a holistic view of the Indian Ocean littoral and the unique aspects of Indian Ocean security rather than a narrow one of the separate PACOM, CENTCOM, and AFRICOM theaters, is long overdue.

A comprehensive regional strategy would encourage more rapid and extensive infrastructure development in concert with partners in the region. The United States must augment its regional knowledge, enhance coordination, and, for the first time, consider the Indian Ocean as a whole, as a vital strategic space, with a networked basing arrangement at its core.

Notes

This is a significantly revised version of an earlier article that appeared as Andrew S. Erickson, Walter C. Ladwig III, and Justin Mikolay, "Diego Garcia and the United States' Emerging Indian Ocean Strategy," *Asian Security* 6, no. 3 (Autumn 2010): 214–37. The authors acknowledge with appreciation the constructive comments of Kent Calder; Alexander Cooley; Thomas Culora; Timothy Hoyt; Matthew Jenkinson; Cdr. James Kraska, USN; William Murray; Michael O'Hanlon; Andrew Winner; and Toshi Yoshihara, as well as two anonymous reviewers. Opinions and conclusions are solely those of the authors and in no way reflect the policies or estimates of the U.S. military or any other organization of the U.S. government.

1. The number of land-based U.S. forces in the Middle East and South Asia is expected to shrink over time, even as counterinsurgency activities there remain a long-term priority. U.S. Defense Department, *Quadrennial Defense Review* (Washington, D.C.: February 2010).
2. Alexander Cooley and Daniel Nexon, "Globalization and the Politics of U.S. Overseas Basing," paper presented at International Studies Association conference, San Francisco, 26–29 March 2008.
3. "BP Statistical Review of World Energy," *BP Global*, June 2009, 6, http://www.bp.com/liveassets/bp_internet/globalbp/globalbp_uk_english/reports_and_publications/statistical_energy_review_2008/STAGING/local_assets/2009_downloads/statistical_review_of_world_energy_full_report_2009.pdf.
4. Mihir Roy, *Maritime Security in South West Asia* (Tokyo: Institute for International Policy Studies, 2002), available at www.iips.org/; and "Indian Ocean," in *CIA World Factbook* (Washington, D.C.: Central Intelligence Agency, 2007), available at www.cia.gov/.
5. "Persian Gulf Oil and Gas Exports Fact Sheet," *Energy Information Administration Country Analysis Brief, June 2007*, http://www.marcon.com/print_index.cfm?SectionListsID=20&PageID=773.
6. Robert Kaplan, "Center Stage for the 21st Century: Power Plays in the Indian Ocean," *Foreign Affairs* 88, no. 2 (March–April 2009): 19.
7. Sureesh Mehta, "Shaping India's Maritime Strategy: Opportunities and Challenges," speech presented at Indian National Defense College, November 2005; and Anand Mathur, "Growing Importance of the Indian Ocean in Post–Cold War Era and Its Implication for India," *Strategic Analysis* 26, no. 4 (October–December 2002): 556.
8. C. Uday Bhaskar, "Regional Naval Cooperation," *Strategic Analysis* 15, no. 8 (November 1992): 736.
9. Kaplan, "Center Stage for the 21st Century," 20.
10. Ministry of Defense, *Indian Maritime Doctrine* (New Delhi: Integrated Headquarters [Navy], 2009), 57.
11. United Nations, *Review of Maritime Transport 2008* (New York: United Nations Conference on Trade and Development, 2008), 23.
12. Halford J. Mackinder, "The Geographical Pivot of History," *Geographical Journal* 23, no. 4 (April 1904): 421–37.

13. For an affirmation of the relevance of Mackinder's ideas, see Colin S. Gray, "In Defence of the Heartland: Sir Halford Mackinder and His Critics a Hundred Years On," *Comparative Strategy* 23, no. 1 (2004): 9–25. For a Cold War–era appraisal that the Indian Ocean is the new "heartland of the world," see Rocco M. Paone, "The Soviet Threat in the Indian Ocean," *Military Review* 50, no. 12 (December 1970): 49.

14. Kaplan, "Center Stage for the 21st Century," 16.

15. *Indian Maritime Doctrine* (2009), 58.

16. Thomas Barnett, *The Pentagon's New Map* (New York: Putnam, 2004), 4.

17. "The Failed States Index 2010," *Foreign Policy* (June 2010), http://www.foreignpolicy.com/failedstates2010.

18. James R. Holmes, Andrew C. Winner, and Toshi Yoshihara, *Indian Naval Strategy in the Twenty-First Century* (Oxford: Routledge, 2009), 120.

19. Kaplan, "Center Stage for the 21st Century," 23.

20. Mihir Roy, "India's Place in the Ocean of Destiny," *Indian Express*, 9 June 1996.

21. Christopher Layne, *The Peace of Illusions: American Grand Strategy from 1940 to the Present* (Ithaca, N.Y.: Cornell University Press, 2006), 27, 45.

22. White House, *The National Security Strategy of the United States* (Washington, D.C.: The White House, March 2006), http://georgewbush-whitehouse.archives.gov/nsc/nss/2006/.

23. J. T. Conway, G. Roughead, and T. W. Allen, "A Cooperative Strategy for 21st Century Seapower," October 2007, http://www.navy.mil/maritime/MaritimeStrategy.pdf; repr. *Naval War College Review* 61, no. 1 (Winter 2008): 7–19.

24. Ashley Tellis, "American and Indian Interests in India's Extended Neighborhood," *India in Transition*, 25 June 2007, http://casi.sas.upenn.edu/iit/atellis.

25. "Iran Tests Anti-Ship Ballistic Missile," *Jane's Defence Weekly 2012*, 19 July 2012, www.janes.com; and Secretary of Defense Leon E. Panetta, "Joint Press Conference with Secretary Panetta and Secretary of State Hammond from the Pentagon," 18 July 2012, *Department of Defense*, www.defense.gov/transcripts/transcript.aspx?transcriptid=5079.

26. "Risky Business," *Economist*, 10 June 2006, 49–50; and Caitlin Talmadge, "Closing Time: Assessing the Iranian Threat to the Strait of Hormuz," *International Security* 33, no. 1 (Summer 2008): 82–117.

27. Ronald L. Burgess Jr., "Annual Threat Assessment," statement before the Senate Armed Services Committee, United States Senate, 16 February 2012, www.dia.mil/public-affairs/testimonies/2012-02-16.html.

28. Sudha Ramachandran, "China Moves into India's Back Yard," *Asia Times*, 13 March 2007.

29. G. S. Khurana, "Maritime Security in the Indian Ocean," *Strategic Analysis* 28, no. 3 (2004): 414.

30. Holmes, Winner, and Yoshihara, *Indian Naval Strategy*, 108.

31. Conway, Roughead, and Allen, "Cooperative Strategy for 21st Century Seapower."

32. Kent E. Calder, *Embattled Garrisons: Comparative Base Politics and American Globalism* (Princeton, N.J.: Princeton University Press, 2007), 11.

33. Frederica M. Bunge, ed., *Indian Ocean, Five Island Countries*, 2nd ed. (Washington, D.C.: GPO, 1983), xix–xxii; and Rasul B. Rais, *The Indian Ocean and the Superpowers: Economic, Political and Strategic Perspectives* (London: Croom Helm, 1986), 13–18.

34. Rais, *Indian Ocean and the Superpowers*, 14.

35. This strategy was devised by Adm. Alfonso d'Albuquerque as a means of using sea power to secure Portugal's mercantilist goals in the region. Bunge, *Indian Ocean, Five Island Countries*, 252.

36. The value of these items at the time corresponds with the contemporary value of oil. Ibid.

37. K. S. Jawatkar, *Diego Garcia in International Diplomacy* (London: Sangam Books, 1983), 3.

38. Vytautas B. Bandjunis, *Diego Garcia: Creation of the Indian Ocean Base* (San Jose, Calif.: Writer's Showcase, 2001), 4; Sergei DeSilva-Ranasinghe, Interview with Ray Mabus, *The Diplomat*, 4 December 2013, http://thediplomat .com/2013/12/ray-mabus/.

39. Robert Scott, *Limuria: The Lesser Dependencies of Mauritius* (Westport, Conn.: Greenwood, 1976), 20, 75.

40. R. Price and J. Richmond Smythe, Diego Garcia, to Rawson Hart Boddam, President and Council Bombay, 3 June 1786, Letters and Papers Relating to East India Company, FO 148/6, The National Archives, Kew, United Kingdom [hereafter TNA].

41. As one visitor in 1886 noted, "The labor on the estates is almost wholly supplied from Mauritius; very few of the laborers have been born on the island." Gilbert C. Bourne, "On the Island of Diego Garcia of the Chagos Group," *Proceedings of the Royal Geographical Society and Monthly Record of Geography* 8, no. 6 (June 1886): 387–88.

42. Ibid., 390.

43. Ibid., 385.

44. Bandjunis, *Diego Garcia*, 6.

45. Gary Sick, "The Evolution of U.S. Strategy towards the Indian Ocean and Persian Gulf Regions," in *The Great Game: Rivalry in the Persian Gulf and South Asia*, ed. Alvin Z. Rubinstein (New York: Praeger, 1983), 49–50.

46. Rais, *Indian Ocean and the Superpowers*, 37.

47. Paul Ryan, "Diego Garcia," U.S. Naval Institute *Proceedings* 110, no. 9 (September 1984): 133.

48. Rais, *Indian Ocean and the Superpowers*, 77; and Sick, "Evolution of U.S. Strategy," 53.

49. Bandjunis, *Diego Garcia*, 2–3; and "US Overseas Bases," memorandum, box 27, Records of the Office of the Secretary of Defense, OASD/ISA files 680.1, Record Group [hereafter RG] 330, National Archives and Records Administration, College Park, Md. [hereafter NARA].

50. Quoted in Rais, *Indian Ocean and the Superpowers*, 76.

51. Ryan notes that Burke's "firm advocacy made the acquisition of the atoll an article of Navy faith"; Ryan, "Diego Garcia," 133. On 9 January 1964, Nitze gave a speech warning of a "power vacuum" in the Indian Ocean and the need to acquire base rights in the region to support deployments; Bandjunis, *Diego Garcia*, 9.

52. Jawatkar, *Diego Garcia in International Diplomacy*, 31.

53. Foreign Secretary, Defence Secretary, and Commonwealth Secretary, "Defence Interests in the Indian Ocean," memorandum, 21 January 1965, FO 371/184522, TNA.

54. Sick, "Evolution of U.S. Strategy," 54. See also Komer (National Security Council) memorandum to President Kennedy, 19 June 1963, in *Foreign Relations of the United States* [hereafter *FRUS*], series 1961–1963 (Washington, D.C.: GPO, 1996), 19:614–15.

55. State to British Embassy (Washington, D.C.), note, 25 April 1963, DEF 15 UK-US, RG 59, NACP; and Ball (State) to Bruce (London), deptel 1272, 23 August 1963, DEF 21 US, RG 59, NACP.

56. Defence Planning Staff, "Brief on US/UK Discussions on United States Defence Interests in the Indian Ocean," 6 March 1964, p. 5, document marked "secret," CAB 21/5418, TNA. Early discussions explored the idea of creating additional shared facilities at Aldabra in the Seychelles and on the Australian-owned Cocos Islands to create a "strategic triangle" in the Indian Ocean. See Rusk to President Johnson, "Indian Ocean Island Facilities," 15 July 1964, in *FRUS*, series 1964–1968 (Washington, D.C.: GPO, 2000), 21:92.

57. House of Commons Debate, written answer to question, 10 November 1965, vol. 720, col. 2.

58. Joel Larus, "Diego Garcia: The Military and Legal Limitations of America's Pivotal Base in the Indian Ocean," in *The Indian Ocean: Perspectives on a Strategic Arena*, ed. William L. Dowdy and Russell B. Trood (Durham, N.C.: Duke University Press, 1985), 437–38.

59. U.S. State Department, "Agreement on the Availability of Certain Indian Ocean Islands for Defense Purposes, 30 December 1966," in *United States Treaties and Other International Agreements* (Washington, D.C.: GPO, 1967), 28.

60. Costs included payments to Mauritius and the Seychelles, the purchase of privately held land on Diego Garcia, and the resettlement of inhabitants. Rather than make a direct payment, the United States credited Britain with $14 million toward its share of the research and development costs of the Polaris missile program. David Bruce, U.S. Ambassador to Britain, to George Brown, Secretary of State for Foreign Affairs, 30 December 1966, letter marked "secret" appended to "Exchange of Notes and Agreed Minutes concerning Defence Co-operation in the British Indian Ocean Territory," FO 93/8/401, TNA.

61. D. F. Milton, memorandum to Woodham, "Diego Garcia: Further Research," 2 October 1975, FCO 40/696, TNA; and Bandjunis, *Diego Garcia*, 8.

62. Bruce (London) to Rusk (State), embtel 12335, 4 September 1968, DEF 15 IND-US, Central Files 1967–69, RG 59, NARA; and Secretary of State for the

Colonies, telegram to Governor, Mauritius, "U.S. Defence Interests in Indian Ocean," 6 March 1964, CAB 21/5418, TNA.

63. Bandjunis, *Diego Garcia*, 15.

64. Memorandum, "House of Lords Question by Baroness Lee: Oral Answer on 27 October 1975," 23 October 1975, FCO 40/696, TNA.

65. Milton memorandum, "Diego Garcia."

66. The majority of the workers were Mauritian citizens either by birth or by Mauritian nationality provisions. Bandjunis, *Diego Garcia*, 64–65.

67. This represented seven times the Mauritian per capita GDP ($780 in 1976) for each displaced worker. An initial payment of $1.4 million provided compensation to anyone living on Diego Garcia as of 1965, including those who had relocated prior to the closing of the plantations. A resettlement plan was developed for the evacuated copra workers, but the Mauritian government neglected to distribute the money until 1978. As a result, many of the former copra workers fell into poverty. Despite the fact that the 1972 resettlement agreement was acknowledged by Mauritius to represent "a full and final discharge of British obligations" to the former plantation workers, the UK gave Mauritius an additional $7.2 million ($4,600 per person) in 1982 as a "full and final settlement" for the workers relocated from Diego Garcia; ibid. Also Larus, "Diego Garcia," 442; and Bart McDowell, "Crosscurrents Sweep the Indian Ocean," *National Geographic* 160, no. 4 (October 1981): 440.

68. Bandjunis, *Diego Garcia*, 55; and U.S. State Department, "Naval Communications Facility on Diego Garcia, 24 October 1972," in *United States Treaties and Other International Agreements* (Washington, D.C.: GPO, 1972).

69. Wilson's decision was primarily motivated by the sterling crisis of November 1967, which badly damaged the British economy and indicated to some that Britain could no longer afford to be a world power. However, the nearly simultaneous collapse of the British presence in Aden was also a contributing factor in the decision to draw down British forces in the region. William Rodger Louis, "The British Withdrawal from the Gulf, 1967–71," *Journal of Imperial and Commonwealth History* 31, no. 1 (January 2003): 82–83.

70. See the discussion contained in "Proposal for a Joint US Military Facility on Diego Garcia," memorandum from the Joint Chiefs of Staff to the Secretary of Defense, 10 April 1968, Indian Ocean 323.3, OSD Files FRC 73 A 1250, RG 330, NARA.

71. Sick, "Evolution of U.S. Strategy," 56.

72. Bandjunis, *Diego Garcia*, 54.

73. Sick, "Evolution of U.S. Strategy," 65.

74. Larus, "Diego Garcia," 439. Under the 1976 agreement, facilities on Diego Garcia are intended to support "ships or aircraft owned or operated by or on behalf of either government." "Exchange of Notes Concerning a United States Navy Support Facility on Diego Garcia, British Indian Ocean Territory," 25 February 1976, FO 93/8/438, TNA.

75. McDowell, "Crosscurrents Sweep the Indian Ocean," 423.

76. Bandjunis, *Diego Garcia*, 70; and Rais, *Indian Ocean and the Superpowers*, 81.

77. Rais, *Indian Ocean and the Superpowers*, 86.

78. Rand's study of various basing alternatives is especially relevant in summarizing the competing concerns for overseas basing strategy, including "the costs and deployment timelines for various forward support location options under different degrees of stress on combat support while taking into account infrastructure richness, basing characteristics, deployment distances, strategic warning, transportation constraints, dynamic requirements, and reconstitution conditions." Its 2006 report concludes that Diego Garcia is one of the most important Tier 1 forward support locations. For a review of the report, see Mahyar A. Amouzegar, R. McGarvey, and R. Tripp, "Combat Support: Overseas Basing Options," *Air Force Journal of Logistics* 30, no. 1 (Spring 2006): 3–14.

79. Conway, Roughead, and Allen, "Cooperative Strategy for 21st Century Seapower," 10. Three new maritime priorities arise from the maritime strategy: reliable access to areas of concern, flexible forward-positioning of resources, and a broadened maritime mission, to include humanitarian response. In key ways, the Indian Ocean region drives each of these priorities. The strategy underscores this new reality: "In times of war, our ability to impose local sea control, overcome challenges to access, force entry, and project and sustain power ashore, makes our maritime forces an indispensable element of the joint or combined force. This expeditionary advantage must be maintained because it provides joint and combined force commanders with freedom of maneuver. Reinforced by a robust sealift capability that can concentrate and sustain forces, sea control and power projection enable extended campaigns ashore. . . . The Sea Services will establish a persistent global presence . . . [that] must extend beyond traditional deployment areas and reflect missions ranging from humanitarian operations to an increased emphasis on counter-terrorism and irregular warfare. Our maritime forces will be tailored to meet the unique and evolving requirements particular to each geographic region, often in conjunction with special operations forces and other interagency partners. In particular, this strategy recognizes the rising importance and need for increased peacetime activities in Africa and the Western Hemisphere."

80. U.S. official, personal interview, September 2012.

81. The AOR seams in the Indian Ocean present both planning and operational challenges. See J. Stephen Morrison, *Exploring the U.S. Africa Command and a New Strategic Relationship with Africa*, testimony before the Senate Foreign Relations Subcommittee on Africa, 110th Cong., 1st sess., 1 August 2007. He states, "Unity of effort . . . transcends the present artificial geographic 'seams' that separate Africa into a U.S. EUCOM zone separate from the Horn of Africa that is the responsibility of the U.S. Central Command. [The U.S. Pacific Command is responsible for Africa's Indian Ocean island nations.] It requires stronger leadership, coherence and integration of programs, and more effective management. And it requires confidence that the resources and commitments

needed over the long-term will be there, and that Congress and the American people will be supportive. These are the accumulating concerns that AFRICOM is intended to address."

82. The authors base their selection of the four main military missions described here on a distillation of various sources, the most important of which are personal interviews conducted with various midlevel naval officials between September 2007 and February 2008. The authors gained general insight into planning and operations from Vice Adm. Jeffrey Fowler, USN, superintendent, U.S. Naval Academy, personal interview, September 2007. The authors are also in indebted to various U.S. Navy officers from Submarine Development Squadron 12, Groton, Connecticut, for their insights into CENTCOM operations. For an updated general overview on Diego Garcia's military capabilities, see "Territories, British Indian Ocean Territory," *Jane's Sentinel Security Assessment—South Asia*, 10 October 2012, sentinel.janes.com/. For another general description of the military assets on the island, see "Diego Garcia: Camp Justice," GlobalSecurity.org, http://www.globalsecurity.org/military/facility/diego-garcia.htm.

83. For a review of prepositioning capabilities and a comprehensive look at the rival sea-basing concept of operations, see Massimo Annati, "Naval Assets for Long-Term Deployment," *Military Technology* 31, no. 4 (2007): 84–90.

84. A small portion of the inhabitants of Diego Garcia are the civilian operators of these sealift vessels. The command structure of the sealift ships keeps manning requirements low. For a comparison of the command structures of U.S. Navy warships and MSC ships, see John K. Hafner, "Separate but Equal," U.S. Naval Institute *Proceedings* 134, no. 1 (January 2008): 32–35.

85. See Gary Roughead, Chief of Naval Operations, *Statement on the Cooperative Strategy for 21st Century Seapower*, House Armed Services Committee, 110th Cong., 1st sess., 13 December 2007, 7–9. Admiral Roughead establishes humanitarian assistance and disaster response, collectively, as one of the six primary maritime missions: "Human suffering moves us to act, and the expeditionary character of maritime forces uniquely positions them to provide assistance." In addition, the Congressional Budget Office has considered speeds of deployment to various hot spots in Europe, the Middle East, and Africa, concluding in most African cases that deployment was significantly faster from Diego Garcia; Congressional Budget Office, *Options for Changing the Army's Overseas Basing* (Washington, D.C.: CBO, May 2004), http://www.cbo.gov/sites/default/files/cbofiles/ftpdocs/54xx/doc5415/05-03-armyobasing.pdf, 69. The report concludes: "Furthermore, the time required to deploy heavy units by sea to many potential trouble spots is not significantly shorter from Eastern Europe than it is from Germany. Moreover, for many ports in Africa, it takes much longer to deploy a heavy brigade combat team from Eastern Europe than to deliver the prepositioned set of equipment that is maintained on board ships at Diego Garcia in the Indian Ocean." MSC ships can also rapidly deploy to the site of a humanitarian disaster; see Robert C. Morrow and Mark D. Llewellyn, "Tsunami Overview," *Military Medicine* 171 (October 2006 supplement): 5–7.

86. Plans for a recreation center were included in FY10 budgets under Project 182. The 10,400-square-foot center was envisioned to allow personnel to use computers, call home, and relax away from the ship—all important luxuries for sailors on long deployments in cramped work environments.

87. Ravi I. Chaudhary, "Transforming American Airlift: Effects-Based Mobility, the C-17, and Global Maneuver," *Air & Space Power Journal* 21, no. 1 (Spring 2007): 94.

88. In the early stages of Operation Enduring Freedom in Afghanistan, for example, U.S. Air Force commanders had very few access points close to Taliban targets. As a result, tactical fighters experienced significant difficulty with the long-range flights: "Even in the early days of the war, shorter-range USAF aircraft, such as the AC-130 gunships and F-15E fighters, participated, though they flew a limited number of missions. These aircraft, launched from bases in the Gulf region, could not operate as efficiently as long-range bombers and large support aircraft. . . . The alternative would be to operate tactical aircraft out of distant bases, an activity that requires extensive aerial tanker support. . . . Diego Garcia is secure and particularly useful for attack operations by B-1B and B-52 heavy bombers. However, the British-owned Indian Ocean atoll lies 2,500 miles from Afghanistan. Whiles this poses no problem for bombers, tactical fighters would face prohibitive distances." See Adam J. Hebert, "The Search for Asian Bases," *Air Force Magazine*, January 2002, 52.

89. For a discussion of the relative strength of bombers vis-à-vis fighters in this type of conflict, see Rebecca Grant, "An Air War Like No Other," *Air Force Magazine*, November 2002, 33.

90. Hebert, "Search for Asian Bases," 52.

91. Shore-basing fighters in various CENTCOM areas is discussed in Scott A. Cooper, "We Need Shore-Based Aircraft in Iraq," *U.S. Naval Institute Proceedings* 133, no. 9 (September 2007): 70–71.

92. "Coalition aircraft at Diego Garcia dropped more ordnance on Taliban and Al Qaeda forces in Afghanistan than any other unit during the war on terror." See "Diego Garcia," GlobalSecurity.org, http://www.globalsecurity.org/military/facility/diego-garcia.htm.

93. Controlled pure water is used in nuclear propulsion plants for circulation in chemically sensitive boilers and in the core of the pressurized water reactor itself. Accordingly, the Navy maintains graded water standards and tests for both chemical and mechanical impurities in the water. Such treatment and testing facilities are expensive to maintain and are not ordinarily required for deployed ships that generate and test suitable water while at sea from reverse-osmosis units.

94. The current structural and utility status of the island is discussed in the Navy-funded construction program "Project 182: Wharf Upgrades and Recreation Facility," FY 2010 Military Construction Program Report, DD Form 1391 (13 May 2006), 5. The report describes the aging electrical infrastructure: "The electrical utility system provides electrical service to the western half of the island where most of the U.S. forces are accommodated. The electrical system

consists of two main power plants, North (NPP) and South (SPP), two 13.8 kV
switching stations and a 13.8 kV distribution system, which consists of overhead
lines and underground cables. The existing switchgear in the switching stations
and power plants are old and obsolete. The normal electrical capacity provided
by the two power plants is 15,000 kW. With the addition of the SSGN to the
island, the electrical load for the island is estimated to be 24,800 kW."

95. Historical electrical use for a full air wing and naval contingent averages
approximately 12,800 amp-hours. This ordinarily leaves 4,800 amp-hours
available for the waterfront complex. Electrical loads for shore power to moored
units approach this limit with only a supply ship and one SSN. As planners
intend to expand mooring requirements for the pier, electrical requirements will
proportionately rise. As a result, a major electrical upgrade will need to occur
before the island can simultaneously host multiple SSNs, a T-AKR, or a supply
ship.

96. To maintain the reactor critical at the pier, three times as many operators
are required to monitor indications from the plant as are needed when the
reactor is shut down. Critical operations at the pier would therefore limit
rest—and mental downtime—for the engineering department of the SSN and
would unnecessarily raise radiation exposure, which the Navy attempts to keep
"as low as reasonably achievable" for both operators and shoreside civilian
populations.

97. "Project 182, Wharf Upgrades and Recreation Facility," 5. The addition
of aerators and filtration upgrades will assist in the removal of the THAs.
Wholesale replacement of the existing water treatment plant is not expected
due to cost and time constraints.

98. U.S. naval official, personal interviews, November 2007 and February
2008.

99. Ibid., 7 February 2008.

100. Ibid.

101. According to a U.S. official interviewed by one of the authors, the SSGN
deployment cycle is anticipated to proceed as follows: "Based on experience
gained in SSBN continuity of operations (SCOOP) exercises, an SSGN deployment cycle has been proposed to maximize deployed presence while continuing
to meet the TRIDENT-class maintenance plan. A four-SSGN force would be
used to provide 365 days of 154-TLAM CENTCOM presence and 365 days
of global SOF availability per year, while meeting all periodic TRIDENT crew
certification requirements and providing SOF training opportunities. Typically, an SSGN would alternate between CENTCOM strike and EUCOM or
PACOM SOF availability. After a 50-day refit, for example, Kings Bay SSGNs
would transit to the CENTCOM AOR, where they would provide the CINC
with strike presence in CENTCOM for 65 days while also being available for
SOF-mission tasking. This would be followed by a 14-day in-theater crew exchange and upkeep period, after which the SSGN would transit to the EUCOM
AOR, where it would be available to the CINC for 65 days, primarily for SOF
missions, but for strike taskings as well. After a return transit to Kings Bay, a

crew exchange, and another 50-day refit, the cycle would repeat. At the end of every third cycle, the ship would conduct a periodic certification for SOF missions. Pacific SSGN cycles would be similar. A four-ship SSGN force with 2 LANT and 2 PAC SSGNs can maintain a 1.29 presence in CENTCOM and an overseas SOF presence in EUCOM and PACOM of 0.49 and 0.45, respectively." Specific figures obtained from www.globalsecurity.org/military/library/report/1999/ssgn.htm.

102. U.S. naval official, personal interview, November 2007.

103. For a full discussion of the unpredictability of the foreign basing environment, see Franklin D. Kramer, chair; C. Richard Nelson, rapporteur, *Global Futures and Implications for U.S. Basing*, Working Group Report (Washington, D.C.: Atlantic Council of the United States, May 2005). The report reiterates the importance of flexible access: "Current surveys show a wide-spread international disquietude with at least some U.S. policies—and with a spill-over into a general anti-U.S. sentiment. If anti-U.S. sentiments become prevalent in much of the world, foreign leaders may face insurmountable domestic opposition to allowing the United States to maintain or to use bases on their territory" (17).

104. For each Suez transit of a naval vessel, Egypt charges the United States a significant cash fee for security services.

105. Ashley Jackson, "The British Empire in the Indian Ocean," in *Geopolitical Orientations, Security and Regionalism in the Indian Ocean*, ed. Dennis Rumley and Sanjay Chaturvedi (New Delhi: South Asian, 2004), 35.

106. Peter J. Brobst, *The Future of the Great Game: Sir Olaf Caroe, India's Independence, and the Defense of Asia* (Akron, Ohio: University of Akron Press, 2005), 13.

107. Keshav B. Vaidya, *The Naval Defence of India* (Bombay: Thacker, 1949), 101.

108. Kavalam M. Panikkar, *India and the Indian Ocean: An Essay on the Influence of Sea Power on Indian History* (London: George Allen and Unwin, 1945), 16.

109. Ibid., 84.

110. This policy has been characterized as "neo-Curzonian"—an allusion to the British imperial viceroy Lord George Curzon.

111. Ministry of Defense, *Strategic Defence Review: The Maritime Dimension—A Naval View* (New Delhi: Indian Navy, 20 May 1998), 34.

112. *Indian Maritime Doctrine*, 56.

113. Ibid., 64.

114. Manjeet S. Pardesi, *Deducing India's Grand Strategy of Regional Hegemony from Historical and Conceptual Perspectives* (Singapore: Institute of Defense and Strategic Studies, 2005), 55.

115. "India," in *CIA World Factbook* (Washington, D.C.: Central Intelligence Agency, 2007).

116. Sureesh Mehta, "India's Maritime Diplomacy and International Security," speech presented at "India as a Rising Great Power: Challenges and Opportunities," New Delhi, India, 18–20 April 2008, www.iiss.org/.

117. Nations in the South Asian region are India, Pakistan, Bangladesh, Sri Lanka, Bhutan, Nepal, and the Maldives.

118. Government of India, *Annual Report 2007–2008* (Delhi: Ministry of External Affairs, 2008), i.

119. Carin Zissis, "Backgrounder: India's Energy Crunch," *Council on Foreign Relations*, 23 October 2007, http://www.cfr.org/india/indias-energy-crunch/p12200.

120. Arun Prakash, "A Vision of India's Maritime Power in the 21st Century," *USI Journal* 136, no. 4 (October–December 2006), http://www.usiofindia.org/Article/?pub=Journal&pubno=566&ano=406.

121. *Indian Maritime Doctrine* (2009), 50.

122. "'Look West' Policy to Boost Ties with Gulf," *Financial Express*, 28 July 2005.

123. "System on Foreign Trade Performance Analysis," *Government of India, Ministry of Commerce & Industry: Department of Commerce*, http://www.archive.india.gov.in/outerwin.php?id=http%3A%2F%2Fcommerce.nic.in%2Fftpa%2Fdefault.asp.

124. P. S. Suryanarayana, "India, ASEAN Sign Free Trade Agreement," *Hindu*, 14 August 2009.

125. "System on Foreign Trade Performance Analysis."

126. Donald L. Berlin, "India in the Indian Ocean," *Naval War College Review* 59, no. 2 (Spring 2006): 58–59; and C. Raja Mohan, *Crossing the Rubicon: The Shaping of India's New Foreign Policy* (New York: Palgrave, 2004), 236.

127. "Indian Navy Chief Admiral Sureesh Mehta Spells Out Vision 2022," *India Defence*, 10 August 2008, http://www.india-defence.com/reports/3954.

128. *Indian Maritime Doctrine* (2004), 52.

129. Devin T. Hagerty, "India's Regional Security Doctrine," *Asian Survey* 31, no. 4 (April 1991): 351–53; and *Indian Maritime Doctrine* (2009), 3.

130. The Indian navy's maritime doctrine explicitly discusses "attempts by China to strategically encircle India" and warns of Chinese encroachment into "our maritime zone." Cited in "India's Naval Posture: Looking East," *Strategic Comments* 11, no. 6 (August 2005): 2.

131. "Chairman's Message," *Gwadar Port Authority*, www.gwadarport.gov.pk.

132. Ching Cheong, "Hostility to Chinese Presence in the Indian Ocean," *Straits Times*, 17 May 2004.

133. See, for example, Gurmeet Kanwal, "Countering China's Strategic Encirclement of India," *Indian Defence Review* 15, no. 3 (July–September 2000): 13; and C. S. Kuppuswamy, "Myanmar-China Cooperation: Its Implications for India," *South Asia Analysis Group*, 3 February 2003, http://www.southasiaanalysis.org/paper596. For a skeptical assessment of such developments, which are in accordance with available data, see Daniel J. Kostecka, "Places and Bases: The Chinese Navy's Emerging Support Network in the Indian Ocean," *Naval War College Review* 64, no. 1 (Winter 2011): 59–78; and Andrew Selth, "Chinese Military Bases in Burma: The Explosion of a Myth," in *Regional Outlook Paper 10* (Nathan, Australia: Griffith Asia Institute, 2007).

134. Vijay Sakhuja, "Indian Navy: Keeping Pace with Emerging Challenges," in *The Evolving Maritime Balance of Power in the Asia Pacific*, ed. Lawrence W. Prabhakar, Joshua H. Ho, and W. S. G. Bateman (Singapore: World Scientific, 2006), 191.

135. Joel Larus, "India's Nonalignment and Superpower Naval Rivalry," in *The Indian Ocean in Global Politics*, ed. Larry W. Bowman and Ian Clark (Boulder, Colo.: Westview, 1981), 46.

136. Ibid., 44.

137. Ibid., 45.

138. Ibid., 47–48.

139. Ibid., 47.

140. For a discussion of this policy and its implications, see Daniel Twining, "America's Grand Design in Asia," *Washington Quarterly* 30, no. 3 (Summer 2007): 79–94.

141. "Mauritius May Relent on U.S. Base in Diego Garcia," *Times of India*, 12 April 2002.

142. For the text of the letter, see "A Negative International Signal," *Indian Express*, 30 June 2007. The response by the *Times* is "Nuclear Bluster," *Times of India*, 3 July 2007.

143. Zhao Danping, "U.S. Military Presence in East Asia," *Banyue Tan* [Semimonthly Talks], 25 May 1996.

144. Wang Weixing and Teng Jianqun, "Air-Launched Cruise Missiles Are Hanging at Asia's Door," *Jiefangjun Bao* [Liberation Army Daily], 6 September 2000, 12.

145. Jiang Hong and Wei Yuejiang, "100,000 U.S. Troops in the Asia-Pacific Look for 'New Homes,'" *Guofang Bao* [National Defense News], 10 June 2003, 1.

146. Zhao Yiping, "What Are U.S. Intentions in Deploying Cruise Missiles on Guam: Interview with Wang Weixing, Research Fellow of the Academy of Military Sciences," *Guangming Ribao* [Enlightenment Daily], 6 September 2000.

147. See, for example, Nan Li, "The Evolution of China's Naval Strategy and Capabilities: From 'Near Coast' and 'Near Seas' to 'Far Seas,'" *Asian Security* 5, no. 2 (May 2009): 144–69.

148. 徐起 [Xu Qi], "21世纪初海上地缘战略与中国海军的发展" [Maritime Geostrategy and the Development of the Chinese Navy in the Early 21st Century], 中国军事科学 [China Military Science] 17, no. 4 (2004): 75–81.

149. Peng Guangqian and Yao Youzhi, eds., *The Science of Military Strategy* (Beijing: Military Science Press, 2005), 443.

150. 静海 [Jing Hai], "美国海军太平洋舰队五大海军基地和多少" [The U.S. Navy Pacific Fleet's Five Great Naval Bases and Their Relevant Statistics], 人民海军 [People's Navy], 4 March 2006, 4. For a similar analysis that also includes Guam (which Jing's *People's Navy* article fails to provide, perhaps for reasons of sensitivity), see 静海 [Jing Hai], "美国太平洋舰队海军基地" [U.S. Pacific

Fleet Naval Bases], 舰船知识 [Naval and Merchant Ships], March 2006, 27–29.

151. Cai Yongzhong, "'Time Bomb' Hanging in the Sky above Asia-Pacific: U.S.-ROK 'Foal Eagle' Joint Military Exercise in Perspective," *Jiefangjun Bao*, 3 November 1999.

152. Qian Wenrong, "Just Where Does the Focus of U.S. Global Strategy Lie?" *Zhongguo Dangzheng Ganbu Luntan* [China Party Cadre Forum], 1 June 2001. Qian is a researcher at Xinhua News Agency's World Issues Research Center.

153. Liu Jiang and Yan Feng, "United States Adjusts Asia-Pacific Policy," Xinhua, 19 December 2000.

154. Wang and Teng, "Air-Launched Cruise Missiles," 12.

155. Zhang Jiyuan, "The U.S. Air Force Will Make New Moves," *Jiefangjun Bao*, 21 December 2000, 5.

156. Liu Jiang and Yan Feng, "U.S. Adjusts Asia Pacific Policy for New Century," Xinhua, 26 December 2000.

157. Cheng Ying-yao et al., "Arms Budget Is a Counter to China," *Taipei Times*, 29 September 2004, 8.

158. Shan Min, "United States Builds World-Largest Warfare Information Network," *Liaowang* [Outlook Weekly], no. 23, Xinhua Hong Kong Service, 5 June 2001.

159. 润田 [He Hongze and Ren Tian], "美数千特工盯我飞船: 天上拍照地面监听, 派间谍四处打探" [U.S. Secret Services Repeatedly Fix Their Eyes on Our Airships, Taking Photographs from the Air and Monitoring on the Ground while Sending Off Intelligence Agents All Over to Spy], 环球时报 [Global Times], 13 October 2003.

160. Xie Ying, "Who Is Closely Watching *Shenzhou VI?*" *Qingnian Cankao* [Youth Reference], 12 October 2005.

161. Lin Bo, Guan Liyan, and Chen Bingyao, "Dialogue with *Renmin Ribao*'s Guoji Zhoukan: Focus on the Global Military Presence of the United States," *Renmin Wang* [People's Net], 12 June 2003; "U.S. Sends More Warplanes to Gulf Region," Xinhua, 18 November 1997; "Second Wave of U.S.-UK Airstrikes against Iraq," Xinhua, 18 December 1998; Li Yunfei, "Sky over Gulf Is Covered with Dark Clouds," *Renmin Ribao* [People's Daily], 6 February 1998, 6; and Chi Yingjie, "The United States Works Out a Plan of Operations against Iraq," Central People's Radio Network, 21 February 1998.

162. "U.S. Issues Worldwide Vigilance Alert," Xinhua, 13 November 1998.

163. He Chong, "U.S. Deployment of Combat Forces Has Dual Objective," *Zhongguo Tongxun She* [China News Agency], 21 September 2001.

164. Gong Yan, "Analysis: Bush Wants to Use Tomahawk Missiles to Fight a 'War of Financial Defense,'" *Jianchuan Zhishi* [Naval and Merchant Ships], October 2001.

165. Zhao Jianfu, "U.S. Military Base al-Udeid in Qatar: U.S. Military's Outpost for Attacking Iraq?," *Jiefangjun Bao*, 15 July 2002, 11.

166. Wang Fengfeng and Yan Feng, "Wind Rushing through the Tower Heralds a Rising Storm in the Mountains: Commentary on U.S. Intention to Use Force against Iraq," *Renmin Ribao*, 1 August 2002, 3.

167. Wang Jinglie, "Iraq War: The United States Draws the Bow but Does Not Discharge the Arrow," *Shijie Zhishi* [World Knowledge], no. 17 (September 2002): 24. Wang Jinglie is an expert on Middle East affairs. For the quote, see "U.S., UK Military Presence in Gulf," Xinhua, 20 March 2003.

168. Chong Zi, "U.S. Policy Reeking of Unilateralism," *China Daily*, 1 April 2003.

169. Xie Pu, Han Qinggui, and Li Zhishun, "A Glance at U.S. and Iraqi Military Strength," *Renmin Ribao*, 10 February 2003, 3.

170. Yang Hui, "Saber Rattling! Will the U.S. Really Dare to Use Force against Iran?," *Zhongguo Tongxun She*, 10 February 2006.

171. He Yijian, "The United States Is Busy Deploying Troops in Asia," *Liaowang*, no. 20 (13 May 2002): 54–55.

172. Li Xuanliang, "U.S. Military's 'New Guam Strategy,'" *Liaowang Dongfang Zhoukan* [Oriental Outlook], 18 June 2006, 18–19; and Lin Chuan, "The Center of U.S. Navy Activities Has Shifted to the Asia-Pacific Region," *Zhongguo Tongxun She*, 9 January 2005.

173. Weng Hansong, "An Analysis of Adjustments of U.S. Global Military Deployment," Military Observation, *Renmin Wang*, 18 May 2005.

174. Yu Xiaokui, "Dramatic Ending of the 'Missile Incident,'" *Guangming Ribao*, 13 December 2002.

175. Zhao Li, "India Is Not Going to Be an Ally of the United States," *Kuang Chiao Ching* [Wide Angle], 16 May 2002, 24–27.

176. Zhou Qingan, "Japan, Where Is Your Self-Defense Borderline?," *Ta Kung Pao* [Dagong Bao], 3 October 2001.

177. Wei Yan, "Perspective on Japanese-U.S. 'Keen Sword 2003' Combined Exercise," *Zhongguo Guofang Bao* [China Defense News], 13 November 2002, 4.

178. Bing Shan, "Japan Wants to Become a Military Power Worthy of the Name," *Jiefangjun Bao*, 13 May 2002, 12.

179. Kazuya Sakamoto, "The Future of Guam and the U.S.-Japan Alliance," *Tokyo Toa*, 1 March 2006, 2–3. Kazuya Sakamoto is a professor at the Graduate School of Law and Politics, Osaka University.

180. Tan Weibing, "The United States Readjusts Deployment of Military Force around the Globe," Xinhua, 15 June 2003.

181. James Holmes and Toshi Yoshihara, "China's Naval Ambitions in the Indian Ocean," *Journal of Strategic Studies* 31, no. 3 (2008): 368.

182. Barnett, *Pentagon's New Map*, 4.

183. Henry A. Kissinger, "Center of Gravity Shifts in International Affairs," *San Diego Union-Tribune*, 4 July 2004; and Jeffrey D. Sachs, "Welcome to the Asian Century," *Fortune*, 12 January 2004.

184. Office of the Director of National Intelligence, *ODNI Releases Global Trends Projections*, ODNI News Release 19-08 (Washington, D.C.: Public Affairs Office, 20 November 2008).

185. *United States Security Strategy for the Asia-Pacific Region*, 1995, 1998; *United States Security Strategy for the Middle East*, 1995; *United States Security Strategy for Sub-Saharan Africa*, 1995; *United States Security Strategy for Europe and NATO*, 1995.

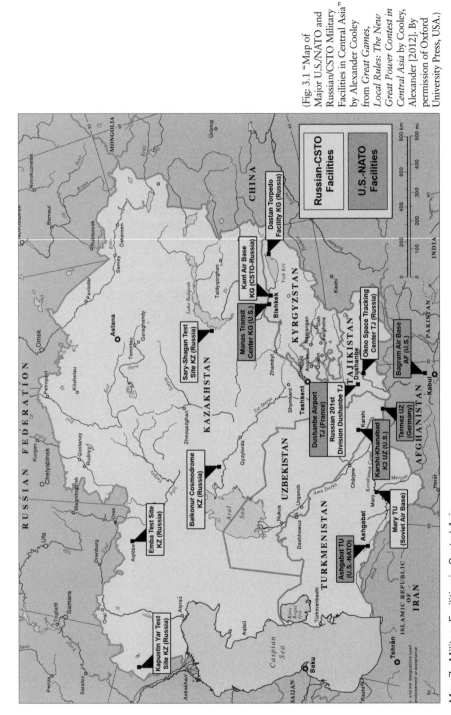

(Fig. 3.1 "Map of Major U.S./NATO and Russian/CSTO Military Facilities in Central Asia" by Alexander Cooley from *Great Games, Local Rules: The New Great Power Contest in Central Asia* by Cooley, Alexander [2012]. By permission of Oxford University Press, USA.)

Map 7. Military Facilities in Central Asia

7

U.S. Bases and Domestic Politics in Central Asia

Alexander Cooley

Most discussions of the current and future U.S. overseas basing network understandably focus on operational needs and strategic context. But in the host countries, overseas bases are also, inescapably, political entities. A cursory examination of the basing issue across Asia over the last few decades suggests that domestic politics inform and even drive the political status and reception of basing issues, often independently of the policies or activities of U.S. forces abroad. For example, in the Philippines during the post-Marcos era, the status of American bases at Subic Bay and Clark became intertwined with democratization backlashes and accusations by legislators and the media that the United States had supported the authoritarian rule of Ferdinand Marcos in order to maintain access to these facilities. Similarly, in Korea since the late 1990s the rise of civil society, the decentralization of power, and the establishment of new media outlets have created a number of new political actors who oppose the U.S. forces in Korea and their underpinning legal arrangements, such as status of forces. In Japan, the enduring presence of the majority of U.S. military facilities on the island prefecture of Okinawa remains a persistent source of tension in relations between Tokyo and the regional government. These examples suggest that basing politics can often play a disruptive role in U.S.–host country bilateral relations and can even escalate to the level of disrupting the legal and diplomatic foundations of the U.S. presence.

The same is true, though rarely acknowledged, of the wave of U.S. bases and facilities established since the end of the Cold War, including those in Central Asia. During the fall of 2001, the United States established bases in the independent states of Uzbekistan and Kyrgyzstan, both former republics of the former Soviet Union, to support military operations in Afghanistan. The bases themselves—at the Karshi-Khanabad (K2) airfield in southern Uzbekistan and the Manas airport near the Kyrgyz capital of Bishkek—were relatively small, not intended to be permanent. The accompanying map depicts these and other relevant facilities in the region. Politically, the U.S. basing presence was initially welcomed by the Central Asian states; however, within a few years host attitudes toward the U.S. presence changed dramatically. In July 2005 the Uzbek government evicted the United States from K2, dealing a major operational and diplomatic blow to American planners. At the same time, the Kyrgyz government demanded and obtained a renegotiation of its basing contract in 2006 before taking initial steps to evict U.S. forces in 2009 and then terminating access to the facility in 2014. What explains this sudden politicization and the contestation of the American basing presence in Central Asia, especially given the continued precariousness of the security environment in Afghanistan?

Media accounts and expert analyses have overwhelmingly focused on current geopolitical changes in Central Asia and, in particular, Russia's new assertiveness in the region. According to this view, a resurgent Russia, along with its new regional partner China, used the Shanghai Cooperation Organization (SCO) to pressure the Central Asian states and convince them that their own national interests and the region's stability would be best promoted through this regional security organization rather than a strategic partnership with the United States. In a seeming new chapter of the "Great Game"—the historical competition among great powers for access and influence in Central Asia—Russia's new offensive appeared to have produced a major diplomatic triumph over the United States. Indeed, in February 2009 Kyrgyz president Kurmanbek Bakiyev announced at a joint press conference in Moscow with Russian president Dmitry Medvedev that he would be closing Manas and would accept a $2 billion emergency economic package from Russia.

These external accounts, however, frequently confuse cause with effect—in fact, domestic political developments within these hosts initially drove changing attitudes toward the base issue, and then the Central Asian states strategically used or invoked Russia and China to justify these domestically based decisions. For example, in the previous example, President Bakiyev skillfully dangled the prospect of closing Manas in exchange for economic assistance that he needed to bridge a domestic budget shortfall and, later that summer, to get reelected. After extracting financial concessions from Russia, Bakiyev double-crossed Moscow by renegotiating a new agreement with the United States. In Uzbekistan in 2005, Karimov's authoritarian regime calculated that its strict domestic political control and repressive tactics amid the so-called Eurasian colored revolutions were threatened by the continued U.S. presence. This regime believed that aligning with Russia and China would be less of a threat, though it has since resumed security cooperation with the United States by playing a critical role in the establishment of the Northern Distribution Network.

Thus, the Central Asian cases demonstrate how authoritarian rulers manipulated the base issue primarily for their own domestic self-interest, not to pursue the publicly stated common security purpose of stabilizing Afghanistan. Although defense planners assumed that the aims of the Afghanistan war are shared with these partners—not illogically, given that failure in Afghanistan and spillover could destabilize the Central Asian region—in practice ruling elites of these new base hosts have always demanded political concessions or quid pro quos from American authorities for accepting U.S. forces. For its part, the United States, quite unintentionally and despite its light footprint and temporary presence, has become embroiled in the internal politics and regime-survival strategies of these hosts. These cases should serve as a caution to American planners who are establishing multiple new bases in politically volatile host countries in other parts of Asia and worldwide.

New Allies and Base Hosts in Central Asia

Shortly after September 11, U.S. officials began planning to topple the Taliban in Afghanistan and eliminate al-Qaeda fighters and training camps. The planning for Operation Enduring Freedom (OEF) was complicated by the fact that the United States lacked forward installations near Afghanistan and had not developed strong security ties with the post-Soviet Central Asian states. Indeed, U.S. planners at first envisioned basing almost exclusively out of Pakistan.

Uzbekistan was the first such state to offer its support for the Afghanistan campaign. It signed on 7 October 2001 an initial agreement that offered basing rights to U.S. forces. The K2 facility—host to Camp Stronghold Freedom—housed several thousand light infantry troops and Special Forces and in December 2001 started trucking supplies to Mazar-e-Sharif in Afghanistan.[1] Much to CENTCOM's irritation, however, Uzbek officials refused to openly allow combat aircraft deployment and insisted that the base be used primarily for "humanitarian purposes." This led the State Department to explore acquiring additional sites among the former Soviet states. Kyrgyzstan was found to host the most suitable possibilities, given that a Japanese-led consortium had just repaved the runway of the Manas airport, near the capital, Bishkek. In December 2001 American negotiators reached an agreement with Kyrgyzstan to establish a coalition airbase at Manas, which was later informally named Ganci (in tribute to Peter Ganci, a New York firefighter who died on September 11). The United States and its coalition partners supplemented these main bases with separate refueling and air-corridor agreements with Tajikistan's, Turkmenistan's, and Kazakhstan's governments, although these were less publicized, for political reasons.[2] The Russian government was not happy to accept American military forces on former Soviet territory but agreed not to oppose the arrangements as long as they were temporary and would be withdrawn after major combat operations in Afghanistan.[3] In addition, Russian intelligence officials—who had been concerned about destabilization in Afghanistan—shared information on and contacts in the Northern Alliance with their U.S. counterparts.[4]

The varying internal political traits and institutional characteristics across these states dictated the types of benefits and quid pro quos that each regime sought from the United States for granting base access. The U.S. basing presence provided an array of benefits to the Uzbek and Kyrgyz regimes. Certainly, these regimes were eager to be associated with a global antiterrorism campaign, both out of a genuine concern for the destabilizing activities of militant Islamic groups such as the Islamic Movement of Uzbekistan and—in the Uzbek case—in order to justify a harsh new crackdown on internal oppositional political movements. The small size of the Kyrgyz economy and its top-down patronage networks made the Kyrgyz regime particularly eager to leverage U.S. base access for its own economic benefit, something it managed with considerable success. On the American side, few officials in the State Department or Pentagon were unduly worried about these states' peculiar institutional characteristics or voiced public concern about their undemocratic tendencies.[5] The compelling need for the United States was to secure by any reasonable means base access for the Afghanistan campaign.

K2 and Uzbekistan: Strengthening Karimov's Dictatorial Grip

Uzbekistan proved the Central Asian country most eager to be associated with Western efforts in Afghanistan. For a decade after independence, President Islam Karimov, a hard-liner who ruled with an iron fist, minimized political and economic reforms and fended off internal political rivals. By the late 1990s the Uzbek regime was most concerned with the growing popularity of Islamic movements, especially in the impoverished Ferghana Valley and the eastern part of the country, and particularly the subversive activities of the militant Islamic Movement of Uzbekistan (IMU). Led by Djuma Namangani, the IMU reportedly had allied itself with Taliban elements in Afghanistan and other radical extremist militant Islamist groups in the region as well as with the group claiming responsibility for a bombing attack in Tashkent in February 1999. During the summers of 1999 and 2000 it skirmished with state security forces in Uzbekistan and Kyrgyzstan after carrying out cross-border kidnappings and raids.[6] Alliance with the United States presented a major opportunity for Karimov to crush the IMU with Western blessing and to justify his regime's tightening grip within the country.

The K2 Base Agreement Terms and Quid Pro Quo

Under the 7 October 2001 status of forces agreement, the Uzbek government offered the United States the right to station up to 1,500 troops at K2, ninety miles from the Afghan border.[7] Uzbek officials had insisted that the United States retain a low profile in some remote part of the country and asked it to conclude a new status of forces agreement (SOFA) that would further specify the U.S. forces' legal status. The United States was granted access to the base and Uzbek airspace for OEF operations, with the duration of the agreement left open-ended. Each side retained the right to terminate the agreement within 180 days after giving formal notice. Officially, the United States was prohibited from deploying combat aircraft at K2 and was limited to humanitarian and surveillance missions.[8]

In terms of quid pro quo, the U.S. side provided a number of benefits to the Uzbek regime. First, and perhaps most important, the United States agreed to target members of the IMU who were fighting alongside the Taliban and al-Qaeda in Afghanistan. Second, by allying itself with Western antiterror coalition members through the agreement, Uzbekistan underscored its autonomy in foreign policy matters and put distance between itself and Moscow. In terms of military assistance and economic quid pro quo, the United States in 2002 provided $120 million in hardware and surveillance equipment to the Uzbek army and $82 million to the security services, as well as $15 million in base-related operating expenses. In the same year, not coincidentally, the U.S. Export-Import Bank granted $55 million in credits to the Uzbek government. American officials did not formally admit that these disbursements were linked to the base, but total U.S. government aid to Uzbekistan increased significantly, from $85 million in 2001 to nearly $300 million in 2002.[9]

The new security relationship was formalized in March 2002 when presidents Bush and Karimov signed the U.S.-Uzbek Declaration on Strategic Partnership. The exact provisions of the accord were kept secret, but the leaked items included a U.S. pledge to preserve the "security and territorial integrity" of Uzbekistan and Tashkent's agreement to support the U.S.-led war on terror and OEF operations. The Uzbek government agreed to undertake an ambitious set of internal political reforms and committed itself to "ensuring respect for human rights and freedoms . . . enhancing the role of democratic and political institutions in the life of society; establishing a genuine multiparty system . . . ensuring the independence of the media . . . [and] improving the judicial and legal system."[10] It is unclear whether U.S. officials viewed these Uzbek commitments as genuine or as political cover to justify the deepening of security ties between the countries.

Karimov's War on Terror and Democratic Retrenchment

In fact, despite this commitment, the Uzbek regime was emboldened by the U.S. presence in K2 to backslide on its democratic commitments and human rights practices.[11] In January 2002 Karimov arbitrarily extended his presidential term until 2007. Later in 2002 Uzbek security services stepped up their internal activities and arrested hundreds of suspects on accusations of fomenting terrorism. In a highly critical report issued after a December 2002 visit, a UN envoy found rampant and systemic torture of terrorist suspects in Uzbek prisons. As part of the Bush administration's policy of "extraordinary rendition," the United States also turned over dozens of suspects to Uzbek authorities in secret flights.[12] For his part, Karimov skillfully used his new coalition position to crack down on all political opposition under the mantra of fighting terrorism, whether these groups actually had ties to Islamic militants or not. Karimov violated democratic norms and reneged on his own international political commitments, calculating that the U.S. government, in order to maintain its base access, would not denounce these actions.

Kyrgyzstan: Akayev's Reprieve and the Depoliticization of the Base Issue

The OEF international coalition offered Kyrgyzstan president Askar Akayev a political reprieve, especially after his backsliding on reforms during the late 1990s. Manas-Ganci became a key coalition facility in the international war on terror, and Akayev was keen to be associated with the effort. By May 2002 the base hosted two thousand coalition troops from nine countries and an array of international cargo aircraft, refuelers, and even some fighter aircraft. In response to this U.S.-led Western presence, the next year Russia established its own air base in Kant, just twenty kilometers away from Manas, making Kyrgyzstan the first country to host officially both a Russian and U.S. military facility.

Like Karimov, Akayev was eager to highlight the potential regional Islamic threat so as to solidify his cooperative partnership with the United States. At times Kyrgyz officials and security services exaggerated and even fabricated terrorist plots to bolster the government's status. The most striking example occurred in November 2003, when Kyrgyz security services allegedly foiled a plot to bomb the base by three members of Hizb ut-Tahir, a regional Islamic group with no actual track record of violence in Kyrgyzstan. The would-be perpetrators were supposedly caught with explosives and a map of the base; they were subsequently tried and convicted. Western and Kyrgyz observers expressed serious doubts about the accuracy of the Kyrgyz government's account of the plot.[13]

Economic Benefits: Patronage and Selective Incentives

For Akayev, the economic dimension was far more important than it was for Karimov. Kyrgyzstan's small population and struggling billion-dollar economy meant that even a small basing presence could have a significant economic impact. The base, which constituted the biggest American economic investment in Kyrgyzstan, from its first year contributed about $40 million annually to the small Kyrgyz economy while employing about five hundred Kyrgyz nationals in various positions.[14]

However, the lion's share of base-related funds flowed not to national agencies but to private Kyrgyz entities with close ties to the ruling regime. Manas

International Airport, legally operated as an independent company partly owned by Aydar Akayev, the president's son, collected $2 million annually in lease payments, plus fees of $7,000 per takeoff, calculated in accordance with civil aviation standards. The airport company won most of the base-related service contracts and charged ad hoc fees for additional parking spaces allocated to coalition aircraft outside of the designated military area.[15] These revenues flowed directly to the Manas airport and were neither accounted for nor taxed by the Kyrgyz government.

But the most lucrative sources of base-related payments were fuel contracts, secured by the airport-run Manas International Services Ltd. and by Aalam Services Ltd., another legally independent fuel company, this one owned by Adil Toiganbayev, Akayev's son-in-law. A *New York Times* investigative story revealed that out of a total of $207 million spent by the U.S. Department of Defense on fuel contracts during the Akayev era, Manas International Services received $87 million and Aalam Services $32 million in subcontracts from the main Western contractors, Avcard (2002) and Red Star (2003–5).[16] The amounts and structure of these payments were kept opaque and were not reported in the Kyrgyz media. A subsequent FBI investigation uncovered that the Akayev clan had embezzled tens of millions of dollars of these base-related revenues through a network of offshore accounts.

Pentagon and State Department officials contend—and they are legally correct—that none of these payments or contracts clearly violated any U.S. laws or DoD tender procedures. But the decision to award such vast sums of money to mysterious offshore companies, with little oversight, did little to encourage transparency or accountability in the contracting procedure.[17] For our purposes, such claims about strict legality do not change the fact that these payments had significant political consequences. Base-related revenues supported the Akayev regime and its political clients, who viewed these contracts as the quid pro quo for granting basing rights to the United States and its coalition partners. Indeed, commenting specifically on the adoption of the seemingly generous landing-rights formula, John O'Keefe, the former American ambassador to Kyrgyzstan, suggested that the fees could have been avoided but were viewed by the American side as an important economic inducement that would secure the Kyrgyz government's commitment.[18] Just as base-related payments had helped keep afloat the patronage machines of other authoritarian figures, such as Ferdinand Marcos in the Philippines in the 1970s–80s, the U.S. military presence in Kyrgyzstan was predicated on providing economic incentives to ruling elites and their cronies in order to maintain their commitment to base access.

The Depoliticization of the Base Issue

These private or selective incentives also served to initially "depoliticize" the base issue in Kyrgyz politics. Not the political parties, the Kyrgyz Parliament, nor the media publicized or overtly criticized the terms of the basing agreement.[19] This depoliticization lasted until Akayev's regime collapsed in March 2005. Much as with foreign assistance and development aid during the 1990s, Akayev and his backers skillfully used external funds both to enrich themselves and pay off key political supporters in the Kyrgyz system. With the exception of Russian-owned newspapers, the Kyrgyz media ran few negative news stories about the base, and neither did they publicize the contracting ties between the U.S. military and the Akayev family.

Changing Domestic Politics and Base Politics: Eviction and Contestation

The year 2005 marked a major turning point in American relations with both Uzbekistan and Kyrgyzstan over the base issue. Domestic political changes in both countries led to the rapid politicization of the U.S. basing presence. Over the period of a few months, U.S.-Uzbek relations deteriorated to the point that on 30 July 2005 the government officially evicted the U.S. military from K2. In Kyrgyzstan the Akayev regime collapsed in March 2005, and the new president, Kurmanbek Bakiyev, questioned the procedural legitimacy of the Manas agreement and demanded a new deal on terms more favorable to the Kyrgyz Republic.

Uzbekistan: Eviction from K2

On 11 May 2005 the Uzbek government ruthlessly cracked down on thousands of demonstrators who had gathered in the town square of the eastern city of Andijon. Uzbek government officials claim that the crackdown was necessary, given that earlier in the day armed militants with Islamic ties had staged a prison break and used automatic weapons to capture a local police station and military barracks.

The Andijon Massacre

International human rights organizations and journalists' accounts maintain that the majority of the demonstrators were peacefully protesting the government's jailing of twenty-three local businessmen accused of militant ties and were generally voicing their opposition to Tashkent's increasingly heavy-handed involvement in local political and economic matters. Local eyewitnesses claim that Uzbek security services in armored vehicles surrounded the demonstrators and then started to fire indiscriminately into the crowd of civilians, mowing down hundreds as they tried to flee the square. Government officials maintain that the death toll of that day was limited to 180, mostly armed insurgents, while international nongovernmental organizations (NGOs) such as the International Crisis Group and Human Rights Watch conservatively estimate the toll at between seven hundred and eight hundred.

Events in Andijon sent shock waves across the region and in the West. In Washington, officials at first reacted tentatively.[20] Initially, the then White House press secretary, Scott McClellan, refused to condemn the Uzbek government's actions, and the Pentagon and CENTCOM were silent about the matter. At NATO headquarters in Brussels, American officials refused to issue a joint communiqué calling for an international investigation into Andijon, purely on the grounds that Uzbek authorities might retaliate by restricting military operations based in K2.[21] Just a few weeks later, however, most major players within the U.S. government adopted a more critical stance. At a U.S. government meeting, according to the memoirs of former defense secretary Donald Rumsfeld, Secretary of State Condoleezza Rice asserted that "human rights trumps security" and publicly backed the formation of an international inquiry.[22] A group of U.S. senators openly called for an investigation into whether Uzbek security forces had used any U.S. military hardware in Andijon. In response to growing criticism by these bodies, Uzbek officials in June restricted nighttime flights and heavy airlift out of the base.

The American position on the subsequent Andijon refugee issue in July 2005 was the final straw for the Uzbek government. Following the violent clashes, 430 refugees fled Andijon and crossed the border into southern Kyrgyzstan. The Uzbek government demanded that Kyrgyz officials forcibly return the refugees, whom they accused of being militants and instigators, to Uzbek security services for interrogation. Instead, the refugees were allowed to remain in southern Kyrgyzstan in makeshift camps run by the United Nations. On 28 July 2005 the United States backed a United Nations decision to move the refugees to Romania and then on to various European nations that had agreed to grant them political asylum. Just a day later, the Uzbek government formally notified the U.S. embassy in Tashkent that it was activating the 180-day termination clause in the SOFA. The last U.S. troops left K2 in November 2005, just four years after their historic deployment to the Central Asian state. Even after the American departure, some base-related tension lingered, as the Uzbek government claimed the United States owed it $23 million for back rent and base-related expenses.

Karimov's Changing Political Calculations and Eviction

Some have pointed to the growing regional influence of Russia and China in Uzbekistan as an underlying cause of Karimov's decision to evict the United States and to realign geopolitically.[23] Certainly, both Russia and China had developed important economic ties to Uzbekistan, especially in the hydrocarbon and electricity sectors. However, Russia and China were also important in that their strong political support in reaction to Andijon ultimately convinced Karimov that his domestic survival and political tenure would be best served by turning to Moscow and Beijing and away from the United States, which had supported three "democratic revolutions" in quick succession in the post-Soviet space (Georgia, Ukraine, and Kyrgyzstan). Immediately after Andijon, Russian president Vladimir Putin and Chinese premier Hu Jintao strongly endorsed the Uzbek president's actions and supported the official Uzbek account of events in the city. In November 2005, following the K2 eviction, the Karimov regime signed a formal security alliance with Russia and proceeded to expel a number of Western NGOs and media outlets from Uzbekistan.

Kyrgyzstan: Regime Change, Quid pro Quo, and the Politicization of the Basing Presence

The political collapse of the Akayev regime was as sudden as it was unexpected. Antigovernment activists and groups had planned a democratic revolution, a "Tulip Revolution," that would be similar to the popular uprisings in Georgia in 2003 and Ukraine in 2004.

The Tulip Revolution and the Fall of Akayev

Few Central Asia political observers or even diplomats in Kyrgyzstan took claims of a planned revolution seriously.[24] But fraudulent parliamentary elections held in late February 2005 sparked uprisings in the southern provinces, and these steadily gathered momentum as various opposition factions and civic NGOs united on an anti-Akayev platform. On 20 March riots erupted in the southern cities of Jalalabad and Osh, and on 23 March demonstrations took place in Bishkek; the security services failed to put down these crowds decisively. Akayev's regime crumbled the very next day, when protesters stormed the presidential White House. Akayev fled to Russia, and on 4 April 2005 he formally resigned the presidency.

Bakiyev's Tough Stance

Kurmanbek Bakiyev, a former prime minister turned critic of the regime, became Kyrgyzstan's acting president in the interim before new elections could be held. In a political pact for national unity, Bakiyev agreed to grant the prime ministership to his main rival, Felix Kulov, who had been imprisoned during the Akayev regime.

The first signs of the growing politicization of the base issue emerged in connection with an early July SCO declaration during the Astana summit, signed onto by Bakiyev a few days before his presidential election, that called for the removal of foreign military bases in member countries. Then, on 11 July, in his very first press conference after his landslide election victory, Bakiyev announced that the Manas base's purpose should be reexamined and that Kyrgyzstan should pursue a more "independent foreign policy."[25] A quick visit by the American secretary of defense, Donald Rumsfeld, on the 26th seemed to quell the issue as the Kyrgyz president reiterated his commitment to hosting the base, but the matter revived when the United States was expelled from Uzbekistan.

Sensing increased bargaining leverage now that Manas was the only remaining U.S. base in Central Asia, and under pressure internally for failing to deliver on his post-Akayev reform agenda, Bakiyev once again raised the base issue during the fall of 2005. In interviews and speeches, he claimed that the terms of the basing presence were not favorable to Kyrgyzstan and that the Akayev regime had embezzled the base's revenue streams. During an October 2005 visit by Secretary of State Condoleezza Rice, Bakiyev demanded increased payments for base rights and insisted on a formal accounting of all base-related payments made during the Akayev regime.

In December the Kyrgyz president called for a "hundredfold" compensation increase from the United States, quoting a figure of $200 million in rent and services, and accused the American side of paying only "symbolic" amounts during the Akayev regime. In January 2006 the Kyrgyz foreign ministry issued a formal request to the U.S. embassy that demanded significant payment increases, including $50 million just for leasing and parking fees for aircraft, as well as separate compensation for base-related environmental damage and the Akayev-era fuel contracts. In April 2006, prior to a visit to Moscow to meet with Vladimir Putin, Bakiyev issued an ultimatum requiring the United States to conclude a new deal by 1 June. American negotiators steadfastly refused to offer such a substantial and explicit quid pro quo, replying to Kyrgyz officials that alternative regional basing arrangements could be secured for well below the new $200 million price tag.[26] In the end, the 1 June 2006 deadline was missed.

The New July 2006 Accord

After months of prolonged negotiations and political brinkmanship, Kyrgyz and American negotiators finally announced a deal on extending U.S. use of the base. The publicly released "joint statement" was a creative and carefully crafted document that appeared to satisfy the main needs of both sides.[27] The U.S. side "expect[ed] to provide over $150 in total assistance and compensation over the next year," thereby allowing Bakiyev to claim that he had extracted a great deal of the $200 million demanded from the Americans. However, American officials could claim that the actual lease payment for Manas rose only from $2 million annually to $17 million and that the "compensation package" included an array of various bilateral assistance programs (many of them already in place) as well as more general base-related economic contributions. To emphasize the point, the statement explicitly emphasized that the base deal was part of a "larger, robust bilateral relationship" between the United States and the Kyrgyz Republic; it also pointed out that since independence the United States had provided more than $850 million in total aid to this Central Asian state. Thus, the same document seemingly acknowledged a total $150 million quid pro quo for U.S. base rights and reaffirmed the broader framework and bilateral relationship.

Bakiyev's Bold New Gambit and the Role of Moscow

Almost immediately following the new deal, however, Kyrgyz officials started to complain openly about its terms. Specifically, Kyrgyz negotiators felt frustrated that American officials were including development assistance, humanitarian projects, and programs like the Peace Corps as part of the $150 million "unofficial" base-rights package.[28] When financial crisis hit Kyrgyzstan in 2008, the Bakiyev government found itself staring at a $125 million dollar budget gap, with little or no prospect of raising money.

In February 2009 the Kyrgyz leader attempted one of the most audacious geopolitical gambits by a small state in recent years. At a joint press conference in Moscow with Russian president Dmitri Medvedev, Bakiyev announced that he would close the "unpopular base," and the Russian leader pledged an emergency aid package of $2 billion in Russian grants and investment in Kyrgyzstan's hydroelectric sector. Although Kyrgyz and Russian officials denied that the Russian aid deal was tied to the closure of Manas, analysts in Washington and Moscow openly made the connection.

Once the $300 million payment was received from Russia in the spring of 2009, the Kyrgyz leader turned to the United States and concluded a new agreement to keep the base open. According to a report on Manas fuel contracting released by a congressional investigation, a representative of Mina Corporation, an offshore-registered company supplying the base with jet fuel, played a key role in the renegotiation by facilitating back-channel discussions between the Bakiyev family and the U.S. Department of Defense.[29] Under the new terms announced in June 2009, the United States would pay $63 million annually in cash to the Kyrgyz government, and the base would be renamed the "Manas Transit Center" as political cover for the Kyrgyz government. Washington considered the 2009 renewal a triumph over Russian meddling; Bakiyev's double-cross infuriated the Kremlin, and Russian-Kyrgyz relations deteriorated to a new low.

In late 2009 and early 2010 Moscow mobilized a soft-power campaign against the Bakiyev regime. Throughout February and March, Moscow-controlled media outlet broadcasts emphasized the regime's corruption, nepotism, and repression. In April the Kremlin stopped shipments of jet fuel from Russian distributors to fuel contractors at Manas and imposed a new duty on Russian fuel exports to the country as a whole. The new excise tax threatened massive price increases in almost all areas of Kyrgyz economic activity. It also initiated a wave of anti-Bakiyev protests in early April in northern cities. On 8 April protesters stormed the presidential White House in Bishkek. The regime collapsed within two days, and the capital experienced disorder and looting and eighty-five people were killed. Bakiyev fled to his stronghold southern city of Osh before leaving for exile in Belarus as a guest of President Alexander Lukashenko.

Renewed Democratization and Political Backlash against Manas

The ouster of Bakiyev once again placed Manas and its underpinning arrangements under political scrutiny.[30] Members of the Kyrgyz interim government claimed that American officials lost all interest in maintaining contacts with Kyrgyz opposition forces or civil society during the last year of Bakiyev's tenure. They were especially critical of Ambassador Tatiana Gfoeller, whom they accused of refusing meetings with Kyrgyz opposition figures and downplaying nonsecurity issues in the U.S.-Kyrgyz relationship. With the annual lease for Manas pending following the change in government, Interim Kyrgyz Premier Roza Otunbayeva in April renewed the Manas lease under the status quo terms of the 2009 agreement but also declared that the Kyrgyz interim government wanted to review the legal and contractual arrangements governing the base in the future.

The most politically significant of these arrangements are the contracts that govern the supply of fuel at Manas. After the collapse of the Akayev regime, it was discovered that the main Western contractors had funneled hundreds of millions of dollars in subcontracts to fuel providers controlled by the president's family. Immediately following the Tulip Revolution, Bakiyev, then interim president, had proclaimed that the fuel contracts would be changed to benefit Kyrgyzstan as a whole, not just the ruling elite. However, it now appeared that Bakiyev maintained exactly the same arrangements. He and his son, Maxim Bakiyev, allegedly raked in huge profits from exclusive control of half a dozen fuel providers, the distribution network, and storage facilities.[31]

In April 2010 the U.S. House of Representatives Committee on Oversight, Subcommittee of Foreign Affairs and National Security, began an investigation into the contracting practices by the main fuel distributors at Manas—Mina Corporation and its predecessor, Red Star.[32] Mina and Red Star had received over a billion dollars in fuel contracts, yet little is known about the origins or practices of these mysterious companies. Although the report found no direct evidence of corrupt arrangements tied to the Bakiyevs, the investigation uncovered the fact that representatives of Mina had actively colluded with Russian fuel suppliers to falsify documents so as to describe the jet fuel as for civilian use, as opposed to military use.[33] It also faulted DoD and the embassy for turning a blind eye to politically damaging allegations of corruption and exercising inadequate oversight over these contracts.

Realizing that the fuel contract issue threatened the legitimacy of the U.S. presence at Manas, American officials scrambled to make amends with the new government. Michael McFaul, director of Eurasia at the National Security Council and President Barack Obama's special envoy, emphasized that Washington wished to expand engagement with the Central Asian country beyond the Manas base. He and Assistant Secretary of State Robert Blake made several trips to Bishkek in an attempt to repair U.S.-Kyrgyz relations. In July 2010 American officials at an international donor's conference pledged $45 million in assistance to Kyrgyzstan and provided funding and technical assistance for the successful parliamentary election in October 2010. In June 2010 the Department of Defense rebid the tender for the fuel contract, a major concession to the Kyrgyz interim government—though in November Mina once again won the contract, to the astonishment of external observers and Kyrgyz politicians. However, over the next year the political tide turned decisively in favor of a new supplier, and in September 2011 the Department of Defense announced that it would be awarding 20 percent of the fuel contract to Gazpromneft-Aero Kyrgyzstan, with the possibility to expand to 50 percent within three months and then potentially to even reach 90 percent.[34] The new company is a joint venture between the Kyrgyz government and Russian-owned Gazpromneft Aero. American officials also took important steps to improve the transparency of the base's contracting practices and its public relations. The U.S embassy began publishing details on its Web site of primary fuel vendors and their contracts as well as a detailed breakdown of U.S. payments to the government of Kyrgyzstan for the use of the airport and related services. The public affairs office also greatly improved its outreach and communications, including a public Web site, about the transit center, its activities, and local relations.

Yet despite these positive steps, the mood among most Kyrgyz politicians and the Kyrgyz media toward the United States ranged from skepticism to hostility. With a precarious coalition government of weak parties under the new Kyrgyz parliamentary system, some of them openly opposed to Manas, a growing tide of Kyrgyz nationalism, and growing Russian pressure to remove the facility, the status of the transit center remained insecure. In June 2013 the Kyrgyz Parliament passed a declaration, signed by Kyrgyz president Almazbek Atambayev, that the base's lease would not be extended past the July 2014 deadline. In October 2013 U.S. officials confirmed that they would honor the deadline and relocate Afghanistan-related transit operations to the Mihail Kogalniceanu Air Base near the Black Sea in Romania.

Central Lessons from Central Asia

The U.S. basing experience in Central Asia has been relatively short but politically tumultuous. Independent of the security situation in Afghanistan, ruling elites in the Central Asian countries have used the U.S. presence to extract political and economic benefits and have contested the basing presence, or even evicted the United States, when they perceived that targeting the U.S. military presence might serve a useful domestic political purpose. Despite public statements of security cooperation and commitment, the cases of Uzbekistan and Kyrgyzstan show how internal political factors, not American strategy or theater developments, frequently drive the political reception and legal status of overseas bases. The fact that the U.S. "footprints" in Uzbekistan and Kyrgyzstan were relatively light and temporary made little difference in terms of their political receptions.

Whatever the strategic merits of basing arrangements, American officials need to be mindful that expanding the network of U.S. military installations, even if they serve purely logistical roles, is likely to create significant and unforeseen downstream political problems and obstacles. Whether they intend it or not, U.S. forces are likely to be enmeshed in the domestic politics of an array of new overseas host, especially in times of democratic transition or other periods of political change. Host governments will, as they have historically, use U.S. military presence for their own purposes, just as political opposition figures will associate the United States with the objectionable practices of previous governments. In this era of media openness, tacit agreements and unacknowledged quid pro quos are more likely than in the past to be publicized, and the globalization of information networks ensures that base hosts and political opponents are likely to learn from each other and imitate successful political campaigns. From a political perspective, the U.S. operating environment is likely to grow more difficult, not less. American defense planners should bear in mind these potential political complexities when calculating future base relocations, expansions, and consolidations.

Notes

1. For operational details, see GlobalSecurity.org. By summer 2002 the base had defined its role as a major supply hub for operations in Afghanistan and hosted 1,000–1,300 U.S. troops, as well as hundreds of contractor personnel. Security was strict; Uzbek security forces guarded a five-kilometer perimeter around the base.
2. See Olga Oliker and David A. Shlapak, *U.S. Interests in Central Asia: Policy Priorities and Military Roles* (Santa Monica, Calif.: Rand Project Air Force, 2005), 11–19; and Elizabeth Wishnick, *Growing U.S. Security Interests in Central Asia* (Carlisle, Pa.: Strategic Studies Institute, Army War College, 2002), 13–14.
3. See Svante Cornell, "The United States and Central Asia: In the Steppes to Stay?," *Cambridge Review of International Affairs* 17, no. 2 (Summer 2004): 245–56; and Rajan Menon, "The New Great Game in Central Asia," *Survival* 45, no. 2 (Summer 2003): 192–94.
4. Celeste Wallander, "Silk Road: Great Game or Soft Underbelly? The New U.S.-Russia Relationship and Implications for Eurasia," *Journal of Southeast European and Black Sea Studies* 3, no. 3 (September 2003): 96.
5. See the apt warning in Pauline Jones Luong and Erika Weinthal, "New Friends, New Fears in Central Asia," *Foreign Affairs* 81, no. 2 (March/April 2002).

6. For an overview of the IMU and its activities, see Ahmed Rashid, *Jihad: The Rise of Militant Islam in Central Asia* (New Haven, Conn.: Yale University Press, 2002).

7. Jim Nichol, *Uzbekistan's Closure of the Airbase at Karshi-Khanabad: Context and Implications*, Report for Congress (Washington, D.C.: Congressional Research Service, 7 October 2005).

8. Cornell, "United States and Central Asia," 241.

9. Shahram Akbarzadeh, *Uzbekistan and the United States: Authoritarianism, Islamism & Washington's Security Agenda* (New York: ZED, 2005), 75, 78.

10. See "Uzbek-U.S. Declaration Kept Secret," *Washington Post*, 1 July 2002.

11. In Freedom House's annual global survey of political freedoms, Uzbekistan remained at or near the bottom, with scores of 7 for political rights and 6 for civil liberties (out of 7, with 7 being the worst). These scores remained unchanged in 2002–4 and declined to 7 and 7 in 2005, placing Uzbekistan among the most repressive regimes in the world.

12. See Stephen Grey, *Ghost Plane: The True Story of the CIA Torture Program* (New York: St. Martin's, 2006), 170–89.

13. U.S. embassy official, interview, Kyrgyzstan, January 2005.

14. Ganci/Manas military officials, presentation and interview, Kyrgyzstan, January 2005.

15. Ganci/Manas military official, interview, Kyrgyzstan, January 2005.

16. David Cloud, "Pentagon's Fuel Deal Is Lesson in Risks of Graft-Prone Regions," *New York Times*, 15 November 2005.

17. For a similar critical assessment and details, see the investigative report U.S. House of Representatives, *Mystery at Manas: Strategic Blind Spots in the Department of Defense's Fuel Contracts in Kyrgyzstan*, Report of the Majority Staff, John Tierney, Chair, Subcommittee on National Security and Foreign Affairs, Committee on Oversight and Government Reform (Washington, D.C.: December 2010).

18. Quoted in Deborah Klepp, "U.S. Needs a Base *Where*?? How the U.S. Established an Air Base in the Kyrgyz Republic" (unpublished essay, National Defense University, National War College, 2004), 8.

19. See Alexander Cooley, *Depoliticizing Manas: The Domestic Consequences of the U.S. Military Presence in Kyrgyzstan*, PONARS Policy Memo 362 (Washington, D.C.: Program on New Approaches to Research and Security in Eurasia, February 2005), http://csis.org/publication/ponars-policy-memo-362-depoliticizing-manas-domestic-consequences-us-military-presence-k.

20. This section draws on Alexander Cooley, "Base Politics," *Foreign Affairs* 84, no. 6 (November/December 2005): 86–88.

21. Personal communication with NATO political affairs officials, Brussels, June 2005.

22. Donald Rumsfeld, *Known and Unknown: A Memoir* (New York: Sentinel, 2011), 634.

23. For an overview of the post-K2 geopolitical environment, see Gregory Gleason, "The Uzbek Expulsion of U.S. Forces and Realignment in Central Asia,"

Problems of Post-Communism 53, no. 2 (March/April 2006): 49–60; Eugene Rumer, "The U.S. Interests and Role in Central Asia after K2," *Washington Quarterly* 29, no. 3 (Summer 2006): 141–54; and Pavel K. Baev, *Russia's Counterrevolutionary Offensive in Central Asia* (Washington, D.C.: Center for Strategic and International Studies, 2005).

24. None of the foreign officials interviewed in Kyrgyzstan in January 2005, just two months before the regime change, considered regime change or a democratic revolution likely.
25. At that conference, on 11 July 2005, Bakiyev stated, "Today it's possible to move toward reviewing the question concerning the expediency of the American military deployment. . . . Time will show when this [U.S. withdrawal] will happen and what specific process [it will follow]." See "Bakiyev Wins Landslide Victory, Courts Controversy with the United States," *Eurasia Insight Report*, 11 July 2005.
26. Personal communications with senior Kyrgyz official from the Ministry of Foreign Affairs, March and May 2006.
27. See Jim Nichol, *Kyrgyzstan and the Status of the U.S. Manas Airbase: Context and Implications*, Report for Congress (Washington, D.C.: Congressional Research Service, 1 July 2009), http://www.fas.org/sgp/crs/row/R40564.pdf.
28. Interviews with Kyrgyz defense official and base negotiators, Bishkek, January 2008.
29. U.S. House of Representatives, *Mystery at Manas*, 29–32.
30. See Alexander Cooley, "Manas Hysteria: Why the United States Can't Keep Buying Off Kyrgyz Leaders to Keep Its Vital Air Base Open," *Foreign Policy* 12 April 2010, http://www.foreignpolicy.com/articles/2010/04/12/manas_hysteria.
31. Edil Baisalov, chief of staff of the interim Kyrgyz premier Roza Otunbayeva, declared that the fuel provider Mina, along with its predecessor Red Star, was "an indirect way for the Pentagon to bribe the ruling families of Kyrgyzstan." Aram Roston, "Fueling the Afghan War," *Nation*, 10 May 2010, http://www .thenation.com/article/fueling-afghan-war-0#.
32. The author of this chapter testified at the inaugural hearing.
33. U.S. House of Representatives, *Mystery at Manas*.
34. Embassy of the United States, Kyrgyz Republic, "Contract Award for the Provision of Fuel to the Transit Center," 27 September 2011, http://bishkek .usembassy.gov/pr_09_27_2011.html.

8

The Role of Sea Basing

Sam J. Tangredi

S ea basing is a strategic concept that has been defined in a variety of often contradictory ways. It is officially a joint concept, but it is widely perceived as a parochial tool to justify budget increases for the Department of the Navy. As an activity, sea basing has been described as both traditional and transformational.[1] Many proponents consider it a specific set of hardware—future platforms, such as the mobile offshore base. Others advocate for additional ships for the Maritime Prepositioning Force (MPF), like the mobile landing platform, which allows for selective off-load of prepositioned material while still at sea.[2] A misperceived exclusive association with amphibious warfare, not currently a priority in the Pentagon, has largely driven sea basing out of policy discussions at the Office of the Secretary of Defense (OSD) level. Ironically, sea basing came to prominence in the past decade under a chief of naval operations (CNO) determined to cut capabilities from the amphibious fleet so as to fund future surface combatants.[3] From 2002 to 2008 sea basing appeared with great frequency and was discussed with great passion in many professional defense journals and reports. But it is not once mentioned in the Quadrennial Defense Review (QDR) 2010 report.

As a grand concept, it appears becalmed, if still visible out on the horizon. However, as a practical reality, U.S. forces engage in sea basing today— and every day. The U.S. Marine Corps—along with a sometimes supportive, sometimes reluctant U.S. Navy—is projected to continue to make incremental improvements.

What Is Sea Basing All About?

There are both broad and narrow views of what sea basing is about. In its broad vision, "sea basing" refers to the capability to use the sea in the same way that U.S. forces use overseas regional bases for deterrence, alliance support, cooperative security, power projection, and other forward operations.[4] This broad vision stems from conceptual discussions that began within the Navy in the 1990s. It is also reflected in the introductory sections of the more recent Marine Corps–Navy–Army *Concept for Employment for Current Seabasing Capabilities,* released on 19 May 2010.

From that perspective, sea basing is decidedly not a new concept. U.S. forces have been sea basing since the Navy became a global force at the turn of the last century—and arguably even before. "The World War II 'fleet train' [auxiliaries, oilers, and supply ships that replenished the combatant ships at sea] that provided the U.S. battle fleet with such unprecedented range and freedom of action" could be considered a sea base since it allowed the fleet to resupply at sea or in isolated anchorages.[5] Likewise, it is easily observed that aircraft carriers are floating air bases that can be positioned and repositioned on a global basis. Surface ships are sea bases for strike systems (Tomahawk land-attack cruise missiles) as well as for theater ballistic missile defense (BMD) sensors and weapons. Submarines are also—depending on tactical employment—strike sea bases. Amphibious warships constitute the components of a base for forces (primarily Marine Corps) that can be rapidly inserted onto land by both surface and air. Combining with the Navy "grey hulls" of the amphibious fleet are the Military Sealift Command's civilian-crewed MPF ships.[6] The Army also operates prepositioning ships.

However, a narrower view focused on improvements to amphibious and MPF ship capabilities—as exemplified in the report of the Defense Science Board's 2003 Task Force on sea basing—currently predominates in operational discussions of joint capabilities. This narrower view is used by the Marine Corps when justifying incremental improvements in naval expeditionary platforms.

As stated earlier, sea basing has never had one generally accepted definition. We see the term rendered as "seabasing," "sea basing," "Sea Basing," "Enhanced Networked Sea Basing," "seabased," "sea base," and other variants. Each connotes a specific nuance designed to distinguish it from the others. It does have an official Department of Defense (DoD) definition, but one that many authorities agree is not complete: "the deployment, assembly, command projection, reconstitution, and reemployment of joint power from the sea without reliance on land bases within the operational area." The entry adds, "See also amphibious operations (JP-3–02)."[7]

This definition is a great improvement over the previous DoD dictionary version (which stated that sea basing was a technique of amphibious operations), but the note betrays the lingering, near-exclusive association with amphibious warfare. This is one reason why significant discussions of sea basing have not appeared in the defense literature in the past five years. In his tenure as secretary of defense, Robert M. Gates—kept in his position primarily to prevail in the "wars we are in"—appeared to discount the likelihood of major amphibious operations in the coming years. As noted, the QDR 2010 final report and the report of the QDR Independent Review panel never mention sea basing. The QDR 2010 report does include the mobile landing platform (MLP) in its listing of desired naval capabilities.[8] But the three contracted MLPs—the first of which, USNS *Montford Point*, was delivered to the Military Sealift Command in 2013—are designed to facilitate the movement of cargo by "connecting" existing maritime prepositioning ships and do not in themselves indicate a strong commitment to more extensive sea basing.

If, however, sea basing is defined as using the sea in the same way U.S. forces use regional land bases, clearly there can be degrees of sea basing in the same way that there are different types of land bases—from austere to well developed infrastructures. Within this range, sea bases currently exist and have existed; a naval task force—depending on its configuration—can provide joint C4ISR,[9] rapid strike capabilities using stealth or nonstealth assets, special operations forces (SOF) insertion, BMD, control of regional air space, search and rescue, emergency medical facilities, space for joint task force command elements, and a means of positioning of infantry, light armor, and artillery ashore beyond the beach.[10] This capability is comparable to that of a regional land base, relative to the size of personnel assigned. Of course, it can move, thereby making enemy targeting more difficult. Its elements can also be widely dispersed throughout a regional sea, an advantage that can be duplicated ashore only by a network of land bases. Depending on operational requirements, sea-basing platforms may not have to operate in close proximity of one another to provide mutual support.

However, physical limits prevent a current sea base from landing heavy-lift aircraft or storing "iron mountains" of supplies. Nor can it land significant amounts of heavy armor ashore or make an Army or Air Force general feel fully in command of things—an unarticulated detriment to the perception of jointness (though the U.S. Army officially supports sea basing). Yet it can be most assuredly joint—and not simply by virtue of, say, operating Army helicopters off aircraft carriers near Haiti.

In a practical sense, its jointness is not new. Army forces participated in amphibious assaults along with the Marines in the Pacific and on their own in the European theater. Although the largest landing force in World War II—that of the D-day invasion—operated across a narrow channel and therefore was well supported by land-based aircraft, such was not true in North Africa or southern Europe.

Since the essence of sea basing appears to be a traditional American capability, the debate of the past decade primarily focused on the following questions:

- Is it an effective method of countering anti-access defenses?
- How much more capable can sea basing be made by applying new technologies and greater resources?
- Considering that the Navy appears simultaneously to oversell the concept and underfund its resources, will the other services continue to support the concept in the joint arena?[11]
- Does the sea-basing concept justify improvements to Navy–Marine Corps amphibious lift, and will it help the Marine Corps in its struggles with the Navy over new ship programs and OSD over the future of MPF ships?
- Could sea basing become a replacement for, not just a supplement to, regional land bases? Unlike overseas land bases, sea basing remains under sovereign American control and does not require other nations' permission.

Sea Control, Sovereignty, and Anti-access

Sea basing is a capability that depends on command of the sea, or sea control. In fact, it cannot exist without sea control. Since the collapse of the Soviet navy in 1991, U.S. sea control has been a given—unlike the situation in World War II, when the Allies had to fight to achieve sea control. Clearly, the People's Liberation Army intends to contest American sea control in the western Pacific. However, China's maritime capabilities have not yet matched its aspirations, and it is unclear whether Chinese efforts at sea denial would be as effective as the more alarmist reports would indicate.[12] American global sea control is not yet broken, presumably ensuring the continued viability of sea basing. But the growing ambition among littoral states for regional denial capabilities—generally referred to as anti-access/area denial strategies (sometimes by the acronym A2/AD)—is itself undeniable.

Because it is dependent on sea control, the U.S. Navy would naturally provide the majority of resources for sea-basing platforms out of its existing fleet and ship-construction budget.[13] Originally the Donald Rumsfeld–era Office of Defense Transformation defined "sea base" as "a noun; the sea and not the things on it."[14] However, the sea base can be more properly thought of as the ships and platforms on which—and by which—the forces are positioned. The ocean is the fluid medium that provides both the terrain upon which heavy objects move and the reduction in friction that allows them to do so—metaphorically, the ocean allows castles to move. These iron castles constitute the sea base. Within the castles are stored and transported the means of military power, including the expeditionary strength of the Marine Corps and resupply for Army land forces. These castles also provide the best available logistical platforms for humanitarian assistance in littoral regions.

As mentioned earlier, a most attractive feature of sea basing is that it offers an overseas base of operation located close to or in a crisis area but that it is completely under the sovereignty of the United States.[15] The strike power that can be projected from the continental United States is just a small portion of that required to affect events on land in combat or crisis. Sea basing provides for a forward presence and thereby produces deterrence effects that might not be achievable through latent conventional capabilities in the continental United States. Sea basing is also a means of providing sustained security cooperation and humanitarian relief. All of this can be achieved without long-term violation of anyone else's sovereign territory under international law.

Proponents of sea basing like to quote British naval strategist Sir Julian S. Corbett's observation (1906) that Britain—then the world's greatest sea power—traditionally favored sovereign ports and bases that made it "independent of uncertain neutrals and doubtful allies."[16] But to justify spending resources on sea basing by the need for such independence is to oversell the concept. America's current allies or partners are for the most part neither weak nor uncertain, and in the current political environment it is doubtful that they would place disabling restrictions on basing in the face of a mutual threat. Indeed, if anything, current trends seem to be in the direction of an increasing willingness on the part even of untraditional allies (such as Singapore) to accommodate an American military presence on their territory. However, it is valid to argue that spending on sea basing should be increased on the grounds that anti-access capabilities of potential opponents (primarily China and Iran) have made fixed regional land bases extremely vulnerable.

Sea basing itself faces an increasing threat but because of its mobility represents a much more difficult targeting problem for opponents. However, can new sea-basing technologies ultimately outpace the anti-access threat? The Navy and Marine Corps are planning incremental improvements in expeditionary off-load from sea to shore. The development of theater ballistic missile defenses and the improved air defense represented by destroyers and cruisers having the Aegis combat system gives additional protection to the sea base. But if future survivability proves increasingly problematic, will a significant investment in improving overall sea basing have been warranted? If it appears that it would, what technological improvements should be prioritized?

Right now technological and engineering improvements are being applied to expeditionary off-load. These are relatively low-cost improvements. But more extensive acquisition—such as the mobile offshore base (MOB), proposed in the 1990s—has lost favor in light of other priorities and anti-access issues. Proposed increases to the naval amphibious fleet are also vulnerable to these concerns. This debate—sea basing versus anti-access—has smoldered for some time and will likely get hotter.

Sea Basing in Sea Power 21

Sea basing (or "Sea Basing," as it appears in Sea Power 21) was touted as one of the pillars of the "Sea Power 21" plan, issued by Adm. Vern Clark as CNO, specifically as a means of "projecting joint operational independence."[17] It was also described "as the foundation from which offensive and defensive fires [that is, strikes from a distance, by artillery, air, missile, etc.] are projected—making Sea Strike and Sea Shield [two other pillars] realities."[18] But the plan omitted any discussion of amphibious ships and emphasized the strike capability of the cruiser-destroyer force.[19] To omit in this way the capability of the sea base to put forces ashore would seem to ignore the most significant means by which the sea base can affect events on land and limits sea basing to fleet strike and defense—unless the omission in fact reflected a predecided budget priority. Clearly, Admiral Clark intended to emphasize the Navy's role in supporting joint forces already ashore; he expressed support for MPF shipping in resupply of those forces. But this role would be a joint supporting capability rather than a joint enabler.

Yet the emphasis on supporting joint forces via a new concept would not seem to have engendered much enthusiasm from other services in the joint arena except as a quid pro quo—"I'll support your program if you'll support mine." In fact, it would seem almost a deliberate provocation of the Marine Corps, which would consider itself a full partner in any new naval concept. These factors resulted in the Navy's overselling sea basing in the sense that it relied on old missions to justify a supposedly new construct. This was not an auspicious way to advance the concept, but it did allow the Navy in 2002 to squeeze some money from amphibious shipbuilding—a decision that, given the length of time required for shipbuilding, directly affects today's fleet.[20] The overall result is that even today it is not clear—Admiral Clark's successors having largely ignored Sea Power 21—what the Navy staff considers sea basing to be.

The Future of the U.S. Marine Corps "Expeditionary Objective"

Since the Navy construct of sea basing did not include the Marine Corps, the Marines did what they do best—declared it an expeditionary objective and took it. Sea basing was turned around from a concept that largely excluded amphibious-assault capabilities to one focused on improving them. Such a focus would seem natural, even within the broad vision. But it did not bank on Secretary of Defense Gates' and his successors' apparent discounting of the need for strong amphibious capabilities—capabilities that were not particularly needed in Iraq or Afghanistan. Succesful OSD efforts to kill the Expeditionary Fighting Vehicle program—and the Marine Corps' previously tenacious efforts to keep it alive despite significant operational limitations and cost increases—may have also colored the secretary of defense's attitude toward amphibious capabilities, MPF, and sea basing.

Consequently, the Marine Corps now views sea basing as a program of incremental improvements in amphibious lift and is primarily interested in developing the ability to use MPF ships without having to off-load them in port. Off-loading at sea, particularly in a combat environment, requires modern connector ships, such as the MLP, which can transfer matériel from cargo carriers of the Maritime Sealift Command to air-cushion landing craft in the sequence that is needed ashore. This approach would increase expeditionary landing capacity without the higher costs of building more amphibious warships.

But although the Marines have experimented with incremental improvements and have received partial QDR endorsement, the Defense Department's "program objective memorandum" for fiscal year 2012 has mandated a drastic cut in the Navy's prepositioning budget. This could put two-thirds of the current MPF into reserve status or eliminate one of the three maritime prepositioning squadrons—specifically MPS Squadron 1, located in the Mediterranean.[21] The decision reflects OSD's perception that the U.S. European Command and NATO will most likely not need the equipment in the immediate future. Nonetheless, a two-thirds cut, as opposed to an incremental reduction, does not bode well for the overall concept of sea basing.

Even as Under Secretary of the Navy Robert O. Work, an expert on sea basing, was outlining a future with more individually capable MPF ships in a 5 October 2010 speech at the National Defense Industrial Association's Expeditionary Warfare Conference, it was becoming apparent that his view might not be shared on the OSD level. At the same conference, Brig. Gen. David Berger, director of the operations division at Headquarters, Marine Corps, described the defense leadership as divided between those who view MPS squadron ships as merely "floating warehouses" and those who see them as a forward crisis-response capability in support of the regional combatant commanders. Gen. James Conway, near the end of his tenure as commandant of the Marine Corps, defended Navy-Marine prepositioning by contrasting it with the Army's view of prepositioning, which he described as simply a fast means of resupplying forces already engaged on the ground. As Conway put it, "The Army uses theirs to support a capability. In many ways, ours [Navy–Marine Corps MPF] *is* the [crisis-response] capability."[22]

Supplementing or Replacing Land Bases?

Whether sea basing can replace land bases, or at least dependence on land bases, raises bureaucratic issues within DoD that contribute to the reluctance to commit to joint sea basing. For one thing, a greater commitment to sea basing— along with a qualitative or quantitative reduction in overseas land bases—might cause allies and partners to question American commitment to mutual defense. To some extent, however, it is a question of foresight. If the future of American war fighting consists of pacifying terror-supporting insurgent groups within land-locked countries or continuing the use of quick-striking SOF units supported by land-based tactical aviation (including unmanned aerial vehicles flown from the continental United States), investment in sea basing would not seem a priority.[23] At times this seems to be the OSD view, but not always.[24] If future wars are going to be dominated by ever more precise global strikes from the continental United States—which would seem to be the U.S. Air Force's preferred future—sea basing would also seem a low priority.

However, if the future involves a range of regional crises in which the United States wishes to retain direct influence, there is a lot to commend sea basing as a primary instrument. As anti-access capabilities of potential opponents expand, the survival of regional land bases becomes problematic. The exact locations of these bases are well known; they can be struck repeatedly by ballistic missiles relying solely on preprogrammed coordinates. But prioritizing sea basing could also mean a future defense posture in which overall DoD force structure is predominantly maritime. Relying primarily on naval assets as the foundation of most joint force regional basing could be seen as a defeat for jointness—which is still largely considered in DoD to mean proportional shares of the pie for all services (and major defense agencies). This is a formula that the Gates and Panetta Pentagons did not break, and as defense cuts are imposed on major acquisition programs, it is likely that they will affect the services roughly equally.

Although the developing planning related to the "Air/Sea Battle" operational concept would seem to be bringing Air Force–Navy cooperation to a peak, the potential for competition for resources between sea basing and global strike in a flat defense budget is obvious. At the same time, the Air Force has not been keen to admit the vulnerability of its long-term regional bases, which are presumed to be required if land-based tactical aviation is to be effectively applied to a regional contingency. The Army has an interest in resupplying its forces—presumably already on the ground—by sea, but it has no interest in becoming a second marine corps. The Army's focus—with program leadership by the Department of the Navy—was on the development of the joint high-speed vessel (JHSV), a ferry-based logistics catamaran built by Austal USA. The JHSV, which is not considered combat survivable, is designed for high-speed insertion of troops in "'soft power' missions—responding to natural disasters, providing humanitarian assistance, conducting port visits and training partner military forces, among others."[25] Subsequent to the construction of the initial JHSV, full responsibility for the program was transferred to the Navy.

Under these circumstances, sea-basing proponents might emphasize supplementing regional bases rather than replacing them. But in a flat or shrinking defense budget, "supplementing" any capability would likely be seen as a luxury.

The Reality in the Asia-Pacific

At the same time there is a practical crosscurrent in the Asia-Pacific region that might force the United States to look to sea basing as a land-basing replacement—the agreed shift of Marine Corps personnel from Okinawa to Guam.

Thus far the question of sea basing versus land bases has been discussed in terms of which posture is more defensible and could deliver more capabilities. But in the Asia-Pacific the most troubling contingencies remain possible conflicts in the Taiwan Strait and Korea. Okinawa is 110 nautical miles (200 kilometers) from Taiwan and approximately 670 nautical miles (1,250 kilometers) from Seoul, Korea. Guam is over 1,470 nautical miles (2,700 kilometers) from Taiwan and 5,900 nautical miles (11,000 kilometers) from Seoul. The greater distances from Guam to either potential point of conflict would appear to require a more extensive amphibious transport operation than would be necessary from Okinawa. That means, first, a need for greater at-sea logistics, more fuel being but one consideration. Second, the force would be exposed to potential standoff attacks for a longer period before it could reach its effective operational area. The decision to base Marine Corps forces on a rotational basis in Darwin, Australia, may bolster America's overall presence in Asia-Pacific as well as supplement Australia's defense posture. But these forces are even further from Taiwan, at 2,246 nautical miles (4,160 kilometers) distance.

Another consequence of the shift is a possible reduction in practical deterrence. A swift Chinese campaign across the Taiwan Strait would likely be intended as a fait accompli that would preclude American reaction. In calculating the potential for success, whether an opposing force is 110 or 1,470 nautical miles away makes a considerable difference. It is unreasonable to argue that air transport can make up for this distance, since airlift cannot move significant amounts of equipment. Although the JHSV could transit quicker than amphibious warships, it requires port facilities for off-loading and has a limited payload. The overall result is a lessening of a previously well-established deterrent to precipitate action.

Three options to overcome this tyranny of distance are to station more heavy equipment closer to the area of potential conflict and rely on the airlifting or "JHSV-ing" of troops into the theater, establish other land bases closer to the area, rely on global strikes from the continental United States, or maintain or be able to quickly assemble a robust sea base within striking distance of the area.

Stationing more heavy equipment in the region and relying on airlifted troops to man it reduces the footprint required by a land base, but the question of where the equipment sets can be located remains. A possibility is Okinawa, if the Japanese government were to agree. Another possibility is on Taiwan itself, but regional political considerations currently make that choice imprudent. Establishing extensive land bases would seem to pose the same problem: Where would they be located? Again, both equipment locations and land bases have fixed coordinates, well known to an attacker.

Strikes from the continental United States simply cannot be relied upon in such a scenario; the nation is not now capable of effective conventional strikes from that distance.

All this leads to the conclusion that the ability to assemble a robust sea base—defined broadly—from forward-deployed joint and naval forces would be the most effective tool and means of practical deterrence in such a conflict. Although anti-access systems can certainly threaten a sea base, targeting moving ships at sea is still a much more difficult problem than is attacking fixed points on land. For example, deception is a much more viable tactic for a sea base than for an unmoving land base.

The Future of Sea Basing: Reality and Recommendations

Thinking about Sea basing: All Ahead Slow is the title of Robert Work's magisterial study of this subject, and it reflects an approach he later espoused as undersecretary of the Navy. It is an apt recommendation for a defense-program environment in which sea basing is not viewed as a priority. Under the constrained budgets of the 1920s and early 1930s, the Marine Corps experimented with amphibious warfare, ultimately developing the concepts and equipment that would enable the great advances in amphibious assault needed in World War II. Experimentation, with modest programmatic investment, might do the same in advancing sea basing until its need is apparent for future contingencies.

However, if one takes the broader view of sea basing, the responsibility for improving the capacity to sea base falls primarily on the Navy—which must also make particular efforts to gain joint support for that broad vision. Dispersed platforms must be netted (securely) together with the overall fleet functioning as a multiple-domain, combined-arms base rather than as a group of independent task forces. Former CNO Adm. Gary Roughead called for greater efforts in developing "revolutionary concepts" for naval information and computing, and his combining the naval intelligence (N2) and C4ISR (N6) branches of his staff indicated his interest in the tighter netting of information. Current CNO Adm. Jonathan Greenert has repeatedly identified operations in the electro-magnetic spectrum, which would include defense of networks as well as offensive operations, as one of his top priorities. Tighter netting of dispersed platforms is indeed a requirement for successful sea basing, but it is obviously not sufficient in itself.[26]

The current Pentagon must deal with a quandary regarding sea basing. Experiences in Iraq and Afghanistan will sour future administrations on extensive commitments of ground forces in crisis-torn states. On the surface, this would seem to refocus DoD on improving naval capabilities, but because sea basing remains associated with putting ashore forces that are larger than SOF units (e.g., Marine expeditionary units), it is unlikely to attract more than incremental investment.

One mission that might increase interest in a tightly netted sea base is naval ballistic-missile defense since reliable information from multiple sources (including land-based) can increase the probability of accurate target solutions. But it is easy to foresee BMD-capable ships as being treated as individual strategic assets that are operationally separate from conventional forces. This would be a mistake. The Aegis destroyer providing ballistic- or cruise-missile defense is as much a part of the sea base as a Patriot battery defending an overseas land base is part of that base's combat infrastructure. At the same time, the ballistic-missile defense provided to the land territory of allies by that same Aegis destroyer is as integral an aspect of the overall sea-base mission as is the capability for landing troops ashore. The logistical network that flows through the sea base—such as fuel delivery by fleet oilers—is the means of keeping the Aegis destroyer on station.

Here are four recommendations for the Pentagon's consideration:

- Examine and experiment with the broad vision of sea basing, particularly in conjunction with developing a joint operational concept for anti-access warfare and elaborating the particulars of Air/Sea Battle.
- If a decision is made to reduce MPS squadrons, a significant portion of the savings should be invested in the Marine Corps' programs for increasing the capabilities of the remaining MPF through new technologies and platforms. This is in keeping with earlier statements by Secretary Gates that the services could keep most of the savings from cuts made. Obviously, current fiscal restraints may obviate retention of any such savings. But enhancing retained capabilities to mitigate part of the reduction is still logical.
- Maintain naval BMD platforms as integral parts of deployed conventional forces—part of the sea base as it exists today—rather than isolate them as an element of strategic deterrence (which may occur in conjunction with the installation of Aegis Ashore in Europe).
- Assess the deterrent effect and responsiveness that sea basing can have in an Asia-Pacific region in which land bases are not close to potential points of conflict. This requires more extensive study of the comparative survivability of sea basing under anti-access conditions.

Defense policy is all about making choices: who or what is the threat; what strategy should we adopt; how should we position or deploy our forces? As noted, it is also about managing resources, even for the United States, with its incomparable military but current fiscal crisis. Since there is no certain answer, risk is always involved, and alternative strategies must always be considered and evaluated. It is the responsibility of defense planners and, especially, the defense leadership to mitigate the risks as much as possible. As a concept, sea basing has the potential to mitigate risks involving overseas basing, anti-access defenses, and regional presence. The priority given to mitigating these specific risks will be an accurate indicator of the future that the defense leadership envisions.

A prudent strategy for the United States that mitigates risk in uncertain times would be to strengthen capabilities that do not rely on nonsovereign overseas basing even while working diplomatically to maintain alliances and access to overseas bases. It would appear best to invest in a balance between SOF capabilities, long-range capabilities based in the continental United States (such as global strike), and highly maneuverable and well-defended sea bases. These capabilities would seem both compatible and complementary. U.S.-based forces can provide extensive firepower but cannot sustain "boots on the ground" in a contested region. Most current American interests overseas lie within range of sea-based forces, our involvement in Afghanistan notwithstanding. In fact, over 70 percent of initial air operations over Afghanistan (before full establishment of the Manas Air Base in Kyrgyzstan) were conducted by naval aircraft flying from aircraft carriers operating in the Indian Ocean and tanked en route.

However, tighter resource constraints usually bring out the worst in organizational rivalries and bureaucratic politics; a clash between sea basing, global strike, planning for future wars "like the wars we are in" (or even recently in), recapitalizing or "resetting" land forces, and expanding special-operations capabilities seems inevitable. Under the current Pentagon leadership and the economic constraints facing the U.S. government, such a clash would likely find sea basing on the short end.

Notes

An earlier version of this article was published as an "E-Note" by the Foreign Policy Research Institute, Philadelphia, Pennsylvania, www.fpri.org, in November 2010, and as the article "Sea Basing: Concept, Issues and Recommendations," *Naval War College Review* 64, no. 4 (Autumn 2011): 28–41.

   1. Robert Work, *Thinking about Seabasing: All Ahead, Slow* (Washington, D.C.: Center for Strategic and Budgetary Assessments, 2006), iv. See also Work, "On Sea Basing," in *Reposturing the Force: U.S. Overseas Presence in the Twenty-first Century*, Newport Paper 26, ed. Carnes Lord, 95–181 (Newport, R.I.: Naval War College Press, 2006). Another excellent study that emphasizes historical continuity of sea basing while crediting its transformational attributes is Gregory J. Parker, *Seabasing since the Cold War: Maritime Reflections of American Grand Strategy* (Washington, D.C.: Brookings Institution Press, 30 June 2010).
   2. One of the strongest proponents of the mobile offshore base (MOB) in the 1990s was Adm. William A. Owens, USN. See his *High Seas: The Naval Passage to an Uncharted World* (Annapolis, Md.: Naval Institute Press, 1995), 163, 165; and William A. Owens and Ed Offley, *Lifting the Fog of War* (New York: Farrar,

Straus and Giroux, 2000), 175–76, 205. See also an excellent discussion in Henry J. Hendrix II, "Exploit Sea Basing," U.S. Naval Institute *Proceedings* 129, no. 8 (August 2003), 61–63. Commander Parker's *Seabasing since the Cold War* study includes one of the best artist's interpretations of the MOB—originally drawn by John Berkey for the April 2003 edition of *Popular Mechanics* (p. 8.)

3. This is my interpretation of Adm. Vern Clark's decisions as chief of naval operations in the early 2000s. Such a motive was never publicly stated. See Work, *Thinking about Seabasing.*

4. Commander Parker has an admirably succinct way of describing what sea basing is about: "It's about Land" (Parker, *Seabasing since the Cold War*, 5). Moreover, it can be described as turning sea into land.

5. Work, *Thinking about Seabasing*, 9.

6. This broad vision interpretation is consistent with sea basing as defined in the U.S. Navy's 2002 policy "Sea Power 21," except that Sea Power 21 made no mention of amphibious ships as part of sea basing—an incomprehensible, albeit deliberate, omission. Work critically discusses this omission, dismissing Navy staff excuses that Sea Power 21 was a "Navy" document not a "naval" document, that was accordingly not intended to include the Marine Corps or, thus, the amphibious ships associated with it (Work, *Thinking about Seabasing*, 163–65). But he does not mention the key factor that the chief of naval operations, Admiral Clark, whose career had been almost exclusively in ships of the cruiser-destroyer type, had little if any interest in expending shipbuilding resources on amphibious ships. Rather, he saw reductions in amphibious capabilities as a "bill payer" for increasing the capabilities of the cruiser-destroyer force. On Sea Power 21, see Vern Clark, "Sea Power 21: Projecting Joint Power," U.S. Naval Institute *Proceedings* 128, no. 10 (October 2002): 32–41.

7. U.S. Defense Department, *Department of Defense Dictionary of Military and Associated Terms*, Joint Publication 1-02 (Washington, D.C.: DoD, 12 April 2001 [as amended through 31 July 2010]), http://wstiac.alionscience.com/pdf/dodmilitarydictionary.pdf, 412.

8. U.S. Defense Department, *Quadrennial Defense Review Report* (Washington, D.C.: February 2010), http://www.defense.gov/qdr/QDR%20as%20of%2029JAN10%201600.pdf, 46.

9. Command, control, communications, computers, intelligence, surveillance, and reconnaissance.

10. Primary stealth assets being cruise and conventional ballistic-missile-launching submarines (SSGN).

11. The development of a Seabasing Joint Integrating Concept (JIC) in 2005 can be seen as joint service support.

12. See discussions in Sam J. Tangredi, "No Game Changer for China," U.S. Naval Institute *Proceedings* 136, no. 2 (February 2010): 24–29; and Craig Hooper and Christopher Albon, "Get off the Fainting Couch," U.S. Naval Institute *Proceedings* 136, no. 4 (April 2010): 42–46.

13. This would not seem as contentious an issue under the broad definition as it does under the narrow one—in which case it seems a more obvious a case of resource trade-offs between surface combatants and amphibious warships.

14. Work, *Thinking about Seabasing*, 8.
15. Sovereignty might be shared with allies or partner nations if they provided ships, platforms, or personnel for the sea base.
16. Quoted in Work, *Thinking about Seabasing*, 17.
17. Clark, "Sea Power 21," 36.
18. Ibid.
19. Work, *Thinking about Seabasing*, 9.
20. See Grace V. Jean, "Marines Question the Utility of Their New Amphibious Warship," *National Defense*, September 2008, http://www.nationaldefensemag azine.org/archive/2008/September/Pages/MarinesQuestiontheUtilityof.aspx.
21. Cid Standifer, "Work: Prepositioning Set for Big Changes," *Inside the Navy*, 11 October 2010.
22. Ibid. Italics supplied, to reflect emphasis as originally spoken.
23. It can be argued that sea basing is also valuable in small, often short-duration operations that can be supported by air based in the continental United States and involve only a small number of troops on the ground, with naval forces providing the logistics, command and control, and quick-reaction "fires."
24. In a 2009 *Foreign Affairs* article, Secretary Gates outlined his plan as being one that maintains balance "between trying to prevail in current conflicts and preparing for other contingencies, between institutionalizing capabilities such as counterinsurgency and foreign military assistance and maintaining the United States' existing conventional and strategic technological edge against other military forces, and between retaining those cultural traits that have made the U.S. armed forces successful and shedding those that hamper their ability to do what needs to be done." While "other contingencies" could indicate operations that sea basing could facilitate, it should be noted that he refers to maintaining "the United States' existing conventional and strategic technological edge" rather than an existing edge in capabilities. Analyses of the article have pointed to "balance capabilities" as meaning a balance across the spectrum of conflict—but that may not be what was meant. In any event, the secretary's natural focus has been on unconventional warfare, counterinsurgency, and counterterror—in which sea basing would play largely a supplemental role, not a critical role. There are no indications that former secretary Leon Panetta or current secretary Chuck Hagel differ in this view. Robert M. Gates, "A Balanced Strategy: Reprogramming the Pentagon for a New Age," *Foreign Affairs* 88, no. 1 (January–February 2009).
25. Grace V. Jean, "Joint High Speed Vessels: Great Potential, But Questions Remain," *National Defense*, March 2011, http://www.nationaldefensemagazine .org/archive/2011/March/Pages/Aluminum%E2%80%98Truck%E2%80%99JointHighSpeedVesselGreatPotential,ButQuestionsRemain.aspx.
26. Andrew Burt, "New Memo from CNO: Roughead Seeks 'Revolutionary' Concepts in Information and Computing," *Inside the Navy*, 11 October 2010.

About the Contributors

Alexander Cooley is professor and chair of the Department of Political Science at Barnard College, Columbia University, in New York. Professor Cooley's research examines the politics of state sovereignty and international military basing arrangements with a focus on U.S. and Russian overseas bases. He is the author of dozens of academic articles and four books, including *Base Politics: Democratic Change and the U.S. Military Overseas* (Cornell University Press, 2008) and *Great Games, Local Rules: The New Great Power Contest in Central Asia* (New York: Oxford University Press, 2012). Cooley earned both his MA (1995) and PhD (1999) at Columbia University.

Walter C. Ladwig III is an assistant professor in international relations at the University of Oxford. He is also a Visiting Fellow at the Royal United Services Institute for Defence and Security Studies and an affiliate of the Corbett Centre for Maritime Policy Studies at Kings College London. Ladwig is the author of nearly a dozen scholarly articles and book chapters that examine aspects of Indian military modernization and its foreign policy in East Asia and Southeast Asia as well as the geopolitics of the Indian Ocean region. Previously he was attached to the speechwriting staff of the U.S. secretary of defense; worked as a consultant to the U.S. Department of Defense in Washington, D.C.; and managed the Afghanistan, NATO, and Central Asia portfolios for the political section of the U.S. Embassy in London. Ladwig holds a BA from the University of Southern California, an MPA from Princeton University, and a PhD from the University of Oxford.

Jack McCaffrie is a visiting fellow at the Australian National Centre for Ocean Resources and Security at Wollongong University, having retired from the Royal Australian Navy (RAN) in February 2003 on returning from his final posting as naval attaché in Washington, D.C. He is also a PhD student at the center. His current and recent work includes coauthoring *Navies of South-East Asia: A Comparative Study* (Cass, 2012) and writing, as a naval reservist, the second edition of the RAN's doctrine publication *Australian Maritime Operations.*

Lt. Justin Mikolay served as speechwriter to the Commander, U.S. Central Command from August 2009 until October 2011. A native of Hudson, Ohio, he graduated with a bachelor's degree in political science from the U.S. Naval Academy, Annapolis, Maryland, in 2001, as a Secretary of the Navy Distinguished Graduate. Lieutenant Mikolay served as electrical officer, damage control assistant, diving officer, emergent dry dock coordinator, and SCUBA diving officer in USS *San Juan* (SSN 751). Tours ashore include senior instructor at the Naval Academy's Political Science Department. Lieutenant Mikolay is a graduate of the Woodrow Wilson School of Public and International Affairs at Princeton University with a master's degree in public affairs, concentrating in international relations.

Chris Rahman is senior research fellow in maritime strategy and security at the Australian National Centre for Ocean Resources and Security (ANCORS), University of Wollongong. He is an academic strategist, researching contemporary issues in maritime strategy, Australian defense policy, China, and the strategic relations of the Indo-Pacific region. He is currently coordinating a major project on the history of the Pacific Patrol Boat Program and manages the ANCORS Vessel Tracking Initiative in collaboration with industry and Australian government partners.

Terence Roehrig is a professor of national security affairs and the director of the Asia-Pacific Studies Group at the Naval War College. He is a coauthor of the forthcoming book *South Korea's Rise in World Affairs: Power, Economic Development, and Foreign Policy* (Cambridge University Press) and has published articles and book chapters on Korean and East Asian security issues, North Korea's nuclear weapons program, and the U.S.–South Korea alliance. He received his PhD in political science from the University of Wisconsin–Madison and is a past president of the Association of Korean Political Studies.

Sam J. Tangredi is the author of *Anti-Access Warfare: Countering A2/AD Strategies* (Naval Institute Press, 2013) as well as three previous books and more than one hundred journal articles and book chapters on defense issues. A U.S. Navy captain now retired from active duty, he is director of San Diego operations for the planning and consulting firm Strategic Insight Ltd. While on active duty, Tangredi served as the head of the strategy and concepts branch of the Office of the Chief of Naval Operations and director of strategic planning and business development for the Navy International Programs Office, as well as in other strategic planning billets. His operational assignments included command of USS *Harpers Ferry* (LSD 49). Dr. Tangredi is a graduate of the U.S. Naval Academy and the Naval Postgraduate School, and he earned his PhD in international relations from the University of Southern California.

Toshi Yoshihara is professor of strategy and the John A. van Beuren Chair of Asia-Pacific Studies at the Naval War College. Previously, he was a visiting professor in the Strategy Department at the Air War College. Dr. Yoshihara has also served as an analyst at the Institute for Foreign Policy Analysis, RAND Corporation, and the American Enterprise Institute. He is author of numerous articles on maritime issues and naval strategy; coauthor of *Red Star over the Pacific: China's Rise and the Challenge to U.S. Maritime Strategy* (Naval Institute Press, 2010), *Indian Naval Strategy in the Twenty-First Century* (Routledge, 2009), and *Chinese Naval Strategy in the Twenty-First Century: The Turn to Mahan* (Routledge, 2008); and coeditor of *Asia Looks Seaward: Power and Maritime Strategy* (Praeger, 2008). Dr. Yoshihara holds a PhD from the Fletcher School of Law and Diplomacy, Tufts University.

The Editors

Andrew S. Erickson is an associate professor in the Strategic Research Department at the Naval War College and a core founding member of the department's China Maritime Studies Institute (CMSI). He is an associate in research at Harvard University's John King Fairbank Center for Chinese Studies. Erickson also serves as an expert contributor to the *Wall Street Journal*'s "China Real Time Report." In the spring of 2013 he deployed as a Regional Security Education Program scholar with the USS *Nimitz* carrier strike group. Erickson is a term member of the Council on Foreign Relations. In 2012 the National Bureau of Asian Research awarded him the inaugural Ellis Joffe Prize for PLA Studies. Erickson has taught courses at the Naval War College and Yonsei University and has lectured extensively at academic and government institutions in the United States and Asia. He received his PhD and MA in international relations and comparative politics from Princeton University and graduated magna cum laude from Amherst College with a BA in history and political science. Erickson is the author of the Jamestown Foundation monograph *Chinese Anti-Ship Ballistic Missile Development* (2013) and coauthor of the CMSI monographs *Chinese Anti-Piracy Operations in the Gulf of Aden* (2013) and *Chinese Mine Warfare* (2009). His coauthored book *Assessing China's Cruise Missile Ambitions* will soon be published by National Defense University Press. Erickson's research is available on his two websites, www.andrewerickson.com and www.chinasign post.com.

Carnes Lord, professor in the College of Operational and Strategic Leadership at the Naval War College, is a political scientist with broad interests in international and strategic studies, national security organization and management, and political philosophy. Lord holds PhD degrees from Cornell University and Yale University and has taught political science at Yale University, the University of Virginia, and the Fletcher School of Law and Diplomacy. He has held senior positions in the U.S. government, including as director of international communications and information policy on the National Security Council staff, assistant to the vice president for national security affairs, and distinguished fellow at the National Defense University. Lord is the author of, among other works, *The Presidency and the Management of National Security* (Free Press, 1988), *The Modern Prince: What Leaders Need to Know Now* (Yale University Press, 2003), and *Losing Hearts and Minds? Strategic Influence and Public Diplomacy in the Age of Terror* (Praeger, 2006); editor of *Reposturing the Force: U.S. Overseas Presence in the Twenty-First Century* (Naval War College Press, 2006); and coeditor of *China Goes to Sea: Maritime Transformation in Comparative Historical Perspective* (Naval Institute Press, 2009).

Index

intelligence-gathering and strategic communications facilities, 93–94

Iran: ballistic missile arsenal of, xiv; overthrow of shah and U.S. interests in region, 141; Strait of Hormuz security challenges, 135; U.S. force positioning and, 132

Iraq: base construction and increase in military presence in, 3–4, 8; Desert Storm operation and interservice debate about responsibility for victory, 57–58; Diego Garcia basing for operations in, 159; Iraqi Freedom operation, 17; number of overseas bases and facilities, 12n12; personnel and resources for war in, 73; U.S. national security interests in, 135

Japan: Aegis-equipped defense platforms, 161; alliance relationship with U.S., 16, 39, 59–60, 72; Chinese military buildup and national security of, 41; Chinese strategy to exploit vulnerabilities of, 41; defense policy and U.S.-ROK alliance, 72; demographic changes and manpower for military service, 40–41; Diego Garcia basing and maritime power projection by, 160–61; earthquake, tsunami, and nuclear meltdown in, 16, 40; economy of, 40; energy needs of, 133; exercises and training facilities for defense force, 21; games and studies on possible war with, xiii; maritime economy and supply chain, dependence on, 41; political and diplomatic relationships between U.S. and, 16; political complications related to U.S. forces in Okinawa, 5, 15, 41, 181; population of, 40; public opposition to U.S. military presence, 41; Taepodong missile launch, 56; territorial disputes between China and, 41, 43; U.S. commitment to security of, 41–42, 43; U.S.-Japan alliance and Chinese missile strike threat, 59–60; weather conditions and challenges, 18. *See also* Okinawa

Japanese bases: air bases, 5; aircraft carrier basing, 25, 42, 43; benefits to Japan, 40, 41–42; Chinese interest in and policy toward, 5–6, 38–39, 42, 43–48, 161; drawdown of U.S. forces, 3; humanitarian and disaster-response operations from, 40; island chain defense perimeter, 45–48; Kure Naval Base, 36, 46; Maizuru base, 46; map of military facilities, 36; Misawa Air Base, 36, 39, 42, 123; missile defense capabilities of, 46–47; missile threat to, 5–6, 28, 38–39, 48–58; naval bases, 5, 42; North Korean threat to South Korea and U.S. forces, 42; number of bases and facilities and forces assigned to, 12n12, 42; Sasebo Naval Base, 36, 46, 47–48, 53; strategic importance of, 5, 39–42, 44–48; Taiwan crisis and support for U.S. operations, 28, 38–39, 43, 46; value of facilities and real estate, 42; Yokosuka Naval Base, 25, 36, 42, 43, 46–47, 50, 51, 53, 56; Yokota Air Base, 36, 42. *See also* Okinawa

Kyrgyzstan: base construction and increase in military presence in, 4, 8, 183–84; base-related payments and economic impact of U.S. base, 186–88, 191–94, 197n31; domestic politics and basing arrangements, 182–83, 194–95; Manas base, 8, 182, 183, 186–88, 190–94, 210; map of military facilities, 180; political and diplomatic relationships between U.S. and, 8, 181–84, 186–88, 190–95; renegotiation of basing contract, 8, 182, 188, 190–92, 197n25; Russian aid to, 8, 182, 191, 192; threat of expulsion of U.S. forces from, 8, 182, 194; Tulip Revolution, 190, 193, 197n24

littoral combat ships (LCS), 7, 120–21

logistics: Australian facilities for, 104–5; global infrastructure for, xiv, 4, 12n13; Guam as hub for, 17, 19, 30;

cruise missiles launched from, 28;
deployment cycle, 149, 173–74n101;
Diego Garcia basing, 131, 146, 148,
149–50, 172n93, 173nn95–96,
173–174n101; Guam basing of,
18–19, 21–22, 23, 30; nuclear reactor
utilization and Pacific transit times,
18; recoring nuclear submarines,
32n12
Suez Canal, 132–34, 138, 150, 174n104

Taiwan and Taiwan Strait: air defense
capabilities, 38; Chinese strategy
toward regional bases and crisis
in, 43; independence of and 1996
missile tests, 58; missile threat to,
28, 37–38, 51, 59; response to 1958
crisis, 55; response to crisis in, assets
and capabilities for, 25, 29; sea basing
and operations related to, 207–8;
Singapore, defense cooperation links
with, 125; tensions related to and
defense of Taiwan, 16, 25–26; U.S.
bases in Japan and crisis in, 28, 38–39;
U.S. carrier and naval deployment in
response to crisis in, 43, 46; warships
and naval piers, Chinese threat to, 38
terrorism: Indian Ocean terrorism and
counterterrorism activities, 135,
163; national security and threat
from, 24, 26; Southeast Asia as front
for fighting, 123; threat from and
transformation of military capabilities
and basing network, 3, 4, 12n9, 73;
threat to bases from, 27, 35n59; threat
to forces in Singapore, 123–24; threat
to sea-lanes by, 16, 29
Thailand, 7, 10n2, 16, 72, 123

United Kingdom–United States (UKUSA)
Agreement, 93
United States (U.S.): alliance relationship
with Australia, 16, 72, 97–98,
106–8; alliance relationship with
Japan, 16, 39, 59–60, 72; alliance
relationship with New Zealand, 72;

alliance relationship with Philippines,
7, 16, 72; alliance relationship with
South Korea, 16, 67–68, 71–73,
82–83; alliance relationship with
Thailand, 7, 16, 72; British-U.S.
treaty arrangements and procedures,
143; defense strategy for Asia-Pacific
region, 15; global power status of, 3;
history of relationship with Australia,
1, 6; humanitarian and disaster-
response operations, 16, 40, 146,
171n85; imperialism and overseas
basing, 2, 10–11n6; maritime strategy
and sea-power status of, 43–48,
62n19, 143, 170n79; military-to-
military contact between China and,
26; Pacific power status of, 1, 10n2,
15–16; Singapore-U.S. relationship,
118–21; SSA partnership, 102; U.S.-
Japan alliance and Chinese missile
strike threat, 59–60
United States (U.S.) territories, 4, 9
unmanned aerial vehicles (UAVs), 106
Uzbekistan: base construction and
increase in military presence in, 4, 8,
183–84; domestic politics and basing
arrangements, 182–83, 194–95;
expulsion of U.S. forces from, 8, 182,
188, 189–90; human rights abuses
and political freedom in, 8, 185–86,
188–90, 196n11; Karshi-Khanabad
facility, 182, 183, 184–85, 195n1;
map of military facilities, 180; political
and diplomatic relationships between
U.S. and, 8, 181–84, 188–90, 194–95

Vietnam and the Vietnam War, 10n2, 18,
70, 80, 118, 123, 140

Wilson, Harold, 140, 169n69
World War II: Korean peninsula division
at end of, 68–69; network of bases
at end of, xiv, 1–2, 3, 9, 10n3; Royal
Navy Singapore Strategy, 89, 90, 117;
U.S.-Australian security relationship
during, 6, 89, 90–92